Dedication

To the youth and the Network of Zambian People Living Positively (NZP+), the unsung heroes of Zambia.

To my family and their continual support.

To fellow volunteers and the spirit of international cooperation

To anybody who ever sent me a parcel or a letter in Zambia. You know who you are.

For my wife, who encouraged me to write and to finish this memoir.

2

Authors note :

Most of this book was sourced from recovered letters and pure recollection, so some inaccuracies may exist. To my regret I did not keep a diary in Zambia so the book does not always follow a strict chronological order.

It must be borne in mind that despite some holiday travels, my reflections and analysis of the situation in eastern Zambia are precisely that ; an analysis of a part of eastern Zambia. I have been sloppy in loosely talking of `Zambia` and even of `Africa`, when at the most general I intended sub-Saharan Africa. Where I have generalised about Zambia these opinions were often formed after discussions with other volunteers in different provinces, or indeed with Bemba colleagues at Chassa, and not usually based on something I saw first-hand. Life could be quite different in other provinces, particularly in Western province I am told, and again to my regret I did not see much of these other provinces myself.

Where I have spoken of `Africa` I have often had my opinions influenced by Kenyan and Ugandan VSOs and Zimbabwean immigrants, as well as various travellers and volunteers passing through Lusaka or Livingstone. Here I would often bump into VSO`s and PeaceCorps from other neighbouring countries and swap stories.

My insights are also limited because I never learnt a Zambian language apart from a few useful phrases. This is another regret and one which may have contributed to any misunderstandings I may have had.

The tone of my account is often critical and indeed even harsh, and it must be kept in mind that the prism through which I viewed events was a developmental agenda. This account is a memoir, but also a reflection on the problems I encountered, and my thoughts on how `development indicators` such as literacy and life-expectancy in Zambia might be improved. Where my personal anger is evident in the writing is it particularly where I have seen poverty and tragedies that I believe were avoidable. If my tone often seems unreasonably impatient it is only because I gained an appreciation of how short life could be in Zambia, and believed every day lived in poverty, rather than life-time, was a tragedy.

To those who would say I have painted an unfairly negative view of life in Zambia, I would retort bluntly that life expectancy there is 34. I travelled to Zambia to help solve problems and so this memoir is naturally focused on such issues rather than any in-depth exploration of native culture.

Finally, whatever difficulties I experienced in Zambia it must always be remembered that I was a guest in the country and usually treated with great courtesy, despite the mixed history between our peoples.

N.b As an idea of the value of money in Zambia, most of my time there saw a US dollar equal about 4 thousand ' kwacha'. This was about the price of 2 loaves of bread. Most public servants in Zambia received about a million kwacha a month (250 U.S dollars), not an extravagant sum, but adequate in a poor rural area where this income was mostly disposable.

Some names in the following account have been changed.

Authors New Foreword (March 2010)

A year since this book was finished I have had some time to put some 'emotional distance' between myself and my experiences as a VSO. This has led me to reflect that I was probably too harsh in many of my conclusions about Zambian society, and unable to detach myself from my prejudice against religion. Many of the books negative conclusions stem from my last four months in Zambia in which a lot happened. If I had left as originally planned in August 2006, I probably would have written quite a different book. I did not however, and rather than change the book I would rather preserve it's original form for the consideration of future and current volunteers. They may well encounter similar difficulties (as many of my contemporary volunteers did) and my record might reassure them that such difficulties are not unique to themselves. Volunteering in the developing world may be challenging in many ways, but I would hate for this book to be interpreted as a recommendation against going. There is still a great deal of work to be done, and despite many inherent problems in the Aid industry individual volunteers can still achieve much, especially by seeking coordination between NGO's , both foreign and domestic.

Likewise I would hate for this book to be interpreted as a recommendation against people travelling to Zambia for other reasons. By and large I am sure the country remains a safe and pleasurable destination, populated by generally warm and friendly people who are welcoming to foreigners. Despite this, visitors should never forget where they are. The recent imprisonment of a Zambian for likening the President to a fool demonstrates the different interpretation of democracy in much of southern Africa. Similarly I would urge volunteers never to be complacent about the work that needs to be done in Zambia. True, the country is largely peaceful and not in as dire straits as many, but the amount of poverty and suffering there should never be underestimated. There are still too many Aid workers sipping beers comfortably in Lusaka and commenting on how much they like the country, whilst out in the rural villages cries go unheard.

Glimmers of Hope : Memoir of a Volunteer in Zambia

By Mark Burke

5

`` Development is a journey with more ship-wrecks than navigators``

-    Eduardo Galeano

TABLE OF CONTENTS

PROLOGUE : THE REASON WHY – August 2003

I remember reading ' The Zanzibar Chest' by Aidan Hartley, and the author commenting that most of the young , screwed up Aid workers he knew in Somalia were there less out of altruism, and more because they were running away from something ; debt, broken relationships etc. Certainly it was for me to some extent. Partly I went to Africa to heal a broken heart, although sometimes afterwards I would wonder if Africa had merely finished if off.

I was a school teacher in London. It was a good school and I enjoyed my job. Having spent most of my life in rural towns I had been itching to get into the capital and it did not disappoint me. I relished the variety and the different nationalities I mingled with. Bowled over by bright lights and the big city, it would be no cliché to say that in my early London years I was young and largely care-free. And yet beneath the surface something began to gnaw at me. Britain seemed to have been changing since my youth, and my third year in London seemed to see these changes crystallise. One obvious change was the violent crime and the general hostility between people that seemed to be on the rise. The recent violent muggings of my three housemates, all on different occasions, sat in the back of my mind and gave me a new caution on the streets at night. Moving out into more suburban London made for a more relaxed setting, but I was still uncomfortable with the increasing drunkenness and general mayhem that made many streets a no-go area on weekends. I was quite a drinker myself but became increasingly discomfited with the brawling and vomiting that appeared now to be the norm for a social night out in Britain. Added to this it seemed that Britain was becoming more angry and casually violent on a societal level. Hardly a week went by without a newspaper story of a well meaning Joe Public being stabbed in a road rage incident or kicked to death for telling a gang of kids to pick up litter.

On a deeper level I felt ever more emptier with what seemed the general aspirations of society. Everybody was striving so hard to get on the property ladder, get a faster car and a bigger TV. In the meantime they contented themselves with celebrity culture. Was this it ? Some might take comfort in their children and a vague optimism in the future, but this sat uneasily with me. I had publicly and only half jokingly proclaimed that my ambition by thirty was to have no car, mortgage or wife. I kept in mind a quote from one of my favourite, cynical poets, Larkin : ` Why did they think adding meant increase ? To me it was dilution`. My aspirations were to travel, to learn and to not be tied down by any material commitments. I was slightly disgruntled with not having a regular girlfriend, but reasoned that there was plenty of time for all that. Life meandered on tolerably enough. And then I met Anna.

Anna was a young Spanish lady and a new teacher at work. Charismatic, charming and with flashing brown eyes, I fell hard for her. Ignoring good sense and any slight nagging doubts I might have, I pursued Anna despite knowing she had a boyfriend. May the best man win I reasoned. My usual caution was thrown to the wind. Anna fell for me too and her boyfriend was soon pushed aside. As our relationship developed my previous disdain for settling down began to ebb away.

Things moved fast with Anna and the end of the year saw us moving in together in east London. For the first time in my life I saw a real future in a relationship and was blissfully happy. Merely to see Anna smile or hear her laugh made me tingle with pleasure. I lived to make her happy and would do anything for her. Marriage and kids seemed to beckon, and I was still more than three years short of thirty. A real contentment settled in me and I felt truly at peace and at ease with myself. I had never really reflected seriously on the meaning of life but now considered that perhaps it was about finding someone and making them happy with your love. But something ominous was on the horizon.

It was not long after moving in together however that cracks began to appear in the relationship. Anna began to pick fights with me for what seemed bizarre reasons. I was nagged endlessly about how I spent my money despite the fact that we did not yet have a joint account and I earned more. On the one hand I was pestered to buy her £50 tennis rackets, and then was mercilessly pilloried for spending an extra £3 on tennis balls because we already had some. She could not get the shower temperature just right (even though it was August) and the melodrama that resulted because I was not a plumber was truly terrible. Another fight erupted when I used tea-bags with a slightly newer best-before date than others. It was only when I kept catching her text someone (whose identity she would not reveal) that I gained a clue into what was going on. As she slept next to me one night I agonised over whether to check her mobile. If I read her texts then a measure of trust was broken and the relationship was irreparably damaged anyway. And yet I had to know. Eventually I slipped out of the bed and tip-toed into the hall with the phone. Breathing hard with the electric blue illuminating my face, I confirmed my fears. She had been texting her ex-boyfriend. He was by all accounts a weak willed dullard, but was from a similar background to Anna (she began to make a big deal out of the fact that I did not smoke and I was not Catholic) and I suspected that above all she wanted someone she could dominate. Her strangely picked fights were a way of forcing a split that she could not yet bring herself to initiate.

The next day after another random argument I packed my bags and in bewilderment headed to a friend's couch in west London. I was truly torn about leaving Anna, but couldn't bear to be around her when I felt like she hated me. I still harboured some small hope that we could be reconciled, but proud Anna soon showed herself to be angrier at the potential embarrassment rather than heartbroken at the split. ` What will my friends say when they find out you've left ?` seemed to be her main worry. A few months later she was back with her ex-boyfriend.

Love did not turn to hate but instead mingled with it. I hated Anna, but at the same time wanted her back ,and yet knew that could never happen. The next time we saw each other was at work, as school recommenced in September. There were a few clipped conversations about picking my stuff up from the apartment but then we never really spoke. She seemed to go out of her way to flirt provocatively with other men in front of me, so I did my best to ignore her. My confusion and despair became absolute. I had thrown my life into making someone happy and had failed. I was back to square one. Grief the like of which I had never known sapped my strength and I felt like a shell of my former self. It was as if someone close to me had died and I fell into a depression. At times it felt like the grief was driving me insane and I was losing my mind. For the first time in my life I suffered panic attacks, something I found most unpleasant. The future, once something vague but at least pleasantly fuzzy, now became a dark blank that I was either apprehensive of, or at best indifferent to.

The breakup with Anna was soon followed by an Ofsted inspection at school, something I cruised through in an emotional stupor. Ofsted did not rate my results or the quality of my explanations but instead focused on how I should type up more of my resources. My particular Inspector was at pains to stress we buy a certain textbook. We checked it out and found she was one of the authors. In all the chaos at school with the Oftsed inspection and the turmoil between Anna and I, all Anna could think of to say to me one day was : ` your shirt looks like it could be better ironed`.

Suddenly my old scepticism of modern life returned with a vengeance. Anna began to personify all that I hated. Modern life was obsessed with appearances at the expense of substance. So many people working to buy new clothes and other crap and forgetting the really important things in life. Whilst the world was destroyed so half the population could have i-pods, the other half starved. A quote from the movie

Fight Club fitted perfectly my newfound attitude of grim humour ; `They got us working jobs we hate so we can buy shit we don`t need`. I was doing what was arguably an important job ; teaching maths to able kids at an elite school. Many of my boys went on to study medicine or other socially useful careers. But even here I increasingly saw pupils opting for the money as opposed to doing something they were interested in ; an example was a talented musician I taught maths to : he opted to avoid university and become an insurance salesman ;   he thought it was easy money.

Life became to me an exercise in crushing mediocrity. Everybody it seemed filled their lives with trivialities and wilfully ignored the real issues. People began to bore me, as I half listened to their minor problems whilst a growing storm raged inside me. With my friends I stopped social drinking and became a quiet, sullen loner on nights out. I would sit stubbornly in a corner and chain smoke with half an ear cocked contemptuously to what I considered the pointless conversations around me. Tiredness and depression became the norm for me and I saw no way out.

During the school holidays throughout the year I wandered aimlessly around Europe, turning up at train stations and randomly choosing my next destination. I took comfort in the change of scenery, and the isolation from others imposed by a foreign language and strange new towns. The wandering prompted me to think that what I needed what was a permanent change of scenery and a fresh start, not just from school but maybe even London and England itself.

And then one day on the underground I saw an advert for Voluntary Service Overseas. I remembered a tale an old history lecturer had told me. A great Victorian social reformer had found their calling in life after the death of their only child. They found that by helping others they could heal their own pain to some extent. Another memory from an ethics lecture surfaced. All this moralising about what was wrong with the world, but who had the balls to actually go out and do something about it ? Somebody had once challenged Mother Theresa on this, and she had considered their point and then left for the developing world. Maybe I too should put my money where my mouth was. That was certainly a big `pull factor`. The big `push factor` of course was that I had screwed up and had an affair with someone at work. I needed a fresh start.

Voluntary Service Overseas needed experienced professionals to work alongside and help teachers amongst others in developing countries. An idea began to form in my mind. Somehow I had always felt isolated from the world`s poor, as if I could do nothing. And yet I was increasingly nagged by that western middle-class guilt of having had opportunities and an easy, sheltered life. But now, with a trade I could ply there was something practical I could do. I could do something really useful with my life and restore some sort of meaning to my existence. Here it seemed people had all the chances they needed and yet wasted their lives striving for a pointless existence in mediocre suburbia, entertaining themselves with pointless celebrity gossip. Meanwhile in the developing world people struggled for very survival with the odds stacked against them. I resolved to apply for Voluntary Overseas and request to be put where I would be most needed, which would likely be sub-Saharan Africa.

Running away to Africa might seem extreme, but I could not merely will myself to be free of Anna. How could I feel something like hate and love for someone at the same time ? I was somewhat haunted. Ridiculously, I felt trapped in some Wuthering Heights-like nightmare where I couldn't get Anna's face out of my mind. London, and of course my workplace now held too many memories. A tune on the radio could remind me of her and was like an instant slap in the face from nowhere. Instinctively I knew that the best way to heal was to relocate and do something so radically different my mind would have no time for the dark introspection I seemed trapped in. Furthermore, by helping people in genuinely difficult circumstances I would appreciate how trivial my own 'problems' were. And rather than complicate my life looking for a personal love, maybe I could find some kind of peace with a more general kind of love for mankind - with of course perhaps some casual relationships on the side. I cannot deny either that I relished the prospect of adventure in a far foreign land, and on a childish level was secretly pleased when people expressed their alarm at my new direction.

So it was that one evening I phoned home and nonchalantly informed my soon sobbing mother that I was packing up my London life and heading for Africa. I could see nothing for me here, and in some way considered my personal life finished. I was no longer even vaguely happy, or more to the point even interested in being so. But my life could still be useful to others.

With such melodramatic and buddhist sentiments running through my mind I applied to Voluntary Services Overseas. I was duly accepted in November 2003, and then there was an agonising wait as the slow wheels of bureaucracy began to turn. Finally in April 2004 I received word that there was a suitable placement in Zambia, due to begin in October in 2004. I didn't know much about the place except that it was in south central Africa and had once been part of Rhodesia along with Zimbabwe. I did some cursory research but not much ; I was satisfied that I was going to sub-saharan Africa, and now desperate to get out of London.

My limited research revealed that at one time Zambia had flourished due to a huge copper industry, but this had collapsed in the late seventies and the country had since fallen on hard times. They were now suffering a huge HIV crisis and average life expectancy had recently plunged to 34. On the positive side, I reassured my friends and family that despite being sandwiched between Zimbabwe, the Congo, Angola and Mozambique, Zambia itself was a historically peaceful and safe nation. My sister had just begun a tour of duty in Iraq and I pointed out that she was the one they should be worried about. Nonetheless, at the airport I was brutally shaken out of my self-absorption when my father's voice failed and he broke down in tears as we exchanged one final hug. A moment later I was ushered through the gate, somewhat shell shocked. At age 28 I had never seen my father cry before. It scared me, and left me shaken. He was a supremely capable, confident ex-air force officer whom I thought could not be ruffled by anything. Only now for the first time did I really consider what I was doing to my friends and family. So wrapped up was I in my own depression and newly acquired self-righteous mission that I had not spared a thought for those that loved me. I considered what I was doing so selfless that I had not reflected that it was actually selfish in other ways ; from the viewpoint of how I was affecting those close to me. Likewise I had left one of my best friends in London, Mary, curiously cold. Whilst she was moved to tears at my departure, I couldn't seem to feel anything except a vague sense of awkwardness and desire to be gone already. I had not seen the big deal at all about uprooting and heading to the African bush. It had seemed self evidently sensible when people there needed assistance. Now that feeling was counter-balanced somewhat by the guilt of leaving loved ones and the effect my indifference had on them. But it was too late now. I shuffled forward helplessly in the queue, swept along in the small human tide to the plane for Lusaka and then rural Africa.

Before boarding I bumped into Liz, a young English teacher I had met on a VSO training weekend. She introduced me to a couple of VSOs before we stepped on the plane, and I felt a bit better as the jet roared away from England.

ARRIVAL IN LUSAKA – October 2004

The national airport we arrived at was tiny. Two Zambian VSO managers were there to meet us ; the short, permanently grinning Maurice, and the tall whimsical George. The heat was oppressive and the sun blindingly bright, but I noted with relief it was not humid. We were bundled into a mini-van and began the drive to the city. The outer suburbs were bare, fields of yellow grass punctuated with the occasional maize field.

Lusaka was a tiny crumbling city in comparison with London. Six of us, all young professionals from Britain, were shunted around dingy immigration offices and bottled up in a hotel for a few days on a short induction programme. The induction programme aimed to educate on cultural differences and outline the major challenges facing Zambia, amongst them poverty, HIV and gender inequalities. The country was about to celebrate 40 years of Independence, although there didn't seem to be much to celebrate at the moment. At least the country had escaped the violence that had wracked it s neighbours. We learnt that Zambia had several different major tribes and almost eighty different languages. Despite this the country had never really seen ethnic or other violence. Christianity seemed to be somewhat of a unifying force here, and Zambians were proud of their peaceful history. Zambia was divided into large provinces and these very roughly reflected the tribal divisions ; the Tongas in southern province, the Lozis in western, the Ngonis in Eastern, the Bembas in northern and so on. The Bembas seemed to be one of the more numerous people, although the language of Lusaka and increasingly more of the country was Nyanja ; a composite of the Eastern languages. North of Lusaka was the roughly urbanised 'Copper-belt' , now in decay, but otherwise much of the country was still characterised by rural subsistence farming.

A group of short, chatty Phillipino volunteers joined us and impressed me with their dazzling smiles and earnest optimism. I was reassured by the friendliness of the VSO Zambia staff, but rather alarmed that there were so few managers to supervise all the scattered volunteers in this vast country. After the induction week we were to be collected by our employers and taken to our respective placements. It seemed that once we were introduced to our employers we basically on our own, with perhaps a VSO manager checking on us every six months. Nonetheless, it was a pleasant week and I formed solid friendships with most of the others, particularly Liz, a witty English teacher also to be in Eastern province, and my roommate Dan, a genial engineer. Tracey the accountant was to be placed in Katete, only 40km from my placement Sinda, so I looked forward to meeting up with her too.

The Zambians we met were uniformly friendly and quite often charming. When we ventured out of the hotel we were always assailed from all directions by shouts of : ' Mzungus ! (whites) How are you ?' . It was uncomfortable to be stared at all the time, but we never felt any hostility, only curiosity. In the hotel bar one night we were approached by a pair of men who introduced themselves as Headmen ; leaders of local villagers. They had figured we were volunteers and wanted to personally thank us for coming to do something for Zambia. A less charming incident foreshadowed some of the troubles I would have later. I happened to pour some water for a smartly dressed Zambian guest at the dinner table. She was an old lady with a church group on a workshop here. She responded to my friendliness by immediately begging me to buy her a beer at the bar. After I politely but firmly declined, she shamelessly persisted, even as the other guests saw what was happening. I eventually had to leave the room and escape to my bedroom. To be so shamelessly begged by a well dressed church goer was a surprise to me, and I should have reflected on it more and what it said about Zambia.

The highlights of that week for me were the guest speakers on the issues of HIV and Gender. An ex-government minister, a tall middle aged lady, related the prejudice she had dealt with in office and the general problem of lack of gender equality in Zambia. But what really made us stand up and listen were the guests who later arrived and talked openly about their HIV status, amongst them one of the VSO managers we had been with all week. The guests described the illnesses they had suffered before diagnosis and treatment, but what seemed to have hurt them most of all was the abandonment they had suffered at the hands of friends and family. In each case they had usually been lucky enough to find just one friend who had accommodated them and helped them until eventually ARV's (Anti-RetroViral drugs) had got them back on their feet. The atmosphere of stigma and discrimination that surrounded the condition not only hampered care for the sick, but also discouraged people from getting tested and so contributed to the spread of the disease.

There was even a session on 'Zambian English' which explained some of the amusing sayings we might come across., many of them with sexual connotations as it seemed Zambians were prudish about discussing such matters directly. ' To present your manifesto' was to chat up a girl. ' Moving up and down' referred to someone who was 'getting around'. Later on we would hear the less charming ' My size !' as a Zambian might shout to a western girl that she was just the one for him. Joking aside, the standard of English in Zambia was often remarkably good, a testament to the education system perhaps, before it had begun to crumble in the eighties. Most Zambians seemed to speak a few tribal languages and have a natural flair for them, although sometimes the use of English was unintentionally funny ; witness the butchers shop that proudly proclaimed : ' Zambeef : Beefing and Porking the Nation' ! Unfortunately we were to receive no language training ourselves. Since we were being sent to different provinces, and most of us would be dealing with bureaucrats and the official language of English, we were left to pursue language studies in our own time. Learning the local tribal language was deemed useful but not essential.

We met some of our employers the Friday before departure. They answered questions and gave us tips on how to conduct ourselves and avoid cultural misunderstandings. One of them seemed particularly friendly after welcoming us, but then with an abrupt hint of menace stressed that on no account should we involve ourselves in politics. Given the history of western involvement here and for our own safety, this seemed fair enough at the time, and I soon forgot about it. Much later in my service however, his comments would return to haunt me.

The volunteers planned a last night out on the town. Unfortunately I was to be whisked away early by a monk from Chassa Secondary school, Brother John. He had arrived earlier and explained we had to leave that evening as he was needed with supplies for the school. Somehow this further increased my feeling of isolation. Whilst the other VSOs had another night to bond, I would be travelling east into the bush. As dusk settled I was bundled into a small but modern red car, where a friend of Johns visiting also sat, and we began the drive out of Lusaka.

Brother John was a short chubby man with a fat neck and restless, gleaming eyes. He reminded me of a cheeky cartoon gofer or a 'chip'monk. He placed an open bottle of beer between his legs then put his foot down. It was not long before we were out of the small city. We hurtled down a narrow road in darkness with little traffic and lots of potholes. Approaching these holes at lethal speed was not a problem apparently because, as John explained patiently to my anxious inquiries, he knew where they all were from previous journeys. I wondered about the new potholes, and the wisdom of overtaking on hills and blind corners with large trucks about. But I was simply too tired and overwhelmed to make an issue of it. I struggled for some conversation and asked about witchcraft in Zambia and how prevalent it still was. John's friend eagerly explained to me that in western province the availability of AK-47s from neighbouring Angola had meant many witch doctors had been gunned down and lost their mystique. It certainly seemed a direct way of countering such superstition, although education would have been somewhat more ideal.

Eventually my tiredness overwhelmed me and I dozed in and out of consciousness on the backseat. After a few hours we stopped at a dimly lit street of roadside stalls. In the hazy orange light I made out straw hats and huge, flat dry fish for sale. John jumped out of the car, picked up a clutch of fish, returned, and floored the accelerator again. We were about to cross the Luangwa bridge into Eastern province.

EASTERN PROVINCE

After a few more hours of driving in almost complete darkness, we finally slowed for the turn off to the school. Even John, with his Mad-Max style of driving, was forced to slow down on the challenging dirt track. When we arrived at the school grounds however I could still see little. We had arrived late at night in almost total, bewildering darkness. A power cut ; the first of many I was to experience. We drove up to the Brothers residence where candles glimmered weakly. Another indication that religion was somewhat different in Zambia was that the first people I bumped into were a group of monks, all drunk, clutching cans of Carlsberg lager, and murmuring excitedly outside their large brick residence. With difficulty I refrained from sarcastically asking them where the kebab house was. After John nipped into the house and returned we jumped back in the car and I was driven the short distance to my house, a solid looking bungalow with a tin roof but otherwise modern looking. After repeated knocking, the existing VSO, a short and chirpy Yorkshire woman in her fifties, let us in, showed me my bedroom and then promptly crashed back into her bedroom making her apologies.

I stood in the large open lounge and contemplated my new home. Crudely built and sparsely furnished, it had large rooms with cracking blue paint on the walls, and polished red floors. To the right, the bedrooms and toilet. To the left the dining room and kitchen. Single bulbs without lampshades glared offensively in each room. Suddenly I felt a twinge in my stomach ; it hadn't been the strongest since my boozing days at University and was now obviously struggling with the new bacteria here. Doxycycline, the anti-malarial I was taking, already seemed to be playing havoc with my guts too. I shuffled off to check out the toilet. It was not functioning (and I learnt that it never did due to low water pressure) and someone had already left a nice floating present in there for me. Somehow given my weak stomach this fact uniquely depressed me. I was going to be living in a house without a functioning toilet. Like a character from 'Trainspotting' I longed to wrap my cheeks around shiny clean porcelain and flush away my problems. Cursing, I bumbled out and went to check out the cooking facilities.

There was a small two ring stove in the gloomy kitchen, and a large water drum surrounded by well buckets. Satisfied, I retreated to my bedroom ; a small room containing only a wafer thin mattress on a slat bed, and a crudely fashioned table and chair. Huge, super fast brown spiders raced around the floor and defied my clumsy attempts to smash them. They seemed to have a sixth sense and know were I was aiming my blows before I did. A cloud of disease-ridden mosquitos buzzed over my bed. Cheeky ghekkos peeped at me from behind walls and then darted out of sight into cracks in the ceiling. Two mangy cats ran in the house with rats clamped between their jaws. They clawed at my bedroom door which didn't shut properly. I wasn't a fan of cats and missed my dog, Champ, already. I was alone. I had left friends and family to live in a poverty stricken, alien environment with strangers for two years. I had been put in a house with another VSO but had had no chance to talk to her yet. She had simply let me in and then after brief introductions returned to bed (Audrey it transpired had already been asleep after working flat out all day. Suddenly I realised I was supposed to be in my own house. After all I was placed with 2 female volunteers. Surely they should share a house ? Nonetheless, I suppose initially I was a little relieved to have someone around, even if I felt a little awkward like an imposing guest in someone else's home.

After spraying liberal amounts of deet to disperse the buzzing mosquito cloud, I wrapped myself in a thin sheet, lay back and sighed. I wondered if I could really hack it here for two years. I had been placed at a boys boarding school in the very backward Eastern province. Although not far from the main road, it appeared to for all intents and purposes to be in the middle of nowhere. In the middle of nowhere, in the middle of Africa. There was nothing around but primitive villages, clusters of mud-huts in the semi tropical forest. My God ! Two years ! ? I wasn't going to make it two weeks here ! A panic began to rise in me as I really for the first time considered what I had done. It had all seemed like a heroic undertaking whilst I was in England. Now the reality was hitting home. For the first time in many years I felt hopelessly crushed by that kind of helpless loneliness that gets you when you're a small child ; that sickening panic that suffocates you when you realise you've lost your mum in the shopping mall and you have no idea what to do. There was no just jumping on a train and going home to get out of this one. I was trapped on the other side of the world. But my mind was so reeling that it couldn't focus on worry and merely spun round in dizzying circles. Eventually the buzzing of insects outside quietened and became calming. I closed my eyes and waited to see what daylight would bring.

The next day I emerged from my house into dazzling sunlight and a hive of activity. It turned out it was not only the Annual General and Parents day but also the fiftieth anniversary of the school, so special celebrations were in order. Most of the activities were at the school field where soccer matches and dancing took place. My VSO housemate Audrey was run off her feet and so I was left to wander bewildered and alone around the celebrations. I had no idea which people in the crowds were my fellow teachers at the school. I was the only white guy around so they must have known who I was, but no one bothered to introduce themselves (Later on I realised in this culture the onus was on the visitor to introduce themselves, indeed I may well have appeared rude by not doing this). I stood awkwardly amongst crowds of Zambians as they watched the days dancing and other activities at the school track, although a large section of the crowd was always staring at me instead. At one point I drifted past the third VSO ; a young, slim pretty blonde, tall and graceful. But she was so busy talking to parents and organising boys however that I couldn't even catch her eye and introduce myself.

At last in the afternoon things settled down a bit for the guests speeches and I managed to sit down next to Audrey. She kindly translated some of the speeches and pointed out some of the staff for me. A lavishly dressed bishop was droning on, praising the 'White Fathers' who had braved malaria and uncertainty to live in the bush and set up a school to benefit locals. Audrey, having been frantically working since 5am, soon succumbed to exhaustion and returned to the house for a nap leaving me painfully alone again. I did however later manage to find pupils presenting projects in a classroom, and I was impressed with them. Grinning, slim young men in white shirts and red ties, they were all friendly, inquisitive and respectful. They had created posters on science topics, and something about the painfully earnest manner in which they ran through their rehearsed explanations touched me. I remembered why I had come here, and vowed that I would remain focused on the job at hand and not wallow in home-sickness. This was not about me. I was here for the pupils.

As night descended the entire campus fell into dim, candle-lit darkness and I stumbled over random bricks and tree roots to the dining hall. There I found ex-pupils who had returned from University. Again I was impressed with their maturity, politeness and curiosity about England. We ate from huge bowls of nshima, the corn-based paste that was the staple food of Zambia, and luckily managed to get our hands on a bowl of heavily salted beef chunks.

After dinner we headed to the small brick bar on the edge of the compound. On the way I bumped into the third VSO who had at last stopped running around. She introduced herself as Sarah and apologised for not being able to talk earlier. We exchanged formal chit-chat but were soon separated at the bar by boisterous ex-pupils getting steadily drunk on bottled lager. A large ex-pupil cornered me and bored me with political talk about the UN. I was tired and had not followed politics in the era he was discussing. I half thought Bhoutras Bhoutras Gali was a Eurovision Song contest winner but was informed several times that he had in fact headed the UN. Fascinating. And for all his apparently intelligent talk, the young man also droned on about Christianity and badgered me about attending an evangelical workshop. It was strange to me that someone so switched on and engaged in world affairs could be so narrow in their spiritual views. I pricked up my ears momentarily however when the earnest young man told me about his mother. She had been a nurse and had died of AIDS. It was the first of many such stories I was too hear, although few were as frank as this boy in admitting that HIV was the killer. After what seemed hours later I stumbled home, somehow still only half-drunk and yet well out of pocket.

MY NEW HOME

The next morning I met Mr. Soko, Audrey's part-time housekeeper. He arrived three days a week to help with the cleaning ; because of the dry soil the surroundings were usually very dusty and a large amount always found its way into the house. Soko also cleaned clothes and helped collect water. Since it transpired there was never running water, this was obviously a vital job (The toilet had to be flushed manually with a bucket of water, and likewise one had to bathe making the best of a bucket of water). Soko was tall and thin, and didn't say much. In fact his main vocalisation was the frequent clearing of his throat ; another suspicious sign of HIV infection. There was also Michael, a young teenage orphan who occasionally cleaned Audrey's yard in return for growing maize on her land. The main job was sweeping around the outskirts of the house, something the children and wives around here seemed to spend a lot of time on. I didn't really see how it was that important, but someone told me later it helped keep away creatures such as snakes ; they preferred to move under cover and also a swept area would make it easier to see their tracks. Michael hardly spoke a word of English however and my Nyanja was minimal, so there was little we could say to each to each other, but with smiles and gesturing we seemed to make ourselves roughly understood. I made my excuses and left to explore my surroundings more.

I stumbled half-dazed around the school grounds. They were beautiful ; small classrooms and dormitories set amongst huge trees and surrounding bush. In the distance massive boulders surged out of the ground. That way, further into the bush, lay Mozambique. Around the school were dotted teachers houses. The general workers had small brick huts lined up behind the dormitories. The most impressive buildings were the huge church and the large Brothers residence where five 'Marist' monks lived in carpeted luxury with Satellite TV and hot water. The Marist monks had originated from France and were now based in Canada. Almost in a Jesuit fashion their mission was the education of young people. They now had headquarters in Nairobi and Johannesburg where they educated and trained locals to university standard to go out and spread the Word. Their disciples here were teachers, and one of their number had recently become the new headmaster. I gathered later from Audrey that this was to the dismay of the other teachers, who perceived a blatant clash of interests. There was a general fear that the school would increasingly be run for the benefit of the Brothers, as opposed to vice versa.

Aside from that there wasn't much else in the school grounds and I was getting hungry. I found a small `tuck-shop` (small convenience store) but it didn't sell much edible stuff apart from stale biscuits and soft drinks that had lost their fizz, as well as the basics such as sugar and flour. Back at the house Audrey was busy cooking and baking but didn't offer any quiche or pizza to me. I wondered vaguely what on earth I was going to live on. I had been snatched up in Lusaka unprepared and had nothing to eat until I figured the place out. I had planned on a wash but was surprised to find a small black scorpion in the bathtub, whom I couldn't flush down the plughole. I remembered something about smaller scorpions harbouring more concentrated poison, so decided not to mess with it for now.

I resolved to hike to Sinda, the local town on the main road. It was only 3km away. Shouldering a day-pack I trudged down the sandy path and tried to stay in the shade of overhanging trees. It wasn't long however before the trees melted away and I was left in the open. To my left sprawled a vast plain with a gleaming dam of water nearby. To my right were dotted villagers huts and the occasional sign of relative wealth ; brick huts with the coveted tin roofs. The road stretched out before me like a hump backed monster ; crooked, sandy, with troughs and small hills. The sun blazed down on me mercilessly, half blinding me and suffocating me with dry heat. I began to breathe hard and my purple shirt darkened rapidly with sweat. Dark continent my ass. Zambians strolled by in raggedy shorts and brightly coloured shirts, some with bizarre pictures of Saddam Hussein and Bin Laden printed on. This made me a little apprehensive. Was there a general anti-American feeling here that would also extend to the British ? Some greeted me with enormous grins. Others stared at me long after we had crossed paths, twisting their necks impossibly around as they walked away. In irritation I too turned around and stared back and so spent some of my time walking backwards trying to stare them down. We must have looked rather strange when this happened, like gunslingers mincing down the road in reverse. Eventually I tired of this and accepted the interest in me. I was the only white guy around and new in town. I suppose for a rural Zambian it must have been quite a curiosity to see a fat white man wheezing his way down the road and rapidly turning a traditional English pink. Some Zambians creaked by on old one-speed bicycles laden with boxes and sacks of flour. Several almost drove off the track and crashed into the bush after twisting round to stare at me. At one point a miniscule old lady speed-walked past me with an enormous bundle of firewood balanced ingeniously on her head. She paused, somehow managed a comical half-bow, clasped her hands in greeting and then shot off again. Small groups of children streamed down to the road from their huts and shouted 'How are you ?' at me, again, again and again. 'I'm fine, how are you ?' I would respond, and they would ask again and again ' How are you ?'. Presumably they wanted to practice their English, and fellow volunteers came to label the game 'How are you Tennis'. Occasionally I would receive the less charming demand : ' Give me money !'. A tiny child would often furrow their brows at me, make this demand, and bark it at me repeatedly as if I was a voice responsive ATM machine. This was amusing at first, but when you never gave money and yet the order was still barked at you two years later, it would become very tiring indeed.

The large man-made dam down in the fields to my left belonged to Sable, the local transport and agricultural company run by Indians, the group of people in most Zambian towns who pulled the strings of power and ran successful businesses (everybody referred to them as Indians but in fact they were often Muslims of Pakistani descent and had been in Zambia for generations). The dam watered their large commercial fields of maize. Apparently villagers had once lived on these prosperous lands, until many years ago a suspect deal between Sable and the local politicians had forcibly shifted the people onto the other, less fertile side. This dam had also cut off Chassa's water supply by strangling the river that supplied our reservoir. Nazir, the head of Sable, had been educated at Chassa and now sent his sons there. I gathered that other schools had rejected the boys and there was some tension here between native Zambians and Indians, as Zambians resented the usual commercial success of the Indians. I later learnt that with some gratefulness to Chassa, Nazir tried to make up for the ancient wrong of the dam with occasional small favours such as ploughing our school fields with his tractor. To his credit too, Nazir took some interest in developing Sinda as a town, and had been responsible for the building of the post office. Apparently he treated his workers fairly and was better regarded than many other Zambians of Indian descent.

To my right were still more small huts built by villagers. Their dwellings ran the length of the road it seemed. The closer I got to town the more often I would continue to see the hallmark of relative prestige ; the tin roof. Unbearable though this might be in the hot season, it would stand up better in the heavy rains than the skilfully crafted but ultimately vulnerable grass roofs. Occasionally I saw strange combinations of the old and new ; a wooden planked door complete with steel padlock wedged into a mud hut. Nearer the end of the road some villagers were attempting the beginnings of brick houses, although there were no glass windows and the bricks looked homemade. At last I came to the junction and turned down towards the market.

It was a new and humbling experience to feel a whole town turn around and start staring at me. I felt like a stranger in a western who gets challenged by a toothless hick with the obligatory' You ain't from round here are yer boy ?'. I scooted particularly quickly past the dingy little bars, where semi-conscious drunks slumped on stools in the heat and watched the world go by with dark liquid eyes. Although nominally a town, Sinda was really just a motley collection of small general stores with a clothes market tacked on. The shops sold mostly biscuits, drinks and sugar. Painted walls everywhere advertised ' Panado : For Fever'. With the prevalence of malaria and HIV, various fevers must have been a common affliction here indeed. In the absence of real health care many Zambians had to make do with a couple of paracetamol for most afflictions. Most of the activity in Sinda was centred around the bus station and takeaway chicken place, where dodgy looking 'bus-boys' and conductors competed aggressively to sell tickets to travellers. In the middle of the tiny town was a food market, but it appeared all the women working there had only onions, tomatoes and cabbage to sell. At least someone was selling potatoes, and there was a place where I could buy meat. I ducked into the tiny red painted shop advertised as the butchers. It was rather rough and ready to say the least ; a carcass was hanging from a hook, and when I asked for a kilo of beef, the butcher simply attacked the dead cow vigorously with an axe. A chunk that dropped to the floor was dutifully wrapped up in plastic and presented to me proudly, although I considered this rather a waste of time as the carcass had already been crawling with flies. I began my weary trudge back to school, noting the small brick post office that I passed. When would the first mail come ?

I stopped halfway at a small wooden stall that had been set up by the roadside. More tomatoes and onions for sale. The lady of the house rushed out to serve me, tightening her chitenge (a sarong) around her waist. A swirling, chattering swarm of children revolved around her, peeping out from behind her back, then shrieking, laughing, and hiding from my curious gaze. Like all the children around here they were delighted to see a white man. ' Mzungu' they would whisper to each other in revered tones. I bought as much tomatoes and onions as I could carry to keep me going, and said my thanks in Nyanja ;' Zikomo Kwambiri'. This provoked great delight amongst my small companions, they repeated it wondrously; the novelty of hearing a white man speak some Nyanja, and no doubt pronouncing it in a humorous way too. Likewise the English version was repeated again and again as I turned my back and walked on. ' Bye bye, bye bye, ... '

FIRST TRIP TO CHIPATA

Before school began on Monday we had a school salary trip to the local provincial capital, Chipata. I welcomed the opportunity to set up a bank account (I needed one to receive wages from VSO) and check out the biggest town around. I duly arrived at the admin at the appointed time. It was a two hour drive and we wanted to arrive soon after the shops opened. We had a long day ahead of us. A few others were there, but no truck. At last I had a chance to meet other teachers, and introduced myself. One man who stepped forward was particularly friendly ; small and energetic with a big grin, bright eyes, and comically big glasses. He was T.T Ngoma, a fellow maths teacher . T.T crushed my hand in his grip and introduced me to some others. J Banda ; a chunky, friendly bear of a man with a reassuring and slow, deliberate manner. The bald Mumba ; wistful, contemplative, drawing on a cigarette and sporting a small beer belly. The young Magomba ; alternately mock scowling and grinning, always jabbering and joking with others. Mashowo; powerfully built but with long eyelashes and strangely effeminate manners. Mr Phiri, the stoical middle aged language teacher who lived opposite me.

Eventually the Toyota Canter arrived, a mini lorry with a small cab. We were all somehow supposed to cram into the back. Rather alarmingly, a large number of women had turned up, all smiles and brightly coloured chitenges (saris) and headscarves . Teachers' wives, they stood apart from the men and chattered excitedly, probably about the things they would buy in Chipata. At last some benches were pulled onto the canter and the back gate of the truck dropped. There was a sudden surge and people piled on. And on. And on. I waited until the dust settled and tried to squeeze on the end, genuinely fearing I would have to be left behind. Eventually, amidst much elbowing, shifting and exclaiming, I somehow popped into a tiny space and was wedged tight. As the truck chugged around the grounds before leaving, more people somehow jumped on and squeezed into spaces that had seemed non-existent before. After picking up empty beer crates at the beer club (which somehow disappeared mysteriously into the cluttered floor of the canter), we started off down the road to Sinda. It was a dusty, bumpy track and the canter bounced irritably around, jolting its occupants painfully. After turning onto the rather ironically named ' Great East Road' (a thin strip of potholed tarmac) we suddenly began to speed up alarmingly. I struggled to twist an arm around and hold onto the side. The over-laden truck swayed like a running drunk. My stomach began to churn with anxiety and I clenched the overhead bar tightly, arm socket jarring with each bump. Suddenly we were braking again, as the first of many large potholes was roughly negotiated. As the canter braked, we all groaned and crushed against each other. Then we were speeding off again and holding on for dear life. The canter lurched dangerously from side to side and swung round corners at astonishing speed. Traffic was sparse on the thin road but when we did meet other trucks we always seemed to be overtaking them around corners and over hills. Green bush and grassy brown huts flashed past. The land rolled away from us in a beautiful green panorama. I would have enjoyed it if I hadn't been in fear for my life. Jittery goats scampered across the road in front of us. The passengers looked at each other and grinned, bearing the journey with remarkable good humour.

We stopped briefly at the petrol station in Katete, this town a veritable metropolis compared to Sinda. Larger general stores were set back from the road with a wide variety of goods. But most strikingly, small crowds of women thronged around the stopped vehicles thrusting bright fruits up at us. Oranges, watermelons, tiny bananas and boiled eggs were pushed into my face and demands were made. Then we were off again, wind ruffling my hair, buttocks smashing up and down on the bench as the driver saw potholes too late and the canter bumped awkwardly up and down. After what seemed a painful eternity of twisting, turning, speeding and braking, I began at last to see more built up houses (with tin as opposed to grass roofs) and finally, the first large warehouses as we entered the outskirts of Chipata. We rounded the long sloping hill and entered what was a real one-horse town. They had one set of traffic lights, which were rather endearingly called 'robots' . I learnt these were relatively new and the residents were extremely proud of them as they apparently designated Chipata as a modern city. The canter pulled up at the Ministry of Education building and I fell out, eventually managing to straighten my back and head to the bank, a local Barclays.

After being informed I couldn't open a bank account with my VSO documentation and Visas, I headed off to the Ministry of Education to get a letter of recommendation. After being redirected several times to various offices, I ended up at a small office where a thin, bald, stern-faced man was looking magnificently important as he methodically finger-typed an official looking letter. Another Zambian, a smartly dressed young man was waiting before me. There was something uncomfortably pleading in the atmosphere. I sensed the Zambian before me was fearful of the all powerful bureaucrat behind the big desk. The man stood slightly stooped before the official, clutching a hat awkwardly between his legs. The conversation between them began in English as it often did in officialdom, but maybe also because Zambians were almost uniformly polite and would talk English in front of foreigners. The bureaucrat was upbraiding the humble young man, whom I gathered had recently qualified as a teacher. ' Why are you here ?!' the official barked, in halting, broken-style English . The young man visibly withdrew into himself, and then mumbled : ' We were told to report at this time for employment ...' ' WHO told you !?' the official snapped. With his lined, bald head, thin physique and thrusting neck he reminded me of a large vulture. ' the government' the young man began, but was cut off : ' We are the government !' the official snapped, spreading his arms expansively around the office. He then crossed his arms and needle-eyed his prey. 'You are wasting my time ! Get out ! ' The official then pointed at me ; ' This sir' he started, looking at me with slightly bowed head and exaggerated deference, 'This sir needs my attention and you are delaying his business!' I was mortified, and tried shrinking back in my seat. I was only a teacher too. The conversation swayed back and forth this way several times, and eventually the unemployed young teacher was sent packing. I squirmed uncomfortably and avoided his eyes guiltily as he shuffled miserably out of the office. I wondered what his situation was at home and how badly he needed the money. The official now turned to me with a fawning grin. He was all sweetness and light for me, and yet knew nothing about me. Except of course that I was white. I smiled back awkwardly and explained my need. He duly typed a letter out, seemingly immensely proud to be helping a mzungu.

I left feeling slightly disgusted with myself ; I should have said something when the official had berated the teacher. I wondered about the general attitude toward the British here. It was great we had left on pretty good terms with the Zambians, but maybe there was an inferiority complex as two decades after independence the economy had gone down the pan. They still seemed to look up to us, even after all we had done was screw them over. We had returned in the guise of helpers as Aid and development workers like myself, but surely the World Bank and IMF were taking more than their share with dodgy loans and privatisation schemes. I remembered travelling a few years earlier in Guyana and listening to taxi drivers wanting the British back. At the time I had been amazed that an ex-colonial people could ever want the return of imperialists. Why exactly had things gone so bad in so many countries the British had left ? Presumably they had withdrawn investment and left little infrastructure, and were notorious for drawing arbitrary territorial boundaries. They didn't seem to have done a lot in Zambia, having concentrated their energies in Harare when the latter was capital of Rhodesia.

I blundered around Chipata for a few hours in the searing dry heat, enduring the usual shouts of : ' Mzungu ! Come here !' At various times complete strangers would clasp my hand in a firm handshake they would not relinquish, and then with the trademark ' Ah, but I've got a problem..' they would explain dying grandparents or similar problems that required 'assistance'. I don't doubt that many of the problems were genuine but I soon began to resent that Zambians never seemed to ask other Zambians for help. Given a choice between a Zambian in a sharp suit and a shambling white man in tattered rags, a Zambian always seemed to ask the white man for help. I suppose a lot of that mentality had to do with the donor and Aid industry of which VSO was a part, but when it ran alongside Christian sermonising and moralising it got very tiresome indeed. All my efforts to explain that I was a Volunteer teacher who was merely paid the same as Zambian teachers were always met with disbelief. These 'devout' Christians could not comprehend why someone like me would leave a rich country and volunteer to work in a poor country for Zambian wages. Or they believed I was being rewarded with a huge payment when I finished my service. Indeed I did get the equivalent of several million kwacha upon completion, but few Zambians seemed to understand that this would not go very far in England. My attempts to explain price inflation and the cost of living in England were met with suspicious scepticism. Eventually I mastered the cold vibe and slight turn of the shoulder that signalled a beggar would be unsuccessful, but it was never entirely successful.

Most of my supplies I simply bought in the modern supermarket 'Shoprite'. Like many western style facilities in Zambia, this was an import from South Africa. I gathered that the Zambian staff were paid pitiful wages and the vast profits returned to South Africa. Like many foreign set-ups in Zambia, Shoprite had tax exemptions and threatened to withdraw its investments if these privileges were withdrawn. The Zambian government found itself in a bind. I later learnt the Chinese were operating similar deals with mining on the Copperbelt. On the one hand the Zambian government had to attract foreign investment, but it also seemed they were commonly held over a barrel when it came to negotiating tax rates for these foreign investors who were backed up by the IMF.

I later learnt that if you really wanted to find something in Chipata you had to leave the high street and find the Indian traders downtown. These guys imported a lot of goods from contacts in Kenyan ports and always seemed to be receiving heavy good vehicles at their warehouses. There was a huge mosque tucked away downtown and interestingly I discerned no religious tensions between the Christians and Muslims. If anything native Zambians seemed to resent the Indians purely for their commercial success. Taking a stroll down to these shops, I was uncomfortable with the way the Indian bosses stood imperiously and ordered around their Zambian minions. It seemed some Zambians had merely exchanged their former white masters for another type of boss. Later on however I realised that even Zambians spoke to each other like this ; anyone in authority seemed to feel that their position necessitated barking loud and aggressive orders and humiliating their 'inferiors'.   Maybe it was mostly harmless, like the barking of a friendly dog, but it sat uneasily with me.

Trailing back in the afternoon to the Ministry of Education, I treated myself to a Coke at a small stall. The girl behind the kiosk looked too young to be working, and I asked her age. She was 14, and when I asked if she went to school she replied no ; both her parents had died and now she had no choice but to work for a living. She was one of the first of many Aids orphans I was to meet.

After meeting at the canter at 3.30pm as agreed, we waited at least two hours for stragglers, and progressively my colleagues crammed so many goods into the vehicle I failed to see how passengers could be added. I was particularly dismayed to see a huge mattress and several chickens stuffed haphazardly into the back. I looked forlornly at the cab passenger's seat which had already been bagged. At last, as the sun began its slow red descent around 6 o clock, we made our way out of Chipata ; a truckload of people sunk in and buried amongst a bewildering variety of red buckets, live chickens and bagged vegetables. As the truck picked up speed I half-contented myself with a beautiful sunset slipping off broad green leaves and disappearing off a vast open horizon. I tried to ignore the chicken shitting on my foot and the terrible cramps in my legs. After Katete, when more villages began to line the roads, I was alarmed to feel the truck swerving and swaying frequently to avoid crossing cattle returning from their evening drink. Dogs, goats and pigs presented a similar problem, but I couldn't see them spilling us out like I was sure would happen if we hit a cow or a donkey. And yet despite the almost constant fear, I continued to be amazed by the beauty of the landscape we raced through ; red sandy paths coloured by the dusk sun, and deep greens sprouting from the ground. Africa, beautiful but painful. I began to think of it as Hell in Paradise – terrible disease and poverty in a land of striking natural beauty. At last, in now complete darkness we pulled up at Chassa and I fell out the back again with my valuable supplies of pasta and oatmeal.

It had been a long, exhausting day. I had feared for my life on the roads and been profoundly unimpressed with Chipata. It was not a trip I wanted to repeat anytime soon. Yet I would have to, in order to collect my salary and buy enough variety of food and staples to keep me healthy. Villagers did cycle by Chassa on a morning on the way to the Sinda market, selling some vegetables such as rape and bananas. This would not be a problem for most of the teachers as they had a wife who could stay at home and organise the house. I however was always teaching. Sometimes locals who knew of my presence would nonetheless try to catch me during the morning hours, like the apple seller who barged into my classroom and tried to extract money from me whilst I was in the middle of explaining gradient functions. No, Chipata would be necessary otherwise the bulk of my diet would be white bread or, when it was available at Chassa, white rice.

I was relieved to get back into the house and have a wash. Our resident scorpion was still sitting smugly in the plug-hole, but today I was in no mood for civilities and promptly smashed him to bits with a frying pan. That night I also sorted my mosquito net out properly. The large net was hung from the ceiling and enveloped the bed. I could tuck it into the mattress and be completely safe from all the bugs, and the cats which seemed to relish jumping on my chest at night. Audrey related how one of the cats had woken her by dropping a large rat in her crotch as she slept. That was definitely something I would like to avoid. With the net tucked in I had a true haven to retreat to and felt like a child hiding from monsters under the duvet. Even during the day I could crawl in here with a book and my walkman and not come out for hours. On a practical level I could also be reasonably confident of avoiding malaria ; I was told the offending parasite was transmitted only by mosquitos biting after 10pm.

Eventually that night I managed to crash on my bed and reflect on the day. How was I going to avoid that awful journey in future ? My bank account, through which VSO paid me, was in Chipata ; I had to go. I was also struggling to find enough of a staple food to keep me going. A few dishes of the native 'nsima' paste had churned my stomach and resulted in deadly flatulence. It also took time and skill to cook. In Chipata I could buy the more convenient oatmeal, pasta and rice that Sinda often ran out of, or sold at extortionate prices as 'novelty food '. I considered the other transport options ; the mini-buses looked like tin cans and I knew of accidents where they had crumpled like cardboard (one of the worst involved a PeaceCorps volunteer ; a huge passing truck had dropped its cargo on top of a minibus. The volunteer at the back was the only survivor. Shell shocked and blood soaked, they looked stunned at the fifteen squashed bodies in front of them). Perhaps however I could go in the larger and safer coaches rather than perched on the back of the staff truck. There were still the infamous ' chicken-buses' on the roads (rickety old school type buses often with goats hilariously balanced on the roofs) but now apparently it was more common to come across relatively modern coaches. The disadvantage of a modern coach however was that its speed capability allowed it to be driven even more dangerously. A rickety but slow 'chicken-bus' might actually be safer in this respect.

My fears about the safety of travel were well justified. A year later I heard about an awful disaster in another province, as a school term ended. A large flatbed truck had crammed about 100 kids into the back and then, speeding around a corner, it had overturned. There were a staggering 45 fatalities. Imagine such a scene of carnage, in a country with no ambulance service. It must have looked like a childrens' battlefield. That terrible accident did later lead to the government banning such modes of passenger transport, or at least stopping such ridiculous numbers travelling in the backs of trucks. I eventually rejected the official school trips to Chipata and instead, when necessary, travelled by coach on the weekend. The large coaches might be speeding, and the minibuses looked as sturdy as tin cans, but both were better options than travelling in the back of trucks. A year later I was in a mini bus when it flew over an unfortunate pig ; luckily for us we held to the road. Looking back, I saw the unlucky pig had somehow been folded in half as we had crunched over it. I reckoned it just might be dead. Likewise the school canter, under the drunken direction of the deputy, later smashed into a donkey one night and survived relatively unscathed, but this time nobody had been in the back.

Whatever my concerns about travel, I now had enough food and money to keep me going for a few weeks. It could be pushed to the back of my mind and I could get on with the job at hand. Tomorrow was a school day and I would finally meet my classes and the rest of the teachers.

The next day school
felt about where I wa
had suspected, the b(
huge, usually about 4
kids were a pleasur(
started their educatic
almost moved me to
punching the air and
a maths problem. It '
made the right choi

discovered referred to a
trivial at the time bu
complaint (Much k
constant luxury,
teachers, and

S. Zul
part

interactive teaching, as they were used to mainly just enjoy e
seemed. Many of these polite and often charming young men had Biblical
names, but occasionally more unique names which often related to the
manner of their birth. A boy who had granted his mother an easy birth might
be called 'Soft' for example , whilst a more difficult entrant to the world
might be called ' Mabvotu' (' Trouble').

Lessons ran from seven to one to take advantage of the day before
the heat sapped too much energy, with a tea break at ten. Adjoined to the
staffroom I was rather surprised to find a huge TV in a sofa-lined tea-room.
Evidently the school was not as poor as some. I loved the tea breaks because
BBC World was on ; I had always been a bit of a news junkie and craved
contact with the 'outside world' from here in the bush. At my very first break
I met all the other teachers, most of whom were middle aged family men. As
they came in they would laboriously trawl around the room shaking hands
with everyone, often with the other hand clasping their shaking hand (this
may have been a old tradition to show you were not concealing a weapon
with your other hand).The absence of women was obvious, and I supposed
most women teachers were in the elementary schools. There was a Japanese
volunteer from JICA, Mr Narita, but his English was poor. He had an
electronic dictionary for translating, but a conversation took about ten
minutes with such methods. Like Audrey, he was soon due to leave and I
gathered that the Japanese were not replacing their volunteers at Chassa. I
quickly established a rapport with Sondashi, a young history teacher and one
of the only single men, as we both agreed the young Indian girl who ran
BBC business news was some serious eye candy. The Zambians would
banter loudly at break times as they invariably heaped around ten spoonfuls
of sugar each in their milky teas. A.G Zulu in particular would usually go for
twelve sugars, at which point the tea would be displaced and start spilling
over the edge of the cup. Most of the teachers would complain loudly about
the lack of 'support' at break times from the administration, which I

absence of buns with the tea. It seemed rather
later I came to see that it was more a symbolic
er I learnt more about how the Brothers were living in
sually off the school budget and at the expense of the other
upils of course !).

he rest of break time was usually spent ribbing the tall and gangly
, whose shenanigens with women (he was on his third wife) were a
cular target for the wry comments of Sondashi. Chiles, the short
ubby, loud business teacher, would usually add to the bantering with his
raucous laughter and baritone voice. He had been crippled by polio as a
child, and left with a club foot, but whilst physically handicapped, seemed to
compensate with a dominating personality. With his bulging eyes, stout neck
and corpulence, the aging teacher resembled a giant bull-frog holding court
in a small pond. When later I learnt that George Lucas had used a Zambian
language in Star Wars for none other than the character of Jabba the Hut, I
almost fell off my chair laughing in recollection of Chiles. (The story of
how I heard this is pretty amusing - apparently a returned PeaceCorps
Zambia volunteer had been half-watching Return of the Jedi and was amazed
to realise he could actually understand what Jabba the Hut was saying
without subtitles). There was also Mr Ziyambo, the humble orderly and
janitor. He also slaved away quietly as a general clerk and collected the mail.
Mrs Banda, the office secretary, was a bright and youthful looking lady and
yet apparently pregnant with her ninth child. Amos Banda was another
orderly and lab assistant, usually loafing around trying to shake off a bad
hangover. Apparently he had once been a gifted student at Chassa but had
found few opportunities and was now busy drinking away his life. After
working as a local cattle herder, he had at last found menial employment at
Chassa. His story highlighted one of the major problems facing the country ;
even if people were well educated there were few jobs for them and little job
creation.

My timetable in the first term was light and I had time to spend in
the staff-room preparing for the odd topic that was on the Zambian syllabus
and new to me. The syllabus was more like a traditional English O-level and
looked challenging, but I gathered it had lost its value as exam leaks every
year were apparently rampant. I often began to day-dream, scarcely believing
I was here, and looked around at the crudely painted walls. Old posters
adorned the staff-room walls, many of them government propaganda that
looked like it had originated during the troubles with South Africa, when
Zambia was aiding Zimbabwe in the war of Independence. Yellowing cards
on the walls warned employees not to take work home or talk idly to
strangers. The newer posters were about HIV, the latest enemy cutting a

swathe through the people Zambia needed most ; experienced teachers and nurses. Being a Catholic institution, there were no posters about condoms ; instead from the walls buxom young girls in pink t-shirts proclaimed their commitment to abstinence.

At one o clock, or thirteen hours as my colleagues would say, I would collapse on my bed and try to sleep through the hottest hours of the day. I was always tired from what was usually a 5am start ; a cacophony of dogs, roosters, wailing children and mewling cats would rudely awake me from a restless, claustrophobic sleep. I would struggle through the mosquito net and go boil enough water for a large cup of cheap, acorn-based coffee to get me through the day. I was struggling with the heat (I had arrived at the hottest time of year – October was labelled 'Suicide month' because of its intensity) and reasoned that afternoon siestas and working later in the evenings would be a wiser use of my time. At first I was denied even this luxury as one day I came home in dismay to find my bedroom and refuge flooded. A heavy morning rain had found a weakness in my rusting tin roof. When I told Audrey and the admin about this they assured me they were well aware of my roof problem ; it happened every year. I had to wonder then why no one had bothered fixing it in the dry season before the rains began. The rains had not yet begun in earnest, but even the occasional short shower was impressive. The huge drops could drench you in an instant, and even these sporadic outbursts were beginning to visibly green up the scrub and bush we lived in.

Usually after my afternoon naps I would awake groggy and disorientated around four o'clock. With time I got into the habit of sleeping through the boys afternoon activities and would awaken to a quietened Chassa. Small children might run giggling around my house with their mothers calling after them, but otherwise with the boys back in afternoon study the grounds were quiet. The wind gently rustled the huge trees around my home and the intense sun had dimmed to a more relaxed golden hue. I would often take a jog around the school track and then finish my marking after a depressingly plain potatoes and tomato dinner. For the first few nights I tried watching satellite TV in the teacher's lounge which was always open, but spectacularly violent thunderstorms would too often knock the power out. The lightning used to rip across the whole dusk sky and sear it orange. The thunder came so loudly and suddenly that at first I mistook it for explosions. If we were lucky enough to be spared such storms and the TV was on, the Zambians were invariably watching Nigerian movies whose plots were pretty much always the same ; a successful businessman's life would go off the rails due to alcohol and witchcraft, and someone would commit suicide at the end by drinking poison. The movie was always punctuated with dramatic pauses that were far too long, and irritating, tinny music. The mosquitos also made the TV lounge unbearable. Somehow they could bite through the thickest clothing and the incessant buzzing would become maddeningly loud as they hovered around my ears.

So instead I would sit around at home, sometimes leaning on the outside back wall with Audrey, cooking by fire in a power cut and watching the sky being lit orange by lightning. The thunder strikes seemed to rip the very air apart and strike like bombs, always making me jump. Later on in the next year I would emerge one morning and find a particularly stormy night had smashed a massive tree down into JL Banda's roof. Half of the tree had fallen through his kitchen roof but thankfully no-one was in there at the time.

Sometimes with the power out I would simply go to bed at around eight and listen to my walkman ; it was difficult to read books by candle-light and there was really nothing else you could do. Most of the music I had brought with me however was Blues and probably wasn't the best thing to listen to as I contemplated my relative isolation in the African bush. After a few nights of this I decided to check out the bar. I wasn't in the frame of mind for drinking or spending money, but knew I had to make more friends if I was going to survive here in the psychological sense. Most of my teaching colleagues were family men and I wouldn't see them around after work. Even Audrey, here for 5 years and active in the church, was rarely invited over to a Zambians house for dinner or socialised with them in the evenings. She was due to leave in a couple of months. Audrey was nice enough, but the old lady seemed to spend most of her time baking, and working at the tuck-shop of which she was the manager. Audrey was also conversant in the local language after 20 years in the congo, and was very pally with the teachers wives at least. Although alone in the evenings, she was in and out of the house with them during the afternoons. With the age gap and her being a devout Christian there wasn't exactly a lot we could talk about ; I felt a bit like a lodger sharing facilities with his conservative landlady.

The other VSO Sarah didn't seem overly friendly. Her manner was famously brusque and snappy, and I had little opportunity it seemed to get to know her as she was always busy. I guess she had already been here for three years and had her own integrated life. She and Audrey had apparently quarrelled, hence the accommodation arrangements. I eventually found out Sarah had also had trouble with the unwanted attentions of the last male volunteer ; another reason I decided to keep my distance. I didn't want to intrude on her like a needy homesick mzungu. Also like Audrey, Sarah was due to leave in December. I was still wary of my own emotional state around attractive women. So the bar it was. Sarah would pass by occasionally as she was the manager, but I aimed to try and make some Zambian friends of my own. It was here that I became particularly friendly with the local police officers.

THE BAR

The bar was a short way up a winding path, nearer the passing road. It was a small, shoddily constructed brick hut with two small patios and low walls. Plastic chairs sat on the patios, and most customers perched on the walls outside. Surrounded by green maize fields and tall grass, it felt nicely cut off from the school. A tinny stereo blasted out rumba, reggae and Zambian r'n'b. Thankfully it was free of gospel music, whose prevailing presence in the area was already beginning to rankle with me. Servy the barman stood silently behind an iron grill, sometimes giggling incomprehensibly at my attempts at conversation. Inside, hilariously run-down sofas beckoned me to fall through to the floor. Bugs of all descriptions were everywhere; clouds of mosquitos, huge beetles, and the spookily fast big spiders I particularly detested. Somehow these particular beasts could sense your incoming blows and jump the other way. Their name in the local language, which I cannot recall now, meant something like : 'That Which Makes Everybody Stand Up'(the volunteers came to label them simply 'Scuttlers' , a name which suitabley captured the creepy manner in which they raced around). And indeed everybody did stand up when these creatures entered ; the conversations would suddenly halt and all would lurch awkwardly out of their chairs to avoid the huge brown arachnids that raced in between our legs. I could never resist the urge to leap after them, and huge cheers went up whenever I managed to successfully plant a foot on one and reduce it to a brown smudge.

The usual bar patrons were a small minority of the school staff ; many Zambians were strictly tee-total. If they did appear at the bar it was only to buy a 'softie' as they called Cokes and Fantas. Mumba would usually be there ; the small, bald, constantly chuckling English teacher with a keen interest in literature and politics. Massina would usually roll up too, a geography teacher and Cadet lieutentant. He would usually arrive much later after drinking cheap stuff in the villages that appeared to make him cross-eyed. A handsome but lanky man, he was instantly likeable with his laidback manner and easy laugh. The Deputy Principal S.Banda and his drinking companion K.Chama occasionally passed by in the battered school pick up. The portly Chama was invariably cradling a bottle of vodka in his lap. S.Banda always peered comically over the rims of coke-bottle glasses. Occasionally when he caught you through the absurdly thick lens you would jump as two huge squid-like eyes fixed on your face. Despite his position of authority he was an easy-going man with a cheeky grin and a menthol cigarette constantly burning in his right hand. Chama and S Banda would especially go on drinking trips when the Head was away. Both men preferred drinking in Sinda, because it was rumoured, of the women. Both had beautiful wives, but I guess that never has anything to do with why men cheat.

Women themselves at the Chassa bar were few and far between ; it was generally considered unacceptable for them to accompany their men drinking or worse go out drinking alone. Many Zambian attitudes in this respect were very Victorian and often seemed the most enduring legacies of colonialism. Children would appear at the bar sometimes ; dark apparitions that hovered nervously on the edge of the light until angrily beckoned to step forth. They would come to spend their measly scrounged money on a penny sweet, or, more usually, to buy handfuls of menthol cigarettes for a parent.

It was quite a time before the other two men I always found drunk at the bar would reveal to me that they were the police. Like a couple of village bobbies wishing they were detectives in the city, they would lounge around the bar in dark sunglasses talking seriously about the latest cheap kung-fu movie they had seen. The police would dress as smartly as their circumstances allowed and sometimes put on fake American accents like Miami-Vice wannabes. We exchanged small talk for a couple of weeks before they admitted they were police. It seemed commonplace in Zambia for those in positions of power to view white volunteer workers as potential spies, whilst on the other hand the general Zambian public were warm and welcoming. It turned out that Max and Sichande were both of the Bemba tribe and from the more urbanised copper-belt. Joe Sichande was tall and athletic with a long and elegant face. He would frequently drink to the point where he would serenade me with random tunes and compile nonsensical poems just for a laugh. This would alternate with periods of mock seriousness where he would ask me my opinions on philosophy, politics, and the sinister machinations of the IMF and witchcraft. Max was broad-faced with a dodgy eighties style moustache. He had less to say, but would imitate my sayings and accent, and thumbs up gestures. ' Cheers, thanks, yeah' he would delight in saying, then hiccup and smile to himself. Maybe they were homesick and that was why they drunk so much. Certainly Sichande didn't think much of the area we lived in. ' Yah, here, …just... bush' he would snort contemptuously, ' One day I will go back home , near Ndola, have a big farm with tractors.'. Max provided a blunter clue as to why he drank so much. ' I'm trying to cut back, but the job….today for instance – we found a dead baby in a latrine. A mother didn't want it, so she threw it down there. And we had to pull it out. So you see - why we drink..'

Generally the police would knock off like me at one o'clock, then head straight to the bar. And there they would remain until the end of the night, sometimes drinking a bottle of spirits and more usually cups of the porridge-like Chibuka beer. Even after nightfall they would sit in their civvies and dark sunglasses, smoking cheap menthol cigarettes and keeping a suspicious eye on all who pottered by on rickety old bicycles. After a couple of weeks of tentative conservations they finally seemed to accept me, and we hung out regularly together at the bar. Eventually it would get to the point when, very sozzled, they would wobble their heads and blurt : ' Burke. We like you.' They would confirm to each other, pointing definitively : ' this one. He's ....real'. Then they would nod solemnly, and belch. Occasionally a distressed villager would burst into the bar and babble out a tale of goat or bicycle theft, and Sichande would fall onto his bicycle and wobble off on one of his 'missions' as he called them. Despite his seemingly permanent drunkenness, he had a reputation for being able to cover large distances very quickly, and was rather amusingly dubbed 'The Phantom' in the local area. The police did occasionally catch criminals, but the offenders seemed to escape the cell at regular intervals. Rather than replace the dubious old lock, the police saw these suspicious escapes as definitive proof of the accussed's involvement in witch-craft.

The other regular customers at the bar included village headmen drinking chibuku beer in their plastic red cups, always extremely drunk but very friendly as well. At various points in the evening they would get up and dance, then usually fall backwards over the wall. This would be the occasion when you would hear them slur out a carefully mastered English phrase ; ' Ah, but me,... I am..... drunk..' They too would nod and grin whimsically to themselves. All was well. Sometimes they felt the need to explicitly point out that they were drunk. Standing over me they would sway, grin sillyly, and then carefully whisper : Burke ! I am.....drunk !'. Small shop owners would sometimes pass by in the usual vehicle of choice ; a battered white Toyota pick up. They too were always delighted to see a white person and would usually insist on buying a beer for me. It was a welcome change from the other clients like Amos Banda who would pester you relentlessly for a cup of chibuku. Some of the younger Brothers and even Father Fanuel (the resident priest) would frequent the bar for a couple of lagers and usually a lot more. Chiza, a small, morose, nervously smirking man would generally whinge about his circumstances (which were basically better than most Zambians could ever dream of), whilst the popular Brother Jumbe would giggle infectiously at anything mildly funny. Father Fanuel, a slight, gentle man, would drink surprisingly heavily then change abruptly from a light-hearted conversationalist into a deeply introspective man, mumbling mysteriously about some past sins about which he would reveal no details. He was suspiciously thin and time revealed he seemed to suffer from malaria even more than the average Zambian.

Father Fanuel and the Brothers it seemed actually talked less about religion than everybody else. Likewise their behaviour was rumoured to be rather less Christian than that of their flock. The brothers were young, as were the neighbouring nuns, and it was said all were far from chaste. Certainly in other aspects their life was far from the humble life a westerner might associate with monk-hood. The brothers lived in relative luxury at the residence, with living standards far above what most Zambians could ever dream of. They had hot showers, satellite television (allegedly paid by the school account) telephones (also allegedly paid on the school account) and three course meals prepared by a cook. Despite their official philosophy of manual labour to humble a person's spirit, they themselves had cleaners and manual labourers to attend to their every needs. They also had their own huge water tank to ensure they never suffered the water shortages which regularly afflicted the rest of us. This water tank had once also serviced a few teachers houses too, but had later been diverted for the sole use of the Brothers. Now the teachers struggled to get enough water for basic needs. Certainly I had to spend mealtimes collecting pumped water so I would have enough to flush my toilet and wash. The Brothers could also use their plentiful water to grow a productive vegetable garden, the fruits of which were not shared with the school. The school gardens and orchards struggled on without such advantages. With the new headmaster being one of their own now, the Brothers also a tight grip on school finances. They always seemed to have plenty of beer in the fridge. As power cuts became more common (and thus water became scarce as it was pumped by electric motor), the comfort the Brothers lived in came to be increasingly resented.

Christianity was a common theme of conversation all round Zambia, but even more so in this area of the country. The most common question after ' How are you ?' was : ' What Church do you belong to ?' Explaining to Zambians that I wasn't really religious was always a hassle and became very tiresome. It was a little bit awkward to ask them why they believed in an ideology foisted upon them by colonial oppressors. Eventually I developed a well-rehearsed response about the advance of science and a secular upbringing etc, but occasionally I got so exasperated that I later explained how many priests in England had been caught sexually abusing boys and this had discredited them. This explanation usually caused enough discomfort amongst Zambians that the conversation changed tack. Zambians were generally very prudish when it came to discussing sex, although what happened behind closed doors seemed quite a different matter. Indeed as time progressed I became increasingly dismayed with the wide discrepancy in Zambia between what was preached in Christianity, and what was practised in the vast majority of cases. Although the Brothers were an extreme example of this, I never ceased to be amazed how people who worshipped at the same church could turn against each other over trivial matters and act so unchristian in so many ways. I suppose a lot of it was simply what tends to happen in small rural societies ; the Italian countryside fifty years ago was probably quite similar.

HILDA AND DEATH IN THE VILLAGES

It was on one of my afternoon walks to Sinda that I was first hailed by villagers and asked to walk up to their homes. Some young women, looking tall and thin in bright chitenges, were shouting at me from their huts, waving their arms at me, maybe fifty yards from the road. I made out they were attempting to say my name : ' Be-cker ! (the closest many ever got to saying Burke) Come... here... Becker ! Come here !'. I relented and walked up through the fields to the central clearing where their mud huts were clustered. A grinning young lady bounced forward and slapped my hand into a vigorous shake. She introduced herself as Hilda. Two other ladies were her sisters, and an ancient grandmother shuffled down from another field. The usual huddle of small children milled nervously around the women's legs. The absence of men was conspicuous. Hilda was fluent in English, unlike the rest of her family. She bantered ceaselessly, asking me about myself and England and then translating my answers to her curiously staring family. As usual, talk centred around Christianity, and I was interrogated about my faith and asked why I was not a fervent believer. The fact that I was white and yet a non-believer seemed to particularly distress them. ' But you people are made in His image, yet it is you who are the non-believers' Hilda agonised. When I pointed out that Jesus was probably dark, if not black, they protested that all the paintings they had seen showed him as a blue-eyed, brown bearded man. I asked them who had done the paintings, and some slight doubt was sown in their mind, but not much. I was given a seat on a small wooden bench and offered a cup of grainy maize sludge.

Hilda and her family struggled by on subsistence farming like most people here. Unlike many villagers however, Hilda had a small crop of cassava too (a relative of the potato) ; a small insurance should the maize fail yet again. I asked the children's ages and was stunned by the answers. What appeared to me were five year olds were actually nine year olds. Their short stature and slight physique belied their poor diet and general lack of protein. I noticed the large rash on Hilda's arm, the tell-tale mouth sores, and the painful thinness of her two sisters. I wondered if they were afflicted by the 'plague' that ravaged so many here. They told me of a cousin who had just died suddenly from meningitis ; a classic HIV related death. I looked around at the dry surrounding brush and asked where they got their water ; they showed me the broken borehole pump and the stagnant well were they now had to draw their supply. The teachers at Chassa might bemoan their relative poverty, but their situation was not comparable to this. I later discovered relative comfort in the teachers houses as they enjoyed VCRs and large screen TVs. This was particularly irritating as they increasingly seemed to be bugging me for loans, catching me alone and shuffling their feet awkwardly whilst they explained they ' had a problem'. Hilda and her family however seemed to live an almost purely seasonal existence and be genuinely threatened with hunger. They had their store of maize, but mainly relied on whatever fruits were around at the time ; guavas, mangos, bananas. People here did not generally die of starvation per se, but the ease with which they succumbed to disease was certainly the result of a consistently poor diet.

Life could be startlingly brief in the villages. A lot of women died in pregnancy, often because they were simply too young, having been married at thirteen. Malaria seemed to hit children particularly hard and caused many fatalities to those under the age of 7 or so. HIV was not well discussed in the villages, but I heard that a suspicious amount of young adults died of lung infections, stomach infections or other common complaints which were typical of compromised immune systems. There was a noticeably high suicide rate ; often amongst young men who had lost a lot of weight and suspected the worst (I seemed to hear quite frequently from Sichande about young men who had hung themselves). Sometimes death manifested itself in bizarre accidents. I heard of a cattle tow over-tipping on our road and a metal drum rolling out and crushing two small children to death.

EARLY DAYS

Sarah would pass by every evening to calculate the takings as she was the bar manager, but though the weeks went by but we still didn't talk much. I didn't really go out of my way to talk to her. I was still a little wary of becoming so close with the other volunteers that it might hinder my relationships with the Zambians. But I have to admit I also stayed out of her way because she was intelligent, attractive and reminded me of Anna with her forceful manner. Here I was in the middle of nowhere trying to heal a broken heart and forget a beautiful woman I became dangerously infatuated with, and VSO placed me with someone like this. Even if had no genuine feelings for her I was now so cautious with women that I was afraid of developing a `situational crush`. For her part I suppose Sarah must have thought me strangely aloof and more at home with the Zambians, and must have been slightly baffled by my apparent indifference to her. And it was true that initially I did get on very well with most of the Zambians. They generally had an easygoing manner and good sense of humour, and I was fairly laid-back and affable myself.

I got on especially well with Sondashi, a young single man with a passion for country music and American politics. He taught history as I once had done, and I tried introducing him to what I believed was the superior, evolved version of country music ; Blues. I threw him Bob Dylan and Chuck Berry as the closest in taste to what we might share and he loved it. I had some of my best history books sent over, collections of essays by AJP Taylor which he also loved. Like the cops, Sondashi was also a Bemba and from the copper-belt and shared a more modern outlook similar to mine, unlike many of the born and bred Easterners. It was usual to stroll into the staff-room and find Sondashi rocking himself with his trademark giggle and fist to his mouth, bantering with his fellow staff. We often shared snobby jokes at the expense of his tribal cousins, the Ngonis. Chief target for Sondashi was A.G Zulu, a real old village boy whose thinking did indeed seem to be slower than everybody elses'. Maybe he just struggled with English, but A.G always seemed full of self-doubt and unable to express himself clearly. He would however perform all tasks with equally painfully slow deliberation. (always with his tongue protruding comically and usually whilst carefully picking his nose). This in itself was not a problem, but like many here it seemed, he always focused on presentation at the expense of substance (That however was a fault common to many Zambians, indeed people in general, in my opinion.) A.G would borrow money off me and actually deliver a formal business letter requesting to do so, with date and references painfully underlined in both red and black ink. It probably took him at least twenty minutes to write it whilst he should have been doing his duties as the Head of

Maths and Senior Academic Teacher. I could just see his tongue trying to reach the tip of his nose whilst he slowly underlined each important point. I knew the presentation was out of respect for me, but the time he wasted on it rankled with me. And indeed his duties were neglected. Our maths departmental meetings were a waste of time. A.G would never follow up anything we agreed on. As senior academic teacher A.G was responsible for coordinating the end of term exams, and these too were always a disaster. Exams would be lost the day before printing in a chaotic Senior teachers office which had no discernible filing system. To his credit however at least A.G Zulu seemed a straighter man than most. I later heard all sorts of stories about the other men teachers concerning stealing school funds and infidelities, but never A.G.

As term passed I became increasingly alarmed at the casualness of the school. I was fairly laidback myself, but this was on a different scale. Teachers would simply skip lessons, maybe sending a boy instead with notes to write on the board for others to copy. As time went on I realised many teachers would sit around in the staff-room all day, passing the newspaper around and complaining about their conditions of service. There was a peculiar obsession with the appearance of cleanliness, but not much concern for learning itself. One teacher complained to me that my tutor group had not swept and cleaned the classroom enough. He had returned to the staff-room and refused to teach them, settling down with the days paper. I high-tailed it back to the classroom and got the boys to clean the place more thoroughly. I returned in ten minutes and happily reported that the place was spic and span and ready for him. But he refused, arguing it was not worth it now. There was almost an hour left of the lesson (My colleagues at Katete hospital suggested this attitude was not limited to the education sector ; the nurses there were apparently far more concerned with keeping their uniforms clean than patient care. There was a marked reluctance to roll their sleeves up and get dirty in the name of duty).

The beginning of the next term saw our secretary off with a pregnancy, and because Michael had refused to pay a decent wage for a replacement, Sarah and I were doing most of the typing. Unlike most British schools, Chassa required that its teachers write a fresh scheme of work every term. I didn't really see the point of this if the exam syllabus didn't change ; surely every year you would follow roughly the same teaching schedule ? Nonetheless I accepted and helped type the schemes in my spare time. I was mildly irked then, when many schemes were returned by indignant teachers pointing out the odd heading or underlining had been done slightly differently on my typed version. They wanted new ones typing and would not accept these. Nonetheless at the time I was at least pleased that the teachers seemed so conscientious, until that is I saw what it was they were conscientious about. Whilst the neatly typed schemes were proudly filed in a smart binder on each teachers desk, the teachers generally then sat in the staff-room that term not actually going to teach. At the end of term we had to fill out records of work detailing how much of the schemes we had covered. Sarah and I were regarded with almost wonderment as we had generally covered our schemes by actually teaching as according to the timetable. The other teachers would usually get half way through a scheme, if that, and then complain of the challenges of teaching a syllabus that was just too long. It was with great irritation then that I received teachers next term who badgered me to write schemes of work that they were never actually going to follow. Furthermore, most resolutely refused to try typing ; they generally regarded it as a something a mzungu was naturally good at and therefore should do. Eventually I compromised and typed mathematics schemes, but insisted other departments take collective responsibility and organise their own.

Deadlines in general were interpreted as largely optional. When exams came in November, staff took an unusual attitude to invigilation. A.G Zulu would sit in the tea-room and complain about an exam he was currently ' invigilating'. The idea that boys would copy off each other with no staff in the classroom was dismissed as unrealistic. When it came to marking, deadlines would generally be missed by about a week and kids would receive their reports, if they were lucky, the day before returning to school after a month long holiday. I didn't see too much of a problem with this actually, but wondered why early deadlines were always set and never met, despite past experience. This attitude applied to everything. At the closing staff meeting, we all sat through a laboriously regimented formal meeting where all issues, academic, pastoral and more usually boarding and living conditions were debated. I had to take minutes at these meetings several times and had to reproduce all names in full and most contributions, despite the fact that it was all ultimately pointless. Never mind that nothing ever got physically done. At least the written records were there. Most of the issues concerned various jobs and repairs that were still pending. Teacher committees and individuals were appointed to deal with the practical logistical problems of running a boarding school, and understandably did so rather half-heartedly. I remember at the first meeting raising the issue of a generator, having been alarmed at grade 12's studying for their Final exams by candlelight, as massive storms had brought down power lines. More than 2 years later at my last ever meeting there was still no generator, despite it being a relatively cheap purchase in the grand scheme of things. Some issues like this were down to simple disorganisation, but as I was to learn later, most of the time it was down to gross 'mismanagement' of funds. As my two years progressed I was to gradually learn that the school was far richer than I thought (it had a yearly income of $300,000 U.S) and was losing an awful amount of money on administration, or more specifically, the personal expenses of the senior management, and even more particularly the expenses of Brother Michael the Headmaster. In the early days however the extent of all this was not yet clear to me, and I was so happy teaching respectful pupils that any misgivings about the administration were pushed to the back of my mind.

In the meantime that first term meandered on uneventfully. When not working or at the bar I welcomed the extra time reading novels and catching up on sleep. Audrey had some old classics and I enjoyed the feeling of having time to catch up on books that I'd always wanted to read but never seemed to get round to. Unlike most people, it actually looked like I really was going to be able to get through 'War and Peace'. I also welcomed the opportunity to have the free time to run myself into shape. The bar was all well and good, but I was wary of becoming dependent on alcohol and my wages were not that ample. Time started to drag a little and I was lonely. The brothers had an internet connection but it was very poor and really only available for emergencies. The landline at the school could receive, but not make international calls. Mobile phones were on the way apparently ; next year a transmitter mast might be erected at Sinda. In the meantime however mail took about two weeks to reach me. Sarah was leaving in a couple of months, another reason I had avoided getting close to her. Sometimes the full 2 years of my service seemed to stretch before me like an eternity. I looked desperately forward to the Christmas holidays when I would catch up with the other volunteers in Livingstone. After Christmas I hoped that 2 new VSO's would arrive. I would look forward to helping them settle in.

At least I was becoming more comfortable with my living conditions and particularly with finding food (although rather irked that Audrey had not even told me of these things ; she had cheerfully waved me off on my speed-walks to Sinda when other sources of food were nearby). I found where the wives baked and sold bread and even potato samosas. I found the Brothers had their own tuck-shop and it was better equipped than the schools ; it usually sold rice and soya pieces. In time I learnt to be opportunist and buy food whenever I saw it ; protein could be found cheaply if you saw someone selling groundnuts as they occasionally did, and you just had to keep your eye out for the odd villager cycling some surplus veg to Sinda.

SAFARI IN MFUWE – November 2004

It was not long after settling that the other volunteers in Eastern took a trip to South Luangwa National park. It was not far as the crow flew, but in order to meet them in the resort of Mfuwe I would have to skirt far around via Chipata and make my way from there, over five hours of very poor road. All in a weekend ; it would be tight. I has stowed away a fifty dollar note to spend at Mfuwe, but now couldn't seem to find it. I was sure I had hidden it at the bottom of my box of anti- malarials by my bed. After hours of searching and turning my room upside down, I was still sure that the money had been there. Someone had stolen it. My immediate thoughts turned to Soko. He was the only one with access to the house who would have time to search thoroughly and find the note. Audrey did let pupils in to borrow books but they were only ever put of her sight for a moment. The chances that one would choose to dart in my room and find the hidden note straightaway were slim indeed. Soko wasn't here at the moment so I discussed the issue with Audrey ; I was sure it was Soko and wanted to ask how I should deal with the matter. Yet Audrey vehemently denied that Soko could have stolen the money. She insisted he would never risk his employment this way. She did mention that years ago he had been suspected in the theft of money from a JICA volunteer, but insisted the theft had probably been a pupil. Eventually she persuaded me to drop the matter and write the money off as lost, probably stolen by one of many pupil suspects. In time my suspicion of Soko lessened and I relaxed again with him pottering around my house. I didn't really consider him necessary, but knew I should keep him on after Audrey had gone, as I was his only source of cash income. Above all, in times of water shortage it was useful to have someone to collect water from elsewhere whilst you had to leave for work (in desperate times we had to scrounge water from the borehole at the neighbouring basic school).

Regardless of the money loss, I got an early start on the Friday afternoon and hoped for the best in Chipata. Arriving at the backpackers there I bumped into a safari jeep driver who was going my way. Albeit at 2am in the morning. At 2am I was duly roused and we set off. An attractive Zambian woman was in the passenger side so I was bundled up into the tourist spotter bench on top. As we left Chipata I must have looked odd indeed, perched on top of the jeep ready to spot game whilst driving through shanty town streets. After a while we turned off for the dirt track and the long bumpy ride really began. We smashed up and down and the jeep rattled incessantly as in headlight darkness we negotiated potholes and puddles. It was a magnificent evening, a small moon and a vast array of bright stars filled the huge sky. A cool night breeze kept me awake, along with clinging to the railings as the jeep lurched and jumped around the gravel track. The scenery soon got old however as I wearied and began to ache with the constant banging around. After what became an agonising four hours we pulled up at dawn at the Flatdogs camp where I thought Liz and Tracy would be. It was a small settlement of huts in a grassy setting. Another jeep was already heading out on an early morning safari. I recognised Tracy with the other tourists perched on the back of the jeep. Her head was down and she was faffing with her camera. I jumped straight off my jeep and bounded up into the other, next to a startled Tracy. Off we went for a four-hour drive in the renowned South Luangwa park.

After crossing a long bridge we were in the park proper. There was a brief pause at the end of the bridge as we spotted a group of hippo wallowing in the river below. I activated my camera and it promptly died. I had lent it to Soko and he had managed to exhaust even the lithium battery. I cursed and sat back, letting Tracy do the photos. The park was overgrown and the truck followed narrow winding paths for some time before we came across animals ; a large herd of elephants crossing the road. They allowed us to get very close ; the few babies were well surrounded by adults and they obviously felt we were no threat. One adolescent male took offence and puffed himself up at us, but contented himself with a mere display of ear wagging and huffing. I was fascinated with a young female who had moved close and was feeding on a bush next to us. When I met her eyes for a moment I had an eerie feeling I was being closely studied by another intelligent being. Was I projecting human qualities onto an animal ? Maybe, but I felt uncannily that the young female was merely pretending to feed near us as an excuse for getting close and monitoring us. More than that, I really felt the elephant was thinking about me, analysing me rather than just observing. I have never had a feeling like that before from any other animal. It sounds horribly cheesy but at the time as we stared into each others eyes it did feel like a bit of a Dian Fossey moment between man and beast.

Some of the stories I subsequently heard about elephants were amazing, and of the less touching and more brutal variety. A couple of hunters I later met related how on foot they had wounded a young bull and pursued it through the bush. Before they could catch up and finish the wounded animal it managed to rejoin the herd, which turned as one against the men. The hunters managed to scramble up a sturdy tree before the enraged herd could catch them. But then they found themselves trapped. The herd would not move on, and seemed determined to wait and finish the hunters somehow. The men then saw the herd conferring; heads together, murmuring low sounds, as if debating what to do. Then the elephants began taking turns to battering ram the tree. Luckily for the men their refuge held fast, shaking violently but obviously not about to fall. After a while it seemed the elephants concluded this wouldn't work, and they stopped. But they appeared to confer again. When the elephants returned they did not ram the tree, but instead began digging up the roots. When the roots had been partially exposed the beasts then returned to ramming the weakened tree, which now at last began to give way. The hunters looked doomed, but at that moment the rest of the hunting party returned in vehicles. They opened up with their considerable armory of semi-automatic weapons and managed to scare the herd off.

Baby Elephant Etosha 2005

Our accommodation at Flatdogs (the nickname for crocs) Camp was unusual to say the least. Many of the budget travellers slept on open tree platforms, something they could have literally rolled off in the middle of the night. I declined this for a bargain mini hut, not just for the convenience but for the safety from hippos. I remembered that a Burke relative years ago had visited Zambia, and on a walking safari had seen a hippo rip a persons head right off their shoulders. There was no physical barrier around the camp and only the river separated us from the reserve. Hence we would get elephants and hippos literally strolling through the middle of our camp (especially at night), as well as of course the obligatory troop of cheeky baboons who would steal whatever food was left unguarded.

The wisdom of my choice was amply demonstrated when we tried to leave the bar for our beds and found the path blocked by an enormous hippo. The beast chewed nonchalantly on bushes that lined the path. There was nothing to do but freeze and wait for it to move on. The dark mass in front of us grunted contentedly and I was ready to bolt ; on my toes with my hamstrings so tense you could have plucked them like a harp. Suddenly out of the darkness shuffled a night-watchman, come to assist us with a lantern. He waited with us for the hippo to move on. It duly did so after a couple of minutes and we were all safely escorted to our beds. Later that night however I was awoken by a hippo snuffling noisily around my hut. At the same time I realised I was bursting for a leak. I lay desperately still until the hippo moved away, then sneakily cracked open the door just a fraction and gyrated my hips manically trying to project the stream as far as possible from the hut.

The next day we were lucky enough to catch a lift with a volunteer couple on holiday from Malawi. In their air conditioned land-cruiser the journey wasn't so bad. At one point we passed over a comically short strip of tarmac ; yet another government project started with foreign help and then abandoned ; a strikingly visual illustration of the piecemeal and hence often useless nature of Aid. The Zambian government said that promoting tourism was one of their priorities, but they didn't seem particularly concerned about access to what was undoubtedly one of the premier safari parks in the world. Most tourists were of the wealthy variety who flew in to the small local airstrip. The vast numbers of potential budget travellers were reduced to the occasional overland tour of Aussies, who rolled up in giant trucks that were capable of dealing with the atrocious roads.

END OF THE FIRST TERM

Arriving as I did in late October, it was soon the end of the school term which saw end of year exams. For the first time I saw how right the teachers were when they said the pupils found maths very difficult. I had taught my boys for about 6 weeks and so now had a vague idea of their overall abilities. I was still stunned however when marking the end of year papers. They were regularly getting things wrong like ' how many sides does a square have' etc. The final scores were generally atrocious ; something I was assured by others was 'the norm' in mathematics here. My VSO maths predecessor had told me he believed I could make little difference ; what would be would be. I was going to have my work cut out. The department was predictably short on books and resources, the teachers were sporadic in their attendance to lessons, and the pupils seemed generally fearful of maths as a subject. Next January was a fresh academic year and I resolved to start addressing these problems in full then.

The end of term saw our goodbyes to Audrey after 5 years of service to Chassa, and some 20 years in the Congo. She was single and in her fifties, and seemed to be a `career volunteer` . I didn't think she would last long in Yorkshire. I reckoned she would return to Africa sooner rather than later. At the Christmas party I saw for the first time the laboriously regimented style of socialising that `polite society` dictated here. Loud music blared out any chance of conservations at the tables, and was only silenced for the speeches from the high table. Soft drinks and packs of biscuits were rigorously rationed, with of course most of the beer being held back for later consumption by those commanding the cooks. Audrey's leaving speech was largely lost in the great hall, but she mentioned something about planting seeds and reaping the harvests of trees. It was a moment for me to reflect on what I wanted to achieve here. Audrey had done an awful lot here and been extremely active in the school and community, but I had my doubts as to how much of it was sustainable, to use the development buzz word. After she had gone, how long would her achievements last beyond her departure ? She had been a conscientious teacher, but what systems and resources had she left behind in the English department ? As VSO's we were here at the expense of the British tax-payer, and we were occupying a job a Zambian could have had. We thus had a duty to bring something `value-added` to the table. Audrey had run the tuck-shop, and with her personal vigilance had stopped the problems of theft that had previously stunted its growth. However it had been handed over to other staff a term earlier to give Audrey more time to prepare for leaving. Already the stock and cash reserves were plummeting. To my dismay, management of the shop was now handed to me ; presumably the administration believed volunteers were more number literate and business minded than most Zambians. Perhaps also since we had no financial worries, they believed we were less inclined to steal. This may have been true (the bar had made a similar recovery under Sarah) but I didn't want to spend my time counting sweets in a tuck-shop when I had more pressing challenges in the maths department. The tuck-shop was staffed by boys however, and I was reassured by Audrey that the previous problems had been due rather to the teaching staff that had managed it. The boys would not steal, and the tuck-shop would be expected to grow well. Perhaps the profits could eventually be used to help pay the school fees of orphans or something else similarly useful. We already had an ex - Chassa pupil, Dr. Chabwera, who supported such pupils with a regular fund.

After a visit from our VSO Manager, the tall, continually chuckling George, Sarah had elected to stay another year. I was relieved, as I had found out the VSO's intended for Chassa were now being diverted to another school. As much as I wanted to integrate with the Zambians, I realised they were staunch family people and not really given to socialising outside church circles. Sondashi and the cops were the only Zambians I regularly socialised with. On the whole they were a friendly bunch, but the odd incident played on my mind and began to cement reservations I might have about them. A typical example was Sarah giving Massina bar money to buy three crates of beer in Chipata. He bought two crates and pocketed money for the third. Sarah obviously found out immediately and asked for the remaining money, but Massina always denied it against the obvious facts. I had to wonder how a colleague of four years could treat another like that. Worse, Sarah didn't seem particularly surprised by it. The tuck-shop and bar were generally accepted to have prospered under the volunteers but suffered under the management of Zambians. The basic reason of course was theft, but nobody seemed to really confront this or talk about it openly. It seemed to be accepted as some kind of inevitability, despite the accompanying Christian moralising that seemed to find its way into most conversations.

I wondered too about Audrey and her attitude to Zambia. She seemed to wilfully ignore some of the problems here and be living in denial. I had been irritated to have her approve my loans to teachers, telling me we were getting paid a lot more, only to admit later that they were paid the same as us. Sarah related that on her way back home after confirming that she was to remain, she had passed Audrey, who looked up at her suddenly with tears in her eyes, and snapped : ' I knew you'd stay again – I don't know how you stand the injustices here !'. I was a little perplexed about this at the time. Audrey hadn't really mentioned any injustices to me. Perhaps she referred to the Brothers and their running of the school, though I had heard little concrete evidence so far that anything untoward was happening.

I finished the first term generally happy with my situation. Teaching eager and respectful pupils was a joy, the staff were friendly, and in general I was far less stressed, and better rested than I had been in a long time. Life might be harder in some ways, but was it simpler too. I might not have had much money and access to luxuries, but on the other hand I had no bills or major worries. Boredom might be an issue, but I was usually content with good books, and having the time and energy to exercise. I'd even stopped listening to Blues so obsessively and was rediscovering my taste for other music. With Audrey gone next term I would have the considerable sized house to myself, which would suit me fine too. The only niggling problem I had was that I was being increasingly bothered for money, often several times a day by teachers, pupils and even random people in the community. It seemed 'Ask and ye Shall Receive' was the most popular quote from the Bible here. I hoped this would ease off in time as people saw my lifestyle and accepted I really was being paid a volunteer wage.

VISIT TO MALAWI –December 2004

After the term ended there was teachers trip to Malawi, generously paid for by the PTA and using the accommodation of the Marist Brothers there (the organisation originated in Canada and had missions all over the world). After being reliably informed that the canter would leave at 6.30 for the long drive to Malawi, I duly arose at 5.30 and was ready at the spot. There were only a few others there though. I soon found out why. Nobody seemed to have planned a damn thing. Had we fuel ? No. Food ? No. Where was the food ? In the canteen. Who had the keys to the canteen ? The workers. Where were they ? Nobody knew, etc...Eventually we started off at 11.30 and arrived 12 hours later in Malawi after what should have been a six hour drive (punctuated with similarly disorganised stops) . Malawi seemed better off than Eastern province. The roads were far better and the shops seemed better stocked. The fields looked better tended and organised. Apparently however Malawi suffered from the same mono-maize culture that blighted Eastern province, and was similar in many ways ; it shared the same language and tribe that was numerous in Eastern ; the Cewa. Indeed during Independence time in the sixties it was touch and go for a while whether Eastern province would be part of Malawi or Zambia. Malawi certainly seemed to be suffering from a similar HIV crisis ; one of the biggest industries seemed to be coffin-building.

The Brothers place was a lodge on the lake belonging to the Marist organisation. It was beautiful, but rather dull and I soon tired of it. After a couple of days lounging around on the beach, interspersed with inevitably disorganised outings, I was relieved to get back to Chassa and set off for Livingstone. A moment on the beach in Malawi had reminded me that I was still a bit of a mess about Anna. It was a moment of cringing cheesiness. Somebody put on the Chris de Burgh tune ' Lady in Red' and something about it had got me. I welled up and felt that sinking low I used to get when thinking of her. It was a moment of doubt and fear for me. Was I any better ? When would I finally be rid of this ? Was the bush the right place ? Even with the work I was doing and in such circumstances – how long would it take ? I had still had my moments at Chassa, those horrible sinking moments when something out of the blue hits you and reminds you of what you've lost. I remember suddenly whirling around at the bar one evening and half snarling to my startled companions :' I wish there was a way to get rid of bad memories !' Meanwhile Sarah had elected to stay another year and I feared I was becoming infatuated with her, whilst at the same time I was sure she was not interested in me. This was certainly something I could do without. I needed to get back to my other VSO friends for a while ; too much brooding isolation was setting me back. I needed busy distraction again.

MTV AND CHEESEBURGERS- Christmas 2004

I headed for Livingstone via Lusaka, and it was a chance for me to get to know the capital city a bit better. It was luxury to crash at the backpackers and find western food. Likewise I could hang out at the VSO office and email, another missed luxury. They had a small library and I stocked up on reading material for what I knew would be the lonely months ahead. The small luxury of free bread and tea in the kitchen was greatly appreciated too, and I began the process of putting a bit of weight back on after my curtailed diet at Chassa.

Later at the backpackers I found one last note from Audrey, and received a nasty shock. Mike, a jovial and powerfully built Canadian VSO who was based in Chipata, was dead. He was our eastern volunteer rep to the VSO office, and we had met him briefly in our induction week where he had radiated positivity and strength. With his booming voice, wide grin and crushing handshake, it was hard to imagine him gone. The circumstances of his death were unsettling. Apparently he had committed suicide, but the reason was not clear yet. It cast an ugly shadow in my mind over what had generally been a positive start to my service here. With no clear news from VSO on what had happened, I tried to push it to the back of my mind and ignore the rumours that circulated about why he had done it.

There appeared to be only really one busy street in Lusaka, Cairo Road. There were embassies and hotels on back roads, but only easily accessible via taxi or long walks. One striking feature of the suburbs were two new modern shopping complexes complete with bowling alleys, fast-food outlets and cinemas. Like Shoprite, I believe they were built with South African investment. To my mind they were also a potent symbol of development in this country ; progress for the wealthy, and investment that was irrelevant to the poor, who were kept at bay by patrolling security guards. I could see that Lusaka, even with it's modern comforts, was somewhere I would tire of quickly. I moved on and bought my bus ticket for the journey to Southern Province.

After my relative isolation and boredom in the bush, Livingstone was like a paradise for me. It was a small town by western standards but had everything you needed ; a variety of restaurants, adventure activities, and lots of western travellers and volunteers from other organisations. The bus journey down was pleasingly safe too, especially compared to the nightmarish journey over the East Road through what I had dubbed the Valley of Death ; twisting roads bordered by steep cliffs. In Livingstone I settled myself down into the comfortable Jollyboys backpackers, and after a viewing of the thunderous waterfalls I waited for the other VSO's to arrive. After my isolation in the bush it was a delight to sit at a bar discussing the latest news with travellers whilst MTV blared away in the background. I was equally relieved to stuff my face with plenty of protein and a variety of food from a modern bar menu. After three months in the bush it was wondrous indeed to sink my teeth into a cheeseburger. I was not alone for long. Dan arrived, and was rather down about his placement. He had discovered a lot of theft in his workshop which was supposed to manufacture furniture for the hospital and make a profit. Despite confronting the hospital and VSO about this, it seemed little was being done. Dan said the thief was a friend of one of the VSO managers and VSO seemed unwilling to take a strong line. I had to laugh disbelievingly as Dan described how when he had confronted the foreman about book discrepancies, the accused had simply run away. A Benny Hill-like chase had ensued, with Dan eventually giving up in the heat and seeing his foreman disappear over the horizon. I myself had yet to experience corruption first-hand and still assumed the school was relatively well run. Certainly it seemed so by reputation, and definitely so compared to other schools. At least our school had relatively well kept buildings and enough desks for pupils ; other schools it seemed lacked even this. It was not unusual to hear of pupils at other schools sitting on bricks in decrepit class rooms that lacked even four walls.

Liz arrived, and was quite happy teaching English, although she found the Luangwa valley heat rather oppressive. She was soon followed by Tracey, placed near me at St. Francis Katete hospital. Tracey had experienced problems similar to Dan's. An accountant in her department had stolen at least 22 million kwacha, a vast sum by Zambian standards, and equal to about 3 thousand pounds sterling. Remarkably the thief had used the money to set up a profitable little shop in town, and no one had thought this suspicious even as money was simultaneously disappearing from the hospital coffers. Or if suspicions had been there, they were not raised in public ; another noticeably Zambian characteristic. After being caught the offender had simply been required to pay back what he could, and was dismissed from his job. But there was no additional punishment, no charges brought or police involvement. This was to be a common occurrence here ; there was rarely any penalty attached to the discovery of theft. Generally the thief just had to pay back what had been stolen. Sometimes they even retained their job or were moved to another position that did not have access to as much cash. Thus there was a positive incentive to steal ; if caught you would only break even. Not bad if the stolen money had been invested wisely and made a profit.

I'M JUST ANOTHER GUY DROWNING TODAY

Livingstone to me was a haze of mild drunkenness and adventure activities. Away from work, I let my hair down a bit. Christmas day was spent in the pool charming Scandanavian women and clutching cold beers. A call from my folks cheered me up ; the first time I had heard their voices in three months. Suddenly I had lightened up and become more comfortable with drinking and socialising again. Only one incident snapped me out of my almost constant boozy merriment. Whilst white water rafting on Boxing Day I had been catapulted out of the raft and quickly held under the water without a chance to take a deep breath. I had been thrown out in an earlier incident and had bobbed merrily alongside the boat. So I was not particularly worried when, as we slid down yet another rapid, a huge wave crashed into the front of the boat and smashed me up into the air. I remember flying through the air backwards and looking at my shoes, the boat and the people beneath me, looking up startled as I flew over their heads. Then I was under. The light quickly faded and I was sucked deep down into darkness. I tried to swim up and out, but soon realised how easily the river kept me pinned under. At first I simply held my breath and waited calmly to pop up, as the raft guides had assured me I would. A few seconds passed, but instead of rising I seemed to be sucked further down. A few more seconds still and I began to panic. My ill trained lungs began to ache. This wasn't going to plan. I was in a highly buoyant lifejacket and was supposed to bob up like a cork. I tried swimming up again, and got nowhere. I realised I was utterly helpless in the grip of the current, as if in the grip of a malevolent giant. Never mind bobbing up gently in a buoyant jacket. I couldn't even swim my way out if I wanted to. As I swirled around helplessly in black waters I began to wonder if I wasn't coming up again.

As this first occurred to me I felt initially only disbelief. I was only 28. How could I be dying now for chrissake? I'd only just started living ! Although I had never wanted kids I remember feeling a specific anger at not having had a chance to pass on my genes. This primeval instinct gave me the strength to start fighting and I frantically pushed my arms up, hoping to grab an oar that maybe someone was pushing down after seeing me go under. My jacket was bright yellow. Perhaps they could see me and were trying to reach me. But my hands did not brush against any outstretched oar, they felt only emptiness. A few seconds more again and my mind raced helplessly .What could I do ? I suddenly felt sadness and then pity for my parents, and guilt. They had devotedly raised me and seen me make it this far. Then I go and get myself killed in a stupid accident in my youth. What particularly made me think of them was the fact that only the day before had been Christmas Day. From England they had called the bar and I had spoken to them for the first time in 3 months since travelling to Zambia. Underwater, I bitterly imagined the phone call my mother would receive in England and her panicky protestation of denial that ' no, he must be ok because I only spoke to him yesterday' . Bizarrely I even found myself wondering who would make the phonecall; a Zambian or a Brit from the embassy ? VSO ? Or even a friend from the backpackers? Who would tell my mother her son was dead ? This terrible thought set me off struggling again and I fought desperately to raise myself out of the blackness. I was being pushed tantalisingly close to light and then sucked back down again. This happened again and again. The white foam would be near but then it would get quieter and suddenly muddy. Then darkness. I realised I must be trapped in some sort of whirlpool. Still my desperate efforts seemed to make no headway against the overwhelming current. Eventually I realised I wasn't going to come up, and nobody could reach me. The air in my lungs was almost done. I wasn't sure if it was getting darker or I was starting to fade out. I couldn't keep the water out much longer. It began to force it's way into my mouth.

And then something weird happened. A strange calm came over me. A rational inner voice began to reason with me. What was so unbelievable about me drowning ? People die every day, right ? And people drown every day. So what was happening here ? I had been unlucky. Many people were probably drowning even right now on planet earth at the same time as me. And I just happened to be one of those people. It wasn't so unbelievable really. Just chance and bad luck. Like many others I was being taken before my time, but it happened to a lot of people. It's not like the world had something personal against me. All you could do was accept it and let go. Thus, somehow bizarrely assured, I relaxed and began to accept the rest of the water into my mouth. I couldn't hold out any longer anyhow. I felt suddenly sleepy and my vision faded. I felt only relief that the panic and fear of death had gone. But as the darkness took me there was a sudden explosion of white foam and the next thing I knew I was back in my world. The real world, with air and noise. I looked around with wonderment at the colours and textures on the canyon wall opposite, the browns and greens in dizzying granite detail that I thought I would never see again. Goggle-eyed, I turned and stared at a kayaker I had surfaced next to. It was a big, dark haired German I had met earlier. He roared with laughter at what must have been the utterly stunned expression on my face. Leaning over, he looked me suddenly in the eye and said in a low voice ; 'Thought you weren't coming up again, eh ? don't worry – they always come up here'. I began to splutter and hack up water and he began laughing again. Looking back, I realised I was quite a way down stream from the rapid. So I had been in a swirl but had been moving forward too, like in a spiral. Much further down my boat moved on, my guide shouting at me to get my ass in gear and swim to the raft before we hit the next rapid.

At the end of the day I arrived in sombre mood at the bar, whilst the other rafters chatted excitedly and downed cold lager. I sat slightly apart from the others, limply clutching a beer that I wasn't drinking. It was a cliche but Mother nature had indeed humbled me and shown how easily she could squash me. Some people report religious revelations after near death experiences. I felt no such thing, only an awareness that my life had been given by the Earth and She could take it back easily any time she pleased. I felt no bigger than an ant that is randomly crushed by a falling stone. Whilst my fellow rafters hungrily ploughed through their evening meal I weakly sipped my beer. Finally we were taken back to the backpackers and I was curious to walk in and find people crowded around the television watching Sky News. It was Boxing Day, 2004. A massive tsnumai had hit Asia. Thousands had drowned at the same time as I had been underwater battling the Zambezi current and contemplating my death. My mood fell further when it became apparent that the considerable amount of river water I ingested had made me quite ill. I spent the next few weeks trying to fight off a virulent stomach bug , no doubt contracted from river water bacteria.

Nonetheless I left Livingstone in good spirits a few days later. It would become a regular haven for me during holidays ; a place where I could temporarily live in relative luxury and above all interact again with other westerners.   I had to wonder again however about the government's commitment to tourism. Livingstone was growing fast because of the troubles in Zimbabwe affecting it's competitor town across the falls. Yet still the roads here were atrocious. Corruption might account for some of that ; later after I left Zambia I learnt that one of the precious white rhinos in the park had been 'mysteriously' poached, despite having a 24 hour guard. But there were also more cultural and political reasons for the relative under-achievement of Livingstone. An ex-pat I chatted to in the backpackers bar told me the area was run by the political opposition and so lost out on a lot of government funding. This seemed like a little like cutting off your nose to spite your face ; surely a booming, successful Livingstone could benefit everybody. But it was an attitude I saw more and more of the longer I stayed in Zambia. I remember being stunned by a newspaper headline in which an official unashamedly told Eastern province that they could not expect help with development if they did not vote for the government. The idea that this was un-democratic didn't seem to occur to many Zambians. Then again, what lessons had they learned from the IMF and World Bank, who made Aid conditional on their own ideological bent being followed ? The IMF had imposed strict budgetary constraints that had not even allowed the Zambian government to employ enough teachers to staff their schools. In addition, though Zambia was now officially a democracy, it had for its first twenty five years of Independence been a one-party state. Democracy was still relatively new here.

2ND TERM AT CHASSA – January 2005

The transformation of Chassa after the rains was quite remarkable. What had previously looked like brush in sandy soil was now a lush, verdant green forest. Particularly striking was the huge tree at the football ground that had blossomed into a stunning mass of bright red flowers. It looked like an explosion frozen in mid-air.

I returned to an empty house. Audrey had gone. The cats, the chunky tabby `Rhino` and the small black `Fink` were not around. They had been left to their own devices during the holidays as Audrey assured me they would take care of themselves. When the pupils returned at the start of the term however so did the cats, presumably knowing the return of 600 noisy boys also heralded the return of their food-providing master. They were tick-ridden after their month fending for themselves in the bush, but otherwise looked healthy (I had left Soko as a house and pet sitter but he didn't seem to have bothered with the cats). Many quiet evenings were spent reading whilst the cats crashed in and out through a side window. They would invariably trot through the lounge with large rats clamped in their jaws. The kills would be taken to their favourite spot on the dining room floor where they were eaten tail and all. Often on a morning I would stumble bleary eyed into the dining room and suddenly jump as I accidently stuck my foot into a cold, slimy set of minature liver and kidneys that had been left behind. I soon tired of the cats shameless begging and mewling whilst I ate too. But after visiting other people's houses I had begun to appreciate my feline friends. At other houses, what sounded like huge rats scrabbled constantly inside the walls, and I'm told, raided the pantries at night. The mere presence of my cats kept rats far away. I was also told cats could deal with deadly snakes, although I found that rather unbelievable. One of the cats, the small black one called Fink, had herself almost been taken by one of the huge owls that swept round the compound at night. It must have mistaken her for a large rat, and she dodged at the last moment and just escaped its huge talons.

Despite their apparent usefulness however, cats were almost universally feared and despised by Zambians, probably because they were night creatures and associated with witchcraft. Owls too I learnt were feared because they were nocturnal and could turn their heads around. Chama, a fellow maths teacher, told me : 'It's not natural for an animal to do those things ; they are evil'. Two beautiful white baby owls nesting near my house were discovered and stoned out of their tree where they died helplessly on the ground ; this despite the fact that their breed were known ratters and snake killers. In another incident two cats had been placed at the dinner hall to deal with the rat problem. Like most half-wild cats here, they had duly done so with awesome effectiveness. As a reward they were stoned to death by the boys, who likewise out of fear would also attack strange dogs if they ever saw them.

With Audrey gone and most people keeping to themselves at night, I began to appreciate the company of the cats and the job they did. I picked the ticks off their faces and began giving them more kapenta (minnow fish caught at the nearby dam) and milk to keep them strong. I stopped Rhinos constant bullying of Fink which had left her with torn ears. I was more of a dog lover, but at Chassa dogs were little more than flea-ridden nuisances who kept me awake at night with pointless howling. Most of them were of the Rhodesian ridgeback variety ; useful guard dogs maybe, but useless against rats and snakes where terriers would have fared better. Fink was a bit difficult, biting and scratching if handled, and would probably always be half-wild. She had also likely been mistreated as a kitten because of her colour and I had caught kids throwing rocks at her before. Cats were bad enough for Zambians, but a black cat was particularly terrifying for them. If she answered the door with me, Zambians would literally shriek and jump back when they saw her. I don't know why, but she began to track me when I walked to the bar at night, waiting patiently in the nearby bush for my return. The first time she did this she scared the crap out of me before I realised it was her, but I came to look forward to it as she would be a useful snake alarm.

Rhino, despite his fearsome reputation (he became notorious for killing the Brother's cat and would regularly chase off packs of dogs) was very trusting of people and took to climbing on and perching on my shoulder in the house, usually before launching himself at gheckos on the walls. He had a comical obsession with lizard hunting which Fink did not share. Whilst Fink was a utilitarian hunter, hunting when she needed to eat, Rhino seemed determined to kill everything he could eat (including thankfully spiders and cockroaches) and to at least beat up everything he could not. One later incident in particular convinced me that both cats were worth looking after.....

FAST FORWARD : AN UNWELCOME VISITOR

It was another violent thunderstorm, the beginning of my second year of service. The rain began hammering on the tin roof and every few minutes it seemed the air itself was torn apart by a savage lightning strike and an ominous rumble of thunder. I was curled up on my sofa reading, with the cats trying to sleep on the opposite seat. Suddenly Rhino got up and stiffened, a low growl emanating from his throat. I recognised it as the warning he gave to dogs, usually before they were chased off or smashed round the face with a claw. Old Benz, the neighbours dog, had probably run over as he sometimes did to shelter on my porch. Rhino jumped down from the seat and padded to the front door. He looked back at me, but I couldn't be bothered to get up. ' Leave it Rhino, its probably just Benz' I murmured. But he persisted, seeming more agitated than usual. Maybe a new dog was in town and Rhino was particularly eager to teach it a lesson. I once seen a large dog, obviously new to the area, trot confidently into the compound and then turn right back again when it saw the world's angriest cat running straight at it. Around here the cats were king, and the dogs learnt to look suitably cowed whenever they met. Now, I sighed and heaved myself up. ' Fine, have him away then..'

I opened the door and suddenly was staring a large snake in the face. It was green, thick and muscular with a broad head. Two cold reptilian eyes seemed to regard me with disdain and contempt. It flicked its tongue out at us and remained otherwise still. The snake had slithered halfway out of the storm gutter onto the porch and was about three feet away. I had no idea what kind of a snake it was, how fast, or how poisonous it might be. I cursed myself for not learning something about snakes after being here over a year. But the snake was big and formidable looking and didn't seem particularly intimidated by me. What I wanted to do of course was close the door and hide in my house, but on the other hand I didn't want to let the snake out of my sight. It was probably attracted by the warmth of the house and looking for somewhere dry to hole up during the storm. If I let it out of my sight it might find another way in. Audrey had once told me of a black mamba that had been found in the bathroom drainpipe. And I didn't want to let it escape. With small children around, this snake would have to die one way or another. My storm-gutters were filled with the torrential rain - the snake was definitely going to haul itself further onto the porch. I looked around for my phone, (halfway through my service mobiles had arrived in Sinda) and thankfully it was right on the table behind me. I twisted around and managed to grab the phone whilst still keeping an eye on my guest. Quickly I messaged the deputy. ' Bloody big snake here. What do I do ?' Rhino suddenly jumped forward onto the porch and puffed himself up. The snake visibly tensed, muscles quivering, and emitted a low growl. I had no idea snakes could growl too! The snake began to inch itself further up the porch, and Rhino promptly gave up and ran behind me. His usually successful bluffing had been called. This was no mere dog. Muscles squirmed and rippled under a diamond skin as the snake hauled the rest of its body onto the porch. The multiple ribs wiggled and shuffled the snake forward like legs in a bag. Suddenly the snake stopped and turned to look at us again. Fink had joined us, and was crouching low, aimed directly at the snake like a missile about to fire. She slowly crept forward until the snake was only a foot and a half away. Something in her manner told the snake that unlike Rhino, this cat was deadly serious about fighting. The snake stopped and turned to focus on

Fink. For all her dimunitive size, she looked far more confident than Rhino in dealing with such a creature. I had seen her bring in giant rats that were almost as big as herself, so wondered if maybe she could pull this off after all. Both animals froze and looked poised to strike at each other. I had to wonder, had Fink done this before ? She looked like she had, but I had no idea if she could really deal with this. But for now she appeared to have halted the beast in its tracks. It was a stand-off.

I took the opportunity to dart into the kitchen and grab a 'slasher' (a kind of long machete for grass cutting) . When I came back nothing had changed. I looked doubtfully at the slasher in my hand. I had no idea how fast a striker this snake was. I didn't want to try, but I would have to intervene if Fink was attacked. Someone had told me that bush cats were immune to snake poison, but I wasn`t going to take the chance. Suddenly Rhino came trotting around the corner of the house. He had gone out the side window to move around the house and approach the snake from behind. He too froze and crouched low waiting for the snake to move. At least the odds were improved. But still no animal moved. I stood frozen as well, slasher held limply in my nervous hand, beginning to tire and feel nauseus from the continual adrenalin.

At last the deputy's boy arrived, shouting a greeting from the end of my path.

' Mr. Burke, where is it ?'

' Right here ! On the porch !' He shuffled forward until he could see the snake clearly. ' Ah, ok, I know these snakes. We will throw bricks! Can I throw these ?' he asked, picking up the bricks that lined my storm gutters.

' Yeah, ok, wait, let me get my cats out the way!' I jumped up and down, shouted, waved my hands until eventually the cats cautiously withdrew to a safe distance. The bricks began to fly, looping down in big arcs on top of the snake, but more often exploding in red powder on my porch as they missed. A big one however soon crushed the middle of the snake`s body and the serpent whipped its head around and bared huge white fangs. It shuffled further up the porch, smearing blood on the concrete as it passed. Now with room to manouevre I jumped forward and began throwing bricks too. Eventually a large one landed on its head and it appeared to stop moving. We kept throwing until the head was suitably flattened. The mouth was jarred open, fangs still exposed in a futile attempt to strike an assailant. I left it on the porch which was now smeared with blood and broken red brick. Rhino re-approached the snake cautiously and sniffed, as if to double-check that it really was dead.

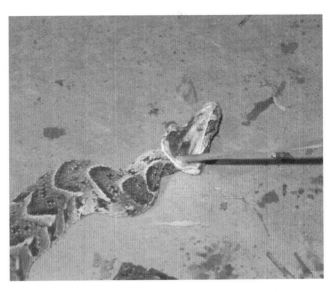

Coincidentally, later that week I received a videotape from mum. She'd video-taped a program on dangerous snakes in Africa. I recognised my porch friend as a puff-adder. Slow moving when it came to getting around, but deadly fast when it came to striking. It injected a flesh destroying poison that literally disintegrated tissue and usually resulted in the affected limb being amputated. If you were unlucky enough to be bitten on the torso then you were usually dead. I was very glad I hadn't tried to tackle it by hand. Later I heard that A.G Zulu's daughter had been bitten by one of these snakes and had to have a finger amputated, as the muscle and skin had wasted away. The bitten finger had literally shrivelled away to become useless bone and skin. It was unnerving to hear that this young lady had been bitten in her bedroom ; the snake must have crawled in there to get warm and struck when disturbed. Unlike other snakes that might try and get away from humans, the puff adder's defence was to lie still and rely on camouflage. Many people were thus bitten by this type of snake after literally accidently stepping on it. Stacy (another volunteer I met later) had met this type of snake before at a PeaceCorps hut. Again a cat had alerted them to the presence of the snake, and they had then managed to kill it with sticks and rocks.

It seemed it was snake season. A few weeks later, Rhino again jumped out of his chair and began growling. I heard some sort of hissing sound, like a sprinkler passing by the front porch. I opened the front door and saw a thin green snake race past me and then head for the tree as it realised it was being chased by a cat. In a moment it had whipped itself around the trunk, slithered into the tree-top and was almost flying around in the branches overhead. Rhino quickly relinquished the pursuit and I was left frantically trying to keep track of the serpent as it camouflaged itself amongst the leaves. I recognised it from the video as a boomslang, extremely poisonous although not aggressive. I still wanted it dead. Mumba was passing and I hailed him. He joined me and we struggled to hit the snake with bricks we threw. We soon lost sight of it however. That did not deter a large group of school boys joining us and lobbing bricks completely randomly into the tree in all directions. In the ensuing chaos we all ended up dodging bricks thrown by each other. And yet no one could see the snake now, or would do again. Later I even ventured into the branches myself with a slasher and cut back the foilage in a vain attempt to find the snake. But it was to no avail. Somehow the sneaky serpent had evaded us.

Apparently a rock python had once taken up residence in the large log on my front yard, but Mr Phiri had managed to burn it out. They were not poisonous, but could bite like a bear. I considered myself lucky in fact never to have met a spitting cobra or mamba. The spitting cobra was notorious for spitting into people's eyes and blinding them. Like the puff adder it tended to attack only when disturbed. The mamba however was the most feared snake around here. It could stand up and strike a man in the face. It also was rumoured to be fast enough to chase a running man, and aggressive enough to do so. The locals were convinced that mambas were territorial and would not even tolerate people in their general vicinity. I wasn't sure of this, but I knew the mamba was an aggressive multiple striker ; if you were unlucky enough to meet one it would bite you several times to just make sure the job was done. J.L Banda related how he had been driving the school truck one day when a mamba had crossed the road in front of him. A villager cycling near him had been so terrified he had swerved straight into the bush and wiped out. I didn't really know if cats could handle snakes like these, but at least they would sense them and alert me to their presence.

There was no doubt the half wild African cats were different to the domesticated cats that western volunteers were used to. They even looked different with larger ears and claws, and were superb ratters ; often catching rats almost as big as themselves. With the exception of a few such as Rhino, they were usually wary of people and seemed very capable of looking after themselves. A U.S Peace Corps volunteer told me of a slain black mamba that her cat dropped at her hut doorstep. Rhino was so confrontational with other animals I wondered how he had survived so long. The Brothers larger but more domesticated cat could not survive repeated battles with him. One night it dragged itself into the Residence and died soon after of its wounds. Apparently this time Rhino had inflicted a particularly nasty wound on its testicles. I regularly saw Rhino chase off packs off dog from my rubbish pit. One dog that decided to face up to him was smashed so hard round the face the sound of the blow echoed off the house opposite. The dog swayed unsteadily on its feet, saw Rhinos shoulder tense for another slap, and decided to leg it. Fink then came flying around the corner, clawing at the terrified dogs back legs as it fled. The dogs here were nothing other than irritating, and I was now a firm convert to cats, at least in this environment.

A Zimbabwean I met in Lusaka told me his cat had once been caught unawares whilst drinking from a water pool at the bottom of the garden. Some elephants had quietly emerged from the bush (they could be unnervingly stealthy when they knew humans were nearby) to also take water. Looking up, the cat had been unsure of how to retreat, and also being viciously territorial had decided to go ahead and charge. The bewildered elephants had actually retreated in confusion, not quite sure of how to deal with such an unusual little attacker. This particularly legendary pet had eventually died whilst trying to battle a large rock python ; one of the few beasts quick and strong enough to kill a bush cat.

PARASITES HITCHING A RIDE

Soon after the second term started I had began to feel unusually tired. My timetable on many days that term was concentrated in the morning and finished at 11.35 after a 7.00 start. Soon after arriving home I would already be asleep before noon. Then again after dinner I might fall asleep again, I was that tired. At first I attributed the symptoms to my struggling with a hot climate and a poor diet based around white bread. It was some weeks later however that I noticed that as well as exhaustion I had to pee all the time. It got so ridiculous that I would pee before going to bed and then have to get up ten minutes later and pee more. Then my sleep would be broken several times during the night by having to pee again. After a few weeks of this, and feeling utterly exhausted, I decided I had to get to the clinic and get some sort of test. I couldn't find anything in the medical book, and doubted I had prostate cancer aged 28. I knew that Lake Malawi had shistoseimiasis (otherwise known as bilharzia), a bladder parasite that flourished in still water where snails (the carriers) lived on reeds. We however had been in an area with quite a vigorous tide ; indeed it had felt like being on an ocean coast rather than a lake. Besides which my medical book listed bilharzia's symptoms as pain in the bladder and blood in the urine. I didn't appear to have that, just the tiredness and the constant to urinate. Yet maybe something else could be deduced from my urine.

Down at the clinic I soon found out that I did indeed have bilharzia. This charming parasite had burrowed through my skin, nestled in my bladder and was now busy producing millions of eggs that provoked my constant urge to urinate. Luckily the treatment was a simple course of drugs that could be bought at the mini chemists in Sinda. The first course seemed to do nothing and I was advised that as I was a big fat white man I would need more. Several liberal doses later I was at last restored to health. I had to marvel that the treatment was relatively new. I shuddered at the thought of Zambians before that just miserably putting up with constant exhaustion and urination. If left untreated the parasite eventually caused bladder cancer. Some degree of immunity apparently existed amongst the natives, but I saw plenty of our boys being sent to the clinic having being infected back home. I learnt my lesson and never swam in an African lake again.

CONVERSATIONS WITH COLLEAGUES....

After months of not much else but reading I had decided I needed a VCR and TV if I was to last two years here. It turned out almost all the teachers had them, and this was often how they occupied their evenings. I figured it would be a wiser use of my time than boozing at the bar and getting bitten by malarial mosquitos. I used the last of my money in my British account and bought a small TV and VCR. I had brought them back from Lusaka after Christmas, but as of yet had no videos and couldn't get TV reception. Evenings were still spent marking books, reading, and a beer at the bar. I planned to ask my mum to send my old videotapes as they'd be obsolete anyway when I returned to England. In the meantime I had moved into Audrey's old room at the back with the one comfortable armchair. As ancient Chicago blues wailed out of my tinny little stereo, I spent many an evening plowing through the heavy classics Audrey had left behind ; Crime and Punishment, War and Peace, and a multitude of smaller classics. I also tried my hand at writing, something I'd always wanted to do, but had only notebooks and really wanted a laptop. There were still weekends for the bar, and I often strolled there at dusk for just a couple of beers and a chat with those who were passing through.

Most of my conversations with Zambians were relatively innocent and shallow, as I was asked the usual questions ' Do you pray ? Do you like nsima ? Are you married ? ' . Most of the time I batted away the religious questions by confirming I was a baptised Anglican. People seemed very relieved to hear this ; at least my soul had a chance. It seemed to not like nsima was an affront to Zambians and so despite my dislike of the soggy, flatulence-inducing paste, I usually told them I did indeed like their national dish. The fact that I was 28 and still unmarried seemed to puzzle many Zambians, and they seemed to regard this as a very strange characteristic of mzungus.

At the bar however, and as time passed, I had the chance to get to know some Zambians, and particularly the teachers, much better. Here we might get past the usual polite formalities and discuss topics a bit more controversial....

WOMEN, CHILDREN AND HUMAN RIGHTS

I now began to find out more about my colleagues. There were some odd conversations indeed at the bar. One for example revealed their extremely sexist attitudes. For starters it seemed to me that the women generally did all the work around here, while the men took things very easy indeed. Perhaps not a lot new there. But where they did shock me was in their attitude to domestic violence. Despite where we were, I had expected, perhaps naively, that they would not harbour these sentiments. Zambians generally had a calm and peaceful manner to them which did not always belie what they were capable of. They thought it perfectly acceptable for instance to beat their wives. ' What choice do you have ?' Chama said , shocking me, as he always seemed so gentle and jovial. With his docile smile, beer-belly and big dome head he was like a Zambian Homer Simpson, albeit an intelligent version.
' If your wife disobeys you..' He continued : 'She must be disciplined as you would a child' . His usually jolly fat face suddenly hardened and all of a sudden Chama looked more like Idi Amin. The attitude to beating of course extended to children. Even the more modern Sondashi and gentle J.Banda asserted : ' An African child is different. They only understand force'.

Likewise my colleagues seemed to have rather casual attitudes to promiscuity, justified by bizarre traditional beliefs. S.Banda nodded comically to his groin, and then looked up at me with his trademark enormous grin : ' Ah, this thing - how can I keep it alive if I feed it only one meat?. I need to be hammering at least a few women to keep this thing strong'. It was difficult to hear such things. His wife, not being capable of having children, had nonetheless taken in several of her husband's relatives and cared for them as if they were her own. That was the problem with my colleagues. They were such pigs to their women but at the same time in other ways so damn likable.

Later at a workshop in Petauke I was cornered in the bar by an unusually fat Zambian who introduced himself as Moses Kajani, a local farmer. He questioned me keenly on western attitudes to women. 'You think Zambia and its government are wrong in the way they treat women?
' Well they're trying to equalise things now , aren't they ?' I replied.
' And what about democracy and human rights ? This government is very behind isn't it ?' Something in his manner was deliberately provocative, so I politely told him that VSO forbade its volunteers to meddle in politics. He grunted with satisfaction at this, and I excused myself to get an early night.

The very same man turned up at school months later to check up on a nephew who was a pupil there. Sondashi was the teacher on duty that they met in the staff-room. There was an unusual tension in the air as the men departed and Sondashi and I watched them trudge back to their vehicle. ' I know that guy' I prompted Sondashi ' A farmer from Petauke, right ?' Sondashi laughed dryly, almost bitterly at this. :' No, no my friend, that is no farmer. They are Intelligence. They know my name. They asked about my father. '
' Your father was in Intelligence ?`
' No, he was in politics once. And my cousin too. But my cousin was murdered.' I stood in awkward silence as we watched the truck pull away.

It turned out we had our own local intelligence officer, though his manner was a great deal less sinister than Kajani's. Kalonde was a drinking companion of S.Banda, and this animated chubby character held the local post 'Office of the President'. When I asked about the function of this office I received vague replies to the effect that it was somehow related to police work. Eventually Sichande told me the job involved monitoring the mood of the people and keeping an eye out for anything that was deemed unpatriotic, rather like the post of a political Commissar in old communist Russia. The boundaries between State and ruling political party were very blurred here to say the least. Kalonde was always personally genial however. He was another Bemba, well educated and witty, and seemed to appreciate that VSO motives here were relatively innocent. I came to nickname him The Brows after his humorous eyebrow raises when talking about women and sex, something he did far more comfortably than most Zambians. Maybe he imagined he looked like Roger Moore's Bond when he did this, but the effect was actually more like Groucho Marx.

WITCHCRAFT AND 'JU-JU'

I was rather stunned at the teacher's attitudes to witchcraft. All of them believed in it totally. It didn't matter if they were science teachers or the deputy head. Stories of witchdoctors crashing naked on people's roofs after magic flights gone wrong were accepted at face value. Witchcraft could be employed to make you rich (this assertion in a country that remained desperately poor didn't seem to strike anyone as odd) or make someone fall in love with you. On a more sinister level witchcraft could be used to harm enemies and when mixed with satanism could involve ritual murder.

Openly, there was a traditional culture of beliefs that involved ' Nyau' dancing and drums etc that seemed quite innocent. It was usual for me to drift off to sleep at night hearing village drums in the distance. Nyau dancing involved the participants dressing up in masks and dancing as if possessed by animal spirits. It was largely harmless and often paraded in the open as entertainment, although I later heard of a frenzied dancer who had bitten a child's ear off. In a later conversation with some Chassa boys, I was also told that anyone who interrupted a Nyau dance at night-time would grow a penis on their head, but at the same time that witchcraft did not really work on mzungus. I decided not to chance it.

There were also traditional healers and medicine men. I once met a man I suppose I would call a shamen. He told me that after meeting a patient he went to sleep and dreamed. In his dream he walked through the bush and was guided to a particular plant. He would then wake and remember his route in the dream to guide him to the required plant, which he alleged, was usually successful in treating his patients.

Beneath the surface at a slightly more secretive level lay the appeals for good luck and wealth that one needed to ask a respected witchdoctor to organise. This could have comic results apparently, as for instance in the story of a Katete man who had danced on a grave and prayed for a Canter (small Toyota lorry). Apparently the man had been less than clear in his pronunciation and in the morning he found on his doorstep - a crate of Fanta (soft drinks).

Then unfortunately there was the bad 'Ju-Ju' – witchcraft that was employed to harm enemies (such as curses that caused illness) . An example of this was when I walked in the staffroom one morning and overheard Masina saying he was going to get his gun. ' Whats going on ?' . I was understandably nervous, as Massina was part of a local defence force that had big trouble in the eighties with rebels crossing from nearby Mozambique, raping and pillaging. Mumba told me how one of their more charming actions had been to machine gun a minibus full of civilians until it blew up. Mozambiquans tended to be feared by the Zambians as hard people. I heard a story of a couple of Zambians who had stolen some cattle from Mozambique . The determined Mozambiquans had tracked down the thieves, sliced the soles of their feet off, and made them walk the cattle all the way back to Mozambique. Eventually the Zambian army had to establish a permanent presence in the area to deter rebel raiders. Luckily I learned that particular trouble had long since gone. ' One of our boys' Massina now explained ' is being haunted by an uncle who does Ju-Ju. He is appearing in the dreams of the boy and threatening him, because the boy left his cousin and came to Chassa. Ah, me, I will go and threaten that guy with my gun if he doesn't stop.' I studied his face closely. Despite his usual jovial appearance it was clear that he was absolutely serious.

I happened to talk later with the Headmaster about this issue and he explained that he himself was protected from Juju because of his faith in Jesus Christ. It was not a question of Christians here not believing in magic. They just believed Christianity was stronger magic. The Head proudly related how a workman the previous year had been fired for stealing. His colleagues had dared not confront him as he was a dabbler in Ju-Ju, but Michael had fired the man knowing that Jesus was more powerful than witchcraft. I thought this was a very revealing comment about Christianity in Zambia. It revealed that some at least may have been motivated into it less out of moral inclination, and more out of fear and perceived gains in power.

There were also the cases of demonic possession that had a Christian element to them. Liz related to me how several girls had been 'possessed' at her school. Liz had been amazed at how all the teachers had accepted that this was indeed some sort of genuine witchcraft. She was relieved when the head of science came to see the girls ' spasming' and said to Liz : ' this isn't witchcraft' . Until he then added : ' No, this is - pure Satanism !'. Oddly enough, when a pastor in the girl's presence recommended that the demon be beaten out of her with a heavy stick, the girl swiftly recovered before the beating could be started.

Then there was the Satanism mixed with 'muti' that could involve ritual murder. The latter was depressingly real, as I found out when a young boy was murdered in nearby Katete. He had gone at dusk to collect water from a pond and never returned. He was found later floating in the pond with his throat slit and genitals cut off. The police were as terrified as everybody else and so it was up to an uncle of the boy to identify the boy and even remove the body. I doubted the story, until I travelled to visit Liz in Katete soon afterwards. 'No, I'm afraid it's real' She affirmed. Tight lipped, she flicked her head towards one of her workers who was strolling past the garden. ' That's the uncle right there'.

Occasionally rumours of witchcraft could result in a hysteria which produced farcical consequences. One lunchtime as I jogged around the track I had been bemused to see three small children I didn't recognise running away from me. I had my shirt off, and was grimacing and turning pink in the heat. I didn't think anything of it until later in the evening when I strolled up to the bar. I found Sarah rocking herself in near hysterical laughter. She practically collapsed when she saw me. Eventually Sarah managed to get control of herself and explain what she was laughing about. Massina and the cops were there, and asked me first if indeed I had been running around the track. They seemed relieved when I confirmed that I indeed had been. Unbeknownst to me, these were kids who had been walking in from the bush, not the Chassa community. As I was the first white man they had ever seen, they had, it turned out, actually been fleeing in genuine terror. I suppose seeing me, huge, tattooed, and rapidly reddening, bearing down upon them must have been quite alarming for the kids. As they fled, one of them had fallen and hurt her leg. They had reported the incident. According to them I had been chasing them down, obviously with the explicit purpose of catching them and eating them (Specifically their hearts of course).

Rumours were currently abounding in the community of Tanzanians who were abducting Zambians and eating their organs. Through the grapevine, the story of my attempted cannibalism had quickly reached the ears of a volatile Para-legal in Sinda. He had stormed up to the school demanding my immediate arrest and detention. The puzzled Sgt. Sichande had taken the Para-legal to the track, and figured out what must have happened ; Sichande knew I ran round the track at lunchtimes. Eventually the enraged accuser was convinced it had been a misunderstanding. When Sarah had heard of the story she had apparently laughed for about three hours straight.

`IF YOU ARE NOT INFECTED THEN YOU ARE AFFECTED`

Rather more damaging than witchcraft were the popular beliefs about HIV/AID's, which seemed to prevail despite the correct information being widely available and pumped into government workers with regular donor-funded workshops. I vividly remember S.Banda turning to me discreetly at the later Nchwala ceremony (a regional celebration of the harvest where a bull was slaughtered in Zulu-like style), as a drunken teacher from another school babbled to me. ' This guy you're talking to' S.Banda whispered in my ear, as the drunk was momentarily distracted ;
' his wife was sleeping with Nkhoma in the holidays'. Nkhoma's wife had died young and was widely believed to have been HIV positive. Nkhoma still seemed healthy himself, but was likewise widely believed to be positive.
' So,.... this guys... dead , basically ?' I responded. Banda grinned ruefully ;
' he's a.... *ghost'*. The guy didn't look too healthy to me, it was true ; pasty and thin. I guess being wasted on chibuku didn't help. And yet surely he was not totally beyond help. ' But he still can get ARV's (Anti Retro Viral Therapy) , live for twenty years maybe ' I asserted. ' maybe someone can talk to him'
' NO, no...' laughed Banda bitterly ; ' once you know you're positive, you 're gone !'. Banda and the others really seemed to believe that having your status confirmed was the beginning of the end ; it was better to struggle on in denial. A year later I heard the young teacher had indeed died. He was in his twenties. He had died a classic HIV death ; TB had weakened him, and then he had fallen prey to a sudden attack of meningitis. He had left several young children, like so many others. And it was utterly preventable. But like many others he had lived in denial until the very end, dying young rather than see his children grow up.

During my time at Chassa I watched another teacher wasting away before my eyes, becoming so painfully thin and slow moving that he started to resemble a stick insect. His first wife had died some years ago, rumoured to be another HIV casualty. And yet like so many others he refused to accept the likelihood that he was infected. Instead he married again and even had a child by his new wife. Almost predictably the child was always sickly. The poor young boy endured four years of almost constant illness, before one holiday I returned to school and learned he had finally been consigned to a tiny grave. And yet his father hung on. By the time I left a year later he seemed to have stabilised his weight and his bouts of illness were less frequent. Perhaps he had finally been tested and had then started ARV's. I remember once when he was hospitalised for some time with a particularly bad bout of malaria, and the rumours had abounded that this would finally be his end. But afterwards he seemed to stabilise and recover. Perhaps this close brush with death had finally convinced him to get tested and access ARVs. It was almost certainly this, rather than the death of his child.

I always wondered how many of my colleagues had the time bomb in their body and had passed it on to their wives. Sichande, the drunken womaniser, looked a likely candidate and I always found it difficult to look his wife in the eye. She was so charming and friendly when she greeted me, and yet in the back of my mind I was always thinking ` your husband has probably given you Aids`. Both Sichande and Max had doubted my claims that condoms were reliable, often with bizarre logic. Max told me he had once 'tested' a condom by filling it with water and hanging it from a tree ; after three days it had begun to leak. My assertion that this was not really a realistic replication of the sexual act was treated sceptically.

Many others left the testing and ARV treatment so late that it could not benefit them, and in their severely weakened state they even suffered a toxic response to the medicine which hastened their death. Hence the belief spread that ARVs merely poisoned a person and killed them quicker. Myths like these gave more ammunition to a masculine culture which looked to find excuses for avoiding testing. Testing would threaten to end a man's sex life and end the possibility of future children which was so crucial to his status and identity. The confidentiality of such testing was also commonly questioned, as was the distribution of ARVs. It was not uncommon to hear of people travelling to Lusaka to get their ARVs rather than risk their neighbours finding out.

There was some evidence that Zambia had recently halted the spread of the disease as a percentage of the population (it now hovered around 17 %), but the increasing emphasis on abstinence as opposed to a comprehensive ABC approach (Abstain, Be faithful, Condoms) was likely to eradicate any recent gains made. On the other hand the increasing availability of ARV's might eventually compensate for this by binding more people into a safer lifestyle. Crucially, ARV treatment could also halt mother-to-child transmission of the disease. Routine testing during pregnancy was at least detecting and resulting in the treatment of a significant percentage of the population.

In the meantime the disease was visibly affecting those in all walks of life. It was common to see people with huge growths on their side of their necks which I'm told was the result of blocked lymph nodes. Skin disorders were also a common sign of HIV infection. A grim tour around Katete hospital with Dan and a doctor revealed that about 70 % of admissions were related to HIV, and putting an intolerable strain on an already degraded health service. A 17% rate in the general population reflected a startling high rate amongst the sexually active, and if you were not infected then your life was likely to have been affected by Aids. The most visible sign of this was the veritable deluge of orphans that seemed to swamp the country. As many as a quarter of our pupils were orphans, or had lost at least one parent. And every teacher in the compound seemed to be looking after nephew and nieces who had been plunged into the same situation. Because AIDS often killed people in their thirties, it was the most productive people that were so often lost. Sometimes it seemed they had shrunk to a minority and Zambia was a nation of orphans and grandparents. The epidemic seemed to be largely driven by a generation of men who refused to change their behaviour, despite their comrades falling all amongst them. Sometimes you would even hear of infected men who were determined to take as many people as possible with them, sleeping around and inflicting revenge on the women in general who represented their downfall.

Attitudes to man-hood were slowly changing, but even educated teachers took pride in the number of children they could produce. A.G Zulu had produced a staggering 15 children and seemed damned proud of it. This of course produced tremendous problems when it came to paying secondary school fees. In the wider context of society the problems were obvious but Zambians would not accept that overpopulation caused poverty. They would invariably argue : ' You need many children in case some die. And we need children to look after us in old age'. I tried to argue that children tended to die precisely because there were too many ; overpopulation lowered living standards and increased poverty. But this argument, probably too broad and abstract in its thrust, was never accepted. I did see a few individuals limit their families which was apparently a new development amongst some. Sichande for instance told me he would have no more then 3 children because of the cost of educating them. Not so for A.G. Every term A.G Zulu would borrow substantial amounts of money off of me to help with the squeeze. It was tempting to rebuff him with the retort that if he couldn't afford the education why did he have so many children ? In VSO training we had solemnly agreed that giving in to these demands would only encourage dependency and the view that VSO volunteers were rich. In practice however we all found it rather difficult to refuse such requests. Our hosts would never believe our protestations that we were paid the same as them. Even if they did, they suspected we had brought hoards of dollars from home. In my more cynical moments I wondered what some of the teachers would do without VSO's being about. The most useful thing we did was probably offer a reliable loan service rather than provide any sustainable development in education.

JL BANDA AND THE ANTI AIDS CLUB

Almost alone amongst the teachers JL Banda was the one who strove continually to battle myths and prejudices about HIV/AIDS. He was the patron of the Anti Aids Club, one of the clubs attended by boys on a Wednesday afternoon. I joined him there in the first term, until later A.G ordered me to run maths club (although no other maths teachers joined me). JL Banda was an authoritative but friendly man, and if Sondashi became like a brother to me I came to regard JL as something of a father figure or' uncle' as a Zambian would call a trusted older colleague. At anti Aids club JL would gently probe the boys about their experiences (many of the attendees were probably Aids orphans) and teach in coded terms about the facts of life (talk I found unintentionally funny – phrases such as ' tasting buns' etc) until the boys became comfortable with more frank sexual terms. There was one major problem of course with Anti Aids club ; it had about 40 attendees because it competed with other clubs on a Wednesday afternoon. JL Banda had pushed repeatedly for some kind of whole school program but the administration didn't seem particularly bothered and offered little co-operation and no money. I raised it numerous times in staff meetings and it was always casually shrugged off. It was a problem that I thought about often, and whilst I made efforts to resolve it, I never satisfactorily solved it. We desperately needed to educate all the boys at the school on this issue.

The ignorance amongst the majority who did not attend the Anti-Aids clubs was worrying. A staggering 25 % of our boys had both lost parents to Aids (we assumed ; unexplained deaths at a young age were usually HIV related) and the general ignorance about sexual matters was stunning. Despite national policies that decreed all basic schools should be taught Sex Ed, it was rarely, if ever done. A chat with my grade 8's revealed that none of them had been taught the facts of life in basic school. It took several hours of registration time over several weeks to clear up the many misconceptions they had. One boy had heard that drinking the blood of white mice cured Aids. The most damaging myth of course was that having unprotected sex with a virgin cured Aids. Such ideas could fuel the child abuse that was apparently quite common. It was a sobering thought to imagine how many young girls had been effectively murdered this way.

The effect of the general lack of sex education and church preaching against condoms showed itself regularly ; in this pious Christian nation the amount of young single women who had children from 'mistakes' in their youth was shocking. A notable example occurred when our Protestant Prefect impregnated the girl who worked at the Brothers Tuck Shop. This led to her ignominious departure back to the villages in an ox-cart.

Rather than reflect on what kind of atmosphere had allowed this to happen in the first place, the admin remained unconcerned about sex education and regarded incidents like this as inevitable human mistakes.

MAIZE, MAIZE, MAIZE

As the seasons passed I began to learn more about the general situation in eastern province. In the bush the villagers seemed to do little else but think about their maize supply. Their lives revolved around the preparation, planting and harvesting of this esteemed crop. The cobs were harvested and usually ground into the flour that made nsima paste. Nothing made villagers happier than tall green maize stalks in a good season. However I was surprised to learn that it was neither drought resistant nor a traditional Zambian crop. It was a crop that was sensitive to the heavy Zambian rains ; every other year it failed due to either flooded fields or drought. It would rot on the vine in a very wet season, or wither to a useless yellow husk in a dry season. Or there would be complications with the timing of planting of the crops. Farmers would often be caught out by early planting, having been deceived by early showers that they mistakenly believed heralded the main rains. They would then plant early and then watch desperately as their fields dried, precious seeds died, and the main steady rains followed some weeks later. Or the reverse would happen ; they would hold back on planting having been caught out the previous year by late rains, only to find that this was the main rains and they had caught it too late. There seemed to be no attempt at any sort of irrigation ; presumably it was expensive and thus only the large commercial fields such as those owned by Sable could afford such systems.

Even a simple drip system using hose pipes seemed beyond the reach of most of the population. I presume borehole water was too scarce to use on crops ; I never saw it used on maize even in the driest conditions. And what of the other crops ? I learned that the traditional native crops had been sorghum and millet ; both drought resistant and reliably farmed for generations by the ancestors of today's Zambians. Perhaps maize was another poisonous colonial legacy ; a crop introduced by the British which now had a strange reverence and status attached to it.

Nsima was regarded by most as the only real food, much like bread had been in eighteenth century England, or rice in Asia. Although maize was refined and made into a paste that was little more than starch, most Zambians regarded it a kind of wonder food. They rejected any notion that it was devoid of vitamins, minerals, fibre and complete protein (as of course it was in its usual refined form). A government minister who had in the 1990's advised Zambians to reduce their reliance on the crop had been mercilessly pilloried and forced out of office. Likewise when I pointed out that the Chinese seemed to be doing pretty well on rice my comments were fobbed off with a belief that Zambians were physically different ; they needed maize to function normally. This particular retort came from a science and agriculture teacher. Not only that, Zambians were immensely proud of maize as their national dish, like an addict who can't see the damage his fix does . After being asked what Church you worshipped at, a Zambian would usually ask you ' Do you like nsima ?'

The over-reliance on nsima probably explained the very short stature and slight physiques of most rural Zambians, despite their strong Zulu heritage. Though the easterner's language was close to cewa – the language of Malawi - their culture was largely of the Zulu-like tribes (such as Ngoni, and in Zimbabwe the Ndebele) that had been forced out of South Africa by the expansion of Shaka's kingdom . There were some good sources of protein such as groundnuts (similar to peanuts) but their value seemed little appreciated. My doctor friends at St. Francis hospital in Katete assured me that constipation was a common complaint (no doubt a result of over-reliance on refined nsima) amongst various other stomach disorders such as ulcers. It was even common for Zambians to vomit whilst travelling and then explain ' I ate nsima before travelling – it always makes me vomit whilst travelling' When I incredulously asked why then did they eat it before travelling I received quizzical replies; it was nsima ; how can you *not* eat it ?

To my mind the obsession with the crop was also holding back the entire development of Eastern province. Some sort of agricultural revolution was necessary for the place to jump forward. Europe had an agricultural revolution in the eighteenth century before it had leaped forward with the industrial revolution. Any pre-industrial society needed to either have more than enough food so they could have hands free for other work, or sell surplus food for extra income. Although the area farmed tobacco and cotton, these were largely dominated by the rich (such as South African immigrants) who invested the profits elsewhere. Year after year the province struggled by as every other season the maize crop seemed to fail. Fortunately it rarely seemed to fail two years in a row, so a bumper harvest one year could tide people over in the next difficult year - either through direct food storage or some capital savings they had made on the previous harvest. Yet this two-year cycle seemed to trap the province in a vicious circle – one which the mentality of the people perpetuated. I remember Sarah and I having a circular argument with the police at the bar about the obsession with maize. After hearing our criticism of the crop and my advocacy of alternatives such as millet, the cops responded :' but maize is the staple food of Zambia'. ' yeah I KNOW ' I exhorted ' THAT'S the problem'. This didn't seem to register and I got the same reply ' but maize is the staple food of Zambia' as if it was something that was eternally fixed. To be fair to Max and Sichande they were drunk as usual ; heads bobbing marionette-like on their shoulders. Even when I asked Nazir of Sable about why he didn't diversify, he explained there was no demand for other crops so the market was trapped in a catch 22. As for improving the reliability of the maize yield it seemed a futile exercise. The crop required a lot of fertiliser as it drained a lot of nitrogen and other minerals from the soil. Most of this fertiliser was of course provided by US AID at subsidised prices and so the economy had a largely subsistence existence, held firmly in place by reliance on outside help. Worse, the donors gave out hybrid seeds which produced a superior yield but could not reproduce. Hence the farmers were completely dependent on getting seeds again off donors the next year. There was also the corruption of ' relief maize'; the government and large buyers would buy extra maize at the beginning of the season and then if things got desperate it would return in dribs and drabs at extortionate prices whilst rumours of large sales to foreign consumers circulated. With a population increasing despite the high mortality rates, the environmental consequences looked grim too. Forests were fast disappearing to make way for fields of nitrogen draining maize.

Whatever the causes, whatever the implications, the immediate results were there for me to see. Round the back of the dinner hall gaunt villagers would queue pathetically for the binned leftovers of the nsima and beans that the boys would leave behind. It would come out in filthy wheelbarrows and they would paw through it eagerly ; skinny, broken-toothed women and small, large headed children dressed in faded charity hand me downs. As I rode out on the school truck one day we turned back to the dinner hall to collect the local electrician. His usual broad handsome face was agitated by the stricken villagers hovering around the backs of the kitchens . The glum expression contrasted weirdly with his comically bright yellow overalls. ' This never used to happen' he complained ' now people are using maize as both a cash crop and food. They sell too much maize to buy soap, other things, send their children to school, and then late in the year..... this happens.'. ' So its getting worse every year ?' I shouted to him as we chugged and bumped along the track. He nodded sadly. And the predictions for climate change were that sub-Saharan Africa would be one of the worse affected areas in the future ; increasing drought alternating with floods. Combined with population increase, this was a situation that was going to get worse, even with increased aid. There was too much structural change that needed effecting and not enough time. Obviously the subsistence farmers needed education on diversification and natural methods of soil renewal if they were to stand a chance. Oil and gas based fertilisers would only get more expensive in the future and the natural fertility of the soil was being degraded. Yet agricultural science was not taught in primary schools and only a few secondary schools, despite the claim of the government that improving agriculture was one its priorities along with promotion of tourism. There was one `agricultural extension` officer per district who had the huge task of getting around literally hundreds of villages to consult on agricultural matters. And if even if they could do that, how to wean people off their emotional attachment to maize? Peace Corps volunteers were here and there trying to teach by example – showing how crop rotation and nitrogen fixing plants could replenish the soil, but convincing Zambians that other foods were just as good as maize seemed impossible. When I talked of this subject with Brother Chiza, he merely suggested that the villagers were lazy. I rather doubted this and had trouble seeing how people could not be bothered to even grow food. Later I would reflect that Chiza`s comments were perhaps more revealing of his own ignorance and unconcern for the rural poor.

I later heard in fact that other provinces had begun to improve, but Eastern province like its neighbour Malawi remained blindly fixated on maize. In northern province the Bembas grew cassava and the Easterners mocked them for this, even as they themselves starved and the Bembas lived comfortably with a drought resistant crop. Likewise I was told that in western province the Lozi people grew millet and sorghum and had a relatively reliable food supply. Articles began to appear more regularly in the papers advocating more crop diversification and I would staple them up in the staffroom. But in eastern province even Banda the agricultural teacher would argue that Zambians needed nsima to survive, as surely as if it was water.

Later when I visited a Peace Corps friend even deeper in the bush, he related how his villagers lived an almost purely seasonal existence ; as one food came to fruition they would live almost solely on that until the next food became available. There were times he said when people staggered around like zombies eating one small meal a day if they were lucky. Hence his work on vegetable gardens for both nutrition and income generation. The Peace Corps were working small miracles with such projects but every village could have done with such volunteers. There were maybe 8 at any one time doing such agricultural work in a vast province that was the size of England.

Meanwhile life continued on at Chassa in its usual routine of births and deaths, although there were the odd comedy incidents...

MONKEYS, HIPPOS AND MACHINE GUNS

A hippo had been spotted nearby at the Sable dam. It was causing some excitement, as a few years ago a hippo had killed a local boy. The story was that after the animal destroyed a farmer's crops, the farmer had procured a shotgun and had camped out at the dam where the hippo was hanging around. He had a son with him who was also old enough to handle the gun. The farmer was no fool, and told his boy that the gun was only capable of killing a hippo with a close head-shot. At some stage the boy had been briefly left alone with the gun and it was tragically at this point that the hippo reappeared. The boy had shot from too far and merely wounded the animal. Enraged, it chased him down and killed him. Despite their appearance it seemed that hippos were amazingly fast and aggressive. The huge teeth were not for show ; they regularly battled and killed each other (most males had terrible scars on their sides) and had been known to kill lions with one bite. .This particular   animal was finished later by local cops armed with their usual AK-47's.

Now at the bar Sichande outlined his drunken strategy for dealing with the new hippo. ' Those things are protected Burke !' he propounded ' But if it makes a nuisance, yah, then - I can get authorisation to kill it. We will go together Burke.'
'Sorry?' My eyebrows raised in alarm ; I hadn't been listening properly and was alarmed to hear 'We'.
' Er, those things are pretty dangerous Joe, I , er, think I'll let you handle it !'
'No Burke, it's ok' he continued ' We just get close, and..... BRRRRRR!' he jumped up, pointing with his fingers and imitating machine gun fire. ' I get close and fire right into it's mouth with an AK. And the meat will be good. Yes, so much meat, and tennnnder. Mmmm.'

I sat silently and sweated. The thought of standing next to a drunken Sichande as he belched and waited for the right head shot in front of a charging hippo was un-nerving. I hoped the call would never come for me to accompany Sichande on a hippo-hunting mission. Thankfully it never did. This hippo stayed a while and then moved on without bothering anyone.

I did however have a real experience of hunting hippo a year later in Livingstone. My parents were visiting and we were in the bar at Fawlty towers, the night before their day trip to Chobe park in Botswana. Richard, the resident boss turned to me in the bar and asked ' what are you doing tomorrow ?

' nothing mate' I replied ' my parents are off to Chobe and I've been before, so I'm staying here just chilling out.'

' Wanna come hippo hunting ?'he prompted
. ' What ? Your're kiddin right ? ' I asked .

' Nope. A local chief had asked us to kill four hippos for the big ceremonies coming up. We killed two but need two more. We're going out in a boat tomorrow. Wanna come ?'

' Well... sure, ok' . I was mildly concerned about stories I'd heard of hippos overturning boats (once a hippo had overturned a boat, crocs would usually finish the occupants off) but decided this was something I just had to see.

So it was that the next morning I found myself sitting in a small tinny boat on the Zambezi river with several men and some giant rifles. We were in a broad part of the river with tall grass lining the banks. The rifles were elephant guns ; very long with sniper scopes and bullets the size of glue-sticks. Our group was led by a huge bearded professional hunter from South Africa, who sat on the seat at the end in the prime position. Richard had hunted before and had a friend from England who was going to try the guns. The friend had shot birds before with smaller rifles but nothing like this. Richard warned him about the elephant guns : ' Watch the kick back mate – its tremendous. When I tried it, the sniper scope slammed back in my eye – the blood was pouring down my face- check out the scar.' He did indeed have a circular scar- in fact a few - ringing his eye socket where the sniper scope had smashed back into his face.

The hippos were being elusive. They had been hunted the day before (successfully – I saw their enormous carcasses strewn and stripped on the riverbank) and now seemed to recognise the particular sound of this boats motor. Their heads were bobbing up briefly in the distance but they stayed down and then reappeared far away whenever we tried to get close to them. All was quiet. There was the occasional splash and we would whirl around only to see some beady eyes and floppy grey ears dip sneakily below the surface. Apparently they could stay submerged for at least five minutes if they wished. During the long day there was only one real chance. A hippo caught us by surprise, lifting his head far out of the water right in front of us. The English guest swiftly levelled his rifle, rocketed off a shot and water sprayed in front of the hippo as it dived. The blast was enormous, for a moment deafening us all. The shooter turned back to look at us ruefully. His eye was streaming with blood. ' Er, yeah , you were right Richard - quite a kickback with that scope' . As for the hippo, the young boy on board thought it may have been hit in the jaw as it dived. But it didn't come up (and they did do when they died) so we faced the prospect of finishing off a wounded and enraged hippo. I looked around nervously again at our flimsy aluminium boat. It looked more like a giant frying pan to me. At one point we pulled up at a bank and the hunters disembarked, taking all the guns with them to try and catch a hippo on land. As the sun descended I sat watchful in the boat as the river gently rocked the boat with a quiet lapping sound. I sure hoped that wounded hippo didn't show up now. The best I could probably do was throw my shoes at it. Eventually the hunters returned empty handed and we headed back, agreeing that the hippos in this area had wised up quickly. Tomorrow the hunters would need to try a new patch.

Most of my safari experiences in Africa were from the safety of a vehicle (although even the open nature of the trucks took some getting used to) but Livingstone amongst other parks provided the opportunities of walking safaris. These were surprisingly safe as long as you kept your distance from elephants and buffalo. Elephants were actually more dangerous outside the parks because they had a peculiar hatred for cyclists, and for cars that did not give way. One unfortunate taxi driver had his cab trashed by an elephant that appeared to have remembered the same car had not waited for its family to cross the previous day. On the other hand the gentle white rhinos in the park would let you get tantalisingly close, partly because their diet was being supplemented by park staff. The buffalos however made me distinctly nervous. One walking safari they had formed up into a herd whilst facing us, and I looked anxiously around for trees to climb. I knew of a VSO who had been attacked and almost killed by buffalo at Livingstone. Despite having their legs shredded, the brave VSO had somehow survived and returned to service after healing. I knew I was looking at her one day in Lusaka when I noticed a young woman at the backpackers with badly scarred legs. I was mortified when Dan strolled nonchantly up to her and stated bluntly : ' Ere, you're that 'buffalo girl', int'ya ?'

Back at Chassa, the monkeys passed through at various times of the year and Sichande was set on hunting them. Again, they provided good meat apparently. Sichande had a shotgun of his own and occasionally at night (especially when he was drunk) I would hear gunshots in the bush which I believe was Sichande hunting monkeys. When I asked him about this he explained that he also let off shots randomly when he heard about local prisoner releases, in order to warn these criminals to stay away from Chassa. He usually required a skinful of beer for this task too. Like snake season, it was yet another good reason not to be wandering around at night here.

For a few days in my second year the area was abuzz with excitement as a breakaway group of lionesses were in the area hunting livestock. At one point they were spotted 8km from Chassa, whilst I was on night duty patrolling the dormitories. That night I turned every dark corner with my breath held, pathetically clutching my best kitchen knife in my pocket. Thankfully the only cat I saw that night was Fink, who was now confident enough to trot by my side if we were alone.

The general beasties and bugs I had become quite accustomed to, although there was still the odd shock. I was mildly disturbed one day to pick up a pile of laundry outside and have a small grey tarantula drop onto my foot. A nearby boy had a look however and assured me it was not poisonous. I was less than pleased however when one evening I found what appeared to be its bigger brother sitting sneakily in one my water buckets. This fellow was palm-sized and could give a nasty bite, poisonous or not. Eventually I plucked up the courage to snap a lid on the bucket and drop the spider outside. I was rather alarmed when the spider appeared to charge by running at me directly, but I made it safely back to the house and tried not to take it personally. There were some other minor snake incidents, such as when a small brown snake was found in my pantry. This breed however were no bigger than large worms and were not poisonous. The offending serpent was chucked harmlessly out and I was only irked that the cats had not found it first.

Later on in the year I would be disturbed by what sounded like an old man wheezing at night outside my house. Was it passing cattle ? A dog ? Even running around the house I could never find anything, and witchcraft stories started to play in my head. Eventually Sondashi passed by one night and upon hearing the wheezing, assured me it was an owl that must have taken up residence in my chimney. Having another rat and snake killer around was fine with me, and the great bird was left undisturbed. I was sorry later one day to see one of the great owls dead by the Brothers Residence. The great talons were at least as big as the cat's claws. I half wondered if it had tried to take my crazy cat Rhino and made a fatal mistake.

DUTY AND MALARIA

It was soon after my return from Livingstone that I had my first turn for a week of 24-hour duty. Since it was a boarding school there was always supposed to be a pair of teachers on duty. Though lessons finished at one o clock, the boys had a busy day right up until lights out at ten. The afternoon and evening had supervised 'prep' sessions and various cleaning duties and sports activities in between. The teacher had to taste the meals and eat with the boys, be available in the staffroom at all times, and make sure lights were out at ten. It was an exhausting week, necessitating a 6.00am start at the latest, and a 10.30pm finish at the earliest.

Unfortunately when it came round to my turn I began to feel rather ill indeed. It started with a nagging back-ache, something Sondashi had warned me could herald the onset of malaria. Some late nights on holiday and sleeping under some holey nets had probably cost me. A couple of days later, when my duty began, the big M hit home. I felt so exhausted I could barely walk. A skull crushing headache seemed to throb constantly deep in my brain. It felt like the worst hangover ever, and it lasted several days, even with liberal doses of doxycycline and painkillers. Trudging around the school on duty chasing up boys was a waking nightmare. At its worst point I could do nothing else but lie still with my eyes closed and wait. After a few days I woke up morning and the illness had gone as suddenly as it had come.

Malaria was a regular illness amongst Zambians. Often lethal to young children, it became more like a bad cold in adulthood as a person developed some degree of immunity. It was not unusual to lose a pupil every year to malaria. The year before I arrived, a young grade 8 had gotten sick and refused to take his medicine. When his condition deteriorated rapidly he was belatedly rushed to hospital but died soon after. His parents suspected witchcraft and tried suing the school. We lost many hours of teaching to malaria ; each member of staff would generally be out for a week every term with the sickness.

I never developed the serious fever and delerium that many Zambians did without access to good drugs. The Zambians in this area seemed far out of date in their allegiance to particular drugs. They usually took a one off dose off an old drug called Fansidar. It had been in use for decades and never seemed to work particularly well. In addition the side effects seemed almost as bad as the malaria. In fact the old classic Quinine still worked well in this area, though Zambians were wary of its side effects. I used it a few times and found it extremely effective, but perhaps I was lucky and tolerated drugs well because I was so much heavier. No one seemed to have heard of doxycycline, though it was cheap and standard issue for volunteers as a preventative. It could also be doubled up as a treatment. I found it peculiar too, how few Zambians actually bothered with an insecticide treated nets. Since malaria was transmitted by mosquitos that were active between 10pm and 4am, a net was indisputably a simple and the single most effective way of avoiding malaria. Nets were heavily subsidised by NGOS and the government, and anybody with even a small cash income could have afforded one (they cost about 2 U.S dollars). Admittedly they were still out of the reach of most villagers. But it was still bizarre to hear later from Stacy for example (a Peacecorps girl I met later on) that a Headmistress down in her village had lost a child to malaria. The victim had not had a net for her children. She could have easily afforded one ; they cost K10,0000 (about 2 dollars) and a teacher had a monthly income of about a million kwacha. Even when nets were given free (as I found they were in Tanzania for example, to women who gave birth in clinics) they were often not used. Many of our boys didn't like nets as they complained they trapped dust and thus caused coughing whilst trying to sleep. I wondered if it was more a case of the apathy and fatalism that seemed to be ingrained in so many peoples attitudes here. They regarded malaria as inevitably a regular illness that just had to be endured. I wasn't sure how many of them knew that malaria was only transmitted by the middle of the night mosquitos. Education campaigns so often seemed to me to miss the crucial point. Mosquitos also loved biting the head, but despite this most men insisted that the only proper hair-cut was a grade one shaving. Whilst my longer hair protected my scalp, I often watched bemused at the bar as the conversations were punctuated by men cursing and slapping their shaved heads.

A WEEK IN THE LIFE OF A CHASSA BOY

Being on duty happened once, maybe twice a term and it gave you an insight into what the lives of the boys were really like at the school. The boys were awakened at 5.30 am with a pupil clanging a makeshift bell that echoed across the entire compound. Various cleaning duties were performed including making the beds and breakfast, which was served at 6.30. Usually the boys ate 'sample' (un-ground corn) mixed with sugar. Like all meals, they were supposed to be eaten in silence and the boys ate hurriedly and snatched brief conversations whilst prefects hovered over them and 'shushed'. Morning assembly was often a real treat as the boys sang beautifully and some might play a makeshift banjo to adapted hymns. When Brother Michael was there it was often to lecture tediously on the latest trend of which he disapproved, usually the 'landmines' which bean laden boys dropped in the surrounding bush. He might also explain his latest travel, often to Lusaka or even Nairobi (the Brothers African HQ) which perhaps he thought impressed us, but actually seemed to irritate most of us who saw him as avoiding his real duties.

Registration was at seven, although few teachers bothered registering boys in the allotted time. Lessons began soon after, but pupils often read through their notes or stared out the windows in the absence of teachers. Often the main activity in the classroom was a 'class monitor' writing teachers notes on the board that pupils had to copy. The assessment of the work was often the teacher just checking that the pupils had finished copying the notes. Some teachers such as Massina might not turn up on a regular basis until break time. Most seemed to teach every other lesson ; one lesson to give notes and the next lesson a few days later to explain the notes in more detail if necessary. At break-time the boys would run up to the bread market and buy the buns, samosas and bread that the teachers and workers wives baked. Though the boys were in lesson until one, these lessons were often interrupted by pupils being taken out to be punished by prefects. Some of us tried to stop this practice, but it was often the only time prefects could nab boys who dodged them at other times in the day. The punishments were manual labour such as cleaning and grass-cutting (tediously done by swinging a slasher). Less conscientious pupils would use the absence of teachers in the classroom to petition the senior teacher's office for something, usually a sick pass or the coveted pass to Sinda. Many would get a pass to Sinda clinic and then slope off into the town. Lunch was usually nsima and beans, a diet that produced flatulence that made Blazing Saddles look like a documentary. The boys were not fond of using the dormitory toilets and would often sneak into the bush to their business. ' Helping themselves' they called it, although they were not helping those who took shortcuts through bush. The results were called 'landmines' and Brother Michael often made endless appeals in assemblies for pupils to stop laying these 'bombs' in the bush.

The afternoons were different every day ; clubs, sports, religious instruction, although there was always one 'house' on cleaning duty. The car park in particular was always being swept by a small battalion of boys with makeshift grass brooms. Many pupils had to work on the school 'Production Unit', our small collection of livestock, chickens and crops. An animal might be slaughtered at the end of term for 'House' parties, and with the maize production at around an impressive 500 sacks a year the school was almost self-sufficient. The teacher on duty was usually based in the staffroom , often dealing with a long queue of boys begging for 'passes', the magic slip of paper that would enable them to run an errand or sleep and yet escape punishment when nabbed by prefects or cadets. There were strict out of bound areas and boys were 'booked' for punishment if caught in the wrong place. Particularly prized were the passes to Sinda that might be obtained off a generous or gullible Teacher on Duty, and the boys came up with all sorts of convoluted reasons why they had to be in Sinda at a particular time. Chassa must have seemed like a prison to these boys at times, and Sinda wasn't much but there was some fast food, bus boys selling daga (the local weed) and of course women. The boys were back in prep in the late afternoon for silent study. Dinner was more beans and nsima, (meat once a week) and then they had more silent study until nine in the evening. Patrolling the dormitories near lights out, one saw how crowded they were in their basic accommodation and the numerous thefts (usually of sugar which boys mixed with water) that so often provoked conflict. There was always a small army of boys protesting at prefects abuses, and allegations of the now outlawed 'beating '. The teacher always had to strike a fine line between maintaining the law and supporting the prefects. The prefects were the people really running the school and I was always careful not to undermine them in public, though I might have to chastise some of them in private for stepping over the line. Prefects tended to clash violently with 'commoners', especially when the former was a village boy and the latter a city boy. Lusaka pupils in particular saw themselves as superior to the village boys and were particularly averse to manual labour, usually having come from privileged families. These pupils often had masses of spare food sent from home or brought by relatives passing through, something which made you feel sorrier for the poorer kids subsisting on beans and nsima and struggling to afford even essentials such as soap.

On weekends the boys had some spare time although most of Saturday was spent cleaning, and Sunday in church. On a Friday or Saturday night the entire school was herded into the hall where they were all forced to watch a proscribed video. The boys seldom had any private time to themselves, but occasionally you might catch them hiding in a corner looking wistfully at photos from home.

The term was long, 13 weeks, and the boys left excitedly at the end on a variety of coaches. The night before they had House parties in which for once they were permitted cakes and soft drinks. There was the usual acrobatic dancing with the traditional hip wiggling, and some skilful modern dancing that would have put Michael Jackson to shame. The next morning some boys might be stranded for a few days as they had blown the transport money their parents had sent. Sometimes no doubt a few parents had encountered genuine difficulties and could not send enough money, but it was nowhere near the multitude of boys that approached me at the end of term demanding inflated sums for the journey home.

STACY AND THE PEACE CORPS

I had met Stacy earlier that year. Since January I had heard that a U.S Peace Corps volunteer was placed not far from me. She had heard the same about me, and one day she rolled up and introduced herself. I had left soon after to return to England for a friend's wedding and enjoy the Easter holidays there, so it was after that we became more friendly. Stacy was a young, tall, auburn haired woman with a southern accent. She helped schools in the area with the building and administration of community schools, and their affiliation with a wind-up radio program ; an ingenious way of supporting and standardising education in an inaccessible country. Lessons from Lusaka would be transmitted all around the country to basic schools whose teachers were helped with how best to use the material.

Stacy's village was rather behind on the building of her hut (it was the responsibility of a host village to provide accommodation for Peace Corps volunteers) ; the roof was unfinished and rainy season was looming. I had plenty of room at my house and Stacy ended up crashing on my couch for what turned out in the end to be six months. It was great to have another westerner to hang around with to lessen the feeling of isolation. Most social events in Zambia revolved around the Church, which I was obviously not party too. I was a regular at the bar but never hung around long ; the volunteers wage stretched surprisingly thin and I could see how regular drinking would suck away my money fast. I was friendlier with Sarah now, seeing as she extended her service for yet another year, but we still didn't see awful lot of each other. She must still have found me strangely aloof from her, yet I still couldn't completely get rid of my awkwardness around her. How could I explain that I found her attractive, when she had trouble with the previous male volunteer ? I might only alienate a valuable ally at work. Sarah was far too valuable as a friend and colleague for me to try anything, besides which I was sure the feeling wasn't mutual. In time I also realised my isolation was exaggerating my feelings and they could not be trusted.

Stacy on the other hand became a regular fixture at my house. Often I would come home at the end of the school day and find her curled up on my couch after yet another epic bike ride to see a far-away village. Stacy was a sharp lady of few words and dry humour. We soon got on famously. Our conversations often centred around fantasies of what we would eat and do when we got back to the West. Stacy was a huge 'Lord of the Rings' fan like me, and we often crashed in front of these movies after a few beers at the bar. As we watched Sam and Frodo struggling in a strange land, somehow the story of bumbling amateurs far from home on a lonesome mission resonated with us. We were hardly at war, but sometimes the environment and obstacles at work were such that it almost felt like it.

Through Stacy I became friendly with the other Peace Corps volunteers in Eastern province. They had a provincial headquarters in Chipata where they met every few months. Through these meetings I formed solid friendships with most of them. When corruption and lack of cooperation in Zambia was driving you nuts you needed another westerner to talk to. It must have been an enormously testing job, psychologically speaking for the Peace Corps ; to go from the richest country in the world and then spend two years in a mud hut. At least I had electricity, albeit sporadically. Adjusting to lower living standards was remarkably easy though ; what was hard was the loneliness as a volunteer was placed in an alien culture. Again, I was at an advantage in that at least I had colleagues who spoke English and had been educated to a similar standard as myself. But to be speaking mostly the local language amongst villagers who had never strayed far – that must have been an extreme culture shock for young American volunteers. Many of them were straight out of university, and yet they usually bore their situation with the sunny optimism that I so admired in the American people. Half the nation might be conservative gun nuts, but they had some real gems too as far as I could see. Their programs focused on improving agriculture, health and HIV, and the education programme that Stacy was involved in. The Peace Corps often attracted criticism as they had a reputation for fleeing the village and partying in the towns. In one notorious incident in Kasama, a provincial meeting and after party had gotten out of hand. Several drunk Peace Corps had climbed the local water tower, and in giant lettering had scrawled on the tank :' Kasama ! Fuck Yeah !' It was a reference to the theme tune in the movie 'Team America'. The Zambian authorities were not impressed. Several volunteers ending up being expelled from the country and the future existence of the provincial headquarters were thrown into doubt. The press inflated the incident with blatant lies. The lettering was barely visible from the ground and the volunteers did not hurl abuse at the townspeople below. Nor did they try and pee in the water supply, which was sealed anyway. The Zambians were paranoid about their water supply, some tanks and wells having being poisoned by Rhodesian invaders as they struggled with the War of Independence in Zimbabwe. Nonetheless, it was a regrettable incident and it gave fuel to peoples' criticisms of the Peace Corps.

Yet from what I could see the Peace Corps were far more effective than many other NGOs. Whilst Peace Corps got down in the dirt with the people on the ground, many other NGO's limited themselves to swanning around towns in air conditioned land-cruisers. The Peace Corps operation was relatively low budget. The volunteers received sparse wages (about the same as a Zambian elementary school teacher – 800,000 kwacha) and the programmes emphasized the sharing of knowledge rather than the donations that encouraged dependency. They learnt the local language and came to understand the nature of problems much better than other volunteers. In the occasional criticism of PeaceCorps I heard from Zambians in Lusaka, I discerned more a jealousy of American power than any valid criticism of the developmental organisation. As much as PeaceCorps volunteers might be effective however, it seemed most of them still left disillusioned with Aid work, and convinced that Aid had to be cut off to wean Zambia off perpetual dependency.

STAFFROOM INVADERS

As I strolled back from the track one afternoon I saw the cats sunbathing outside the house, and then noticed something grey and snakelike near them. The cats woke at my approach and saw it too. They shook themselves to their feet and padded across to it curiously. Whatever it was, it flew down a nearby hole in the ground. I was close enough only to see a thick muscular tale whip down the hole and disappear. The cats gave up their half-hearted chase. I stood some twenty feet away, heart thumping. 'If that's a snake....' I thought nervously. I extrapolated an estimate of its length based on the tail I had seen and was alarmed to 'guesstimate' it was maybe nine feet long. Cautiously I approached the hole, and then hurriedly stuffed a nearby brick in and jammed it as far down as I could. I rapidly stuffed more down, breaking bits up to completely fill the hole. The next morning I stuck my head into the deputy's office and asked his advice. He was confident the cats could deal with it but also suggested I could pour petrol down the hole. I returned to the hole that afternoon and was alarmed to see the bricks had been pushed aside and the hole was clear again. Kids perhaps ? But why ? I bricked it up again, keeping a nervous eye on the trees around me. We were at least half an hour away from a good hospital and I had no idea what anti-venoms were available. And yet the next morning the bricks had again been pushed aside. I mentioned this to Sondashi as I entered the staff room and he said he had in fact seen a monitor lizard entering the hole. ' Those things are very strong. They can push those bricks aside.' ' Dangerous ?' I asked. 'Hmm.. to chickens maybe, and they steal eggs' . Relieved, I thought no more of it. I didn't really know what a monitor lizard looked like but it didn't sound particularly threatening, so I forgot about it.

It was in fact about a year later that I entered the staff room and found staring back at me what appeared to be a small komodo dragon. I stood stunned as the lizard eyeballed me sideways. Suddenly it exploded away from me and towards the corner of the room, knocking over chairs and wobbling tables as it passed. I ran out, breathless, and saw Magomba and Ziyambo talking near the office. ' Hey, there's a huge lizard in there ! ' I gasped, ' take a look at it !' They stood bemused.
' Oh you mean the one that hangs around here ?' Magomba asked, pointing to the path where an iguana or some other medium sized lizard usually hung out.
' No way !' I snorted ' this one is a lot bigger.'
Mrs Banda the secretary got up to see what was going on. Ziyambo and Magomba conferred quickly in Nyanja and I could get the gist ; they still thought I had been startled by the iguana which must have wandered inside. Exasperated, I ran back to get Stacy and her camera.

They still hadn't entered when Stacy and I arrived, gasping for breath. The five of us went in together. I directed them to the corner where I had seen the lizard flee. As we approached the bookshelf it was hiding under, it sensed us coming and suddenly barrelled past, smashing chairs aside again as it flew to the other side of the room. There were shouts and exclamations as we leaped out of its way, and I collapsed in nervous laughter even as I pulled myself onto a table. ' I told you it was big !' I laughed. After more nervous rapid conferring in Nyanja , Ziyambo leaped down from the table and ran to get something. We waited tensly until he returned brandishing a metal rake. He cautiously cornered the lizard behind a bookshelf and soon a running battle ensued, in which Ziyambo repeatedly slammed the rake down onto the beast's head as it dashed from cover to cover. Eventually it stumbled out dazed on to the path outside and Ziyambo bludgeoned it again and again until it was still. In seconds its head was a bloodied mess and it had stopped moving completely. It was a shame to see such an impressive creature killed, but I was assured that a monitor lizard this big would be quite a menace to people's chickens, and had to be dispatched. Secretly I was relieved too ; I didn't want my cats trying to fight such a creature and losing. It had probably only backed down in the earlier incident because there had been two of them and I had been approaching. The lizard was big and looked powerful enough to kill a small dog.

ALLOWANCES AND PENIS CANCER

Early in my first year we headed off to Katete for a weekend on HIV / AIDS. It was my first introduction to the workshop and allowance system. We were all given substantial amounts of cash at the beginning of the workshop to pay for the expenses of accommodation and food. I soon realised that it was a vastly inflated amount. We were told we needed 150,000 kwacha for a bed, but it was in fact 15,000. The allowance for each meal was 30,000 but yet meals could easily be purchased for 10,000. Neither could I discern any advantage from leaving Chassa ; indeed the school was left dangerously unsupervised. So workshops were essentially a practice where large amounts of donor money were used to bribe people into attending an educational weekend. Often however they happened during the week and hence cut further into productivity. Workshops seemed to permeatate every occupation. Donors and NGO's even paid for private companies to have their workers educated on issues of HIV and Gender. And yet they often seemed a colossal waste of money that could be far better spent in such a needy country. People walked away from workshops with slogans and T – shirts, but I had to doubt what else of genuine worth. And how much did they pass on to their children ? Yet there were still many clinics without HIV test kits and many girls missing out on education. Surely donor money could be better spent on more immediate material needs. How many mosquito nets and antibiotics could that money have bought ? I alleviated some of my guilt by giving my leftover workshop money to Mr Ziyambo ; he was re-sitting school exams and was struggling with the fees on his meagre salary.

Whilst some of the weekend was facilitated by JL Banda, the program was principally run by the nun Sister Angela. Whilst J.L's session focused plainly on the facts, Angela raised some more controversial points and revealed some of the bizarre thinking behind some Zambian attitudes to HIV. One of her more alarming assertions was that in general, condoms were unreliable. They were derided as too small for Africans because they were made by Chinese (my assertion that I had seen them fitted on peoples heads at University parties were greeted with incredulous mocking laughter), damaged after travelling in heat, and even in ideal conditions as generally prone to failure. I had heard of the Catholic church spreading doubts about the efficacy of condoms, but didn't think they would really be that irresponsible until I heard it with my own ears. Brother John chimed in with his own idiotic assertion that he had heard condoms cause penis cancer. This was accepted by a solemnly nodding Sister Angela as indeed quite possible. It was only me, Sarah and a couple of Zambian teachers who tentatively challenged this, but for most Zambians it was difficult to challenge the stance of an authority such as a nun. Despite the fact that she had no medical experience, Sister Angela was accepted as an authority on the subject. If many educated teachers accepted this, what of villagers? It didn't bear thinking about. At one point, as Sarah had argued the need for more education, I was amazed to hear Sister Angela respond :   ' But how do we reach these villagers ? There's no point '. I would always remember that comment as a perfect illustration of the comfortable 'elites' contemptuous disregard for the villagers of Zambia.

The workshop was food for thought for some of the teachers who half considered testing. Sondashi asked me discreetly if I had been tested, and I affirmed that I had, in fact twice. He seemed to seriously consider this, especially as he was engaged to be married. His coy comments about women on TV could be amusing sometimes, but I wondered if he had already paid a price if he had womanised recklessly at University.

YOU SNOOZE, YOU LOSE – May 2005

After the first of my returns and friends weddings, my old friend Craig said he would accompany me back and take a holiday in Zambia. I had to go back to work, but he could see where I lived and then head off to Livingstone where he would find plenty of other travellers. After landing in Lusaka early in the morning we decided to head out to Shoprite and stock up before the trip to Eastern province. It was about ten thirty when we arrived at the station. That was bad. It meant we had missed the safer buses and were left with the option of Zoom, the aptly named speeding bus company. This company by far held the record for crashes and fatalities. Apparently in their first six months here they had written off eight coaches in Zambia and had great difficulty in getting insured these days. Their proud logo was ' You snooze, you lose'. Another company countered with : ' Germins. Safety first. Arrive Alive' . Unfortunately the company that so charmingly promised not to kill us were now finished with eastbound buses for the day. I viewed the battered Zoom coach in front of us warily and then looked at Craig. I had travelled on these pieces of crap myself before, but didn't want to put a good friend at unnecessary risk. On the other hand school was starting the next day so I had to leave today. After a brief discussion Craig assured me he would be ok if I was, and we boarded the 12 o'clock service bound for Chipata. As usual of course there was the obligatory 2 hour delay for no clear reason, as the passengers on board slowly cooked in the growing heat. At last however the bus chugged out of the station and we were on our way. Once out of Lusaka there were the usual hairy corners and death wish overtaking, but on the whole I was mildly surprised to find it wasn't much different from other bus journeys. Meaning of course that they were all pretty bad. Three hours later we were on the home straight out of the Luangwa valley, going fast admittedly, but straight at least, and at last I began to relax. Aside from the usual dreadful blaring gospel music, this journey was turning out all right. I un-tightened the tense knots in my stomach and allowed myself to semi-doze.

Suddenly there was a huge bang and the speeding bus shuddered violently as though it had been hit by something. Then, inexorably, it began to slide sideways off the road, even as it was hurtling forward at 80mph. Half of the passengers spontaneously rose together out of their seats and a tangible wave of fear filled the air. It could have been the whiff of a hundred colons about to open. I looked terrified at a fat man opposite me who beckoned me to sit ; ' We're ok ! We're Ok !' he seemed fixated on the driver at the front. ' He s got it !'. And he had. Somehow the driver managed to wrestle with the wheel and just about keep us on the road until the bus eventually spasmed to a halt. I breathed a sigh of relief then looked guiltily at a stunned Craig. We staggered off the bus and gaped at a front tire that was so shredded it looked like it had been hit with a bazooka. Whilst we waited at the side of the road for another bus, the Zambian passengers wandered off and bought sugar cane from curious villagers. I stood and thought uneasily about the situation I had almost put a best friend in. And he still had to go back.

About a year later another bus crashed on this spot and some twelve people were killed, including several teachers from nearby Petauke high school. Crashes became a semi-regular occurrence on this spot as it was a fast downward straight with potholes. Speeding here in combination with bald tires tended to result in blowouts. Every few months with depressing regularity we would hear of a huge coach crash with usually at least ten fatalities. The vehicles would usually leave the road at speed and roll several times. The frustrating thing was for me to see Zambians accept this, as they did many avoidable tragedies, with a kind of fatalism as though it was inevitable. There was nothing inevitable about it all. The drivers drove like lunatics and were frequently drunk. The coaches were badly maintained, despite huge profits by the companies (drivers received K500,000 per Journey, and I knew a regional manager in Chipata who was extremely wealthy). I found 'Marks Motorways ' particularly galling. This self proclaimed ' Christian' bus company would have a group prayer at the beginning of a journey, praying for a safe journey as if it was all in Gods hands. Driving slower and replacing bald tyres never seemed to occur to them. After setting off, the Marks Motorways conductor would always announce that littering, drinking and swearing would not be tolerated on this particularly virtuous coach service. Then they would drive like lunatics and kill ten people. How was that Christian? Making these kind of points in the staff-room I was usually met with awkward silences, though someone more forward thinking like Mumba would usually agree with me. Toward the end of my service, almost completely sick of religion, I heard of yet another crash right outside Sinda. It was the usual simple cause ; speeding and bald tyres on a bad road. A church group had been travelling at high speed from Lusaka to Chipata when a blow-out had led to their swift departure from the road, and for some, existence. There were 6 fatalities and numerous injuries. I could only shake my head whilst hearing of this in the staff-room. ' Where was God ?' I asked T.T. Ngoma. He grinned awkwardly, and I walked out in disgust before he could respond.

The fatalistic attitude was demonstrated by Brother Michael too. Stacy related to me that once before he had given her a lift to Petauake, he had prayed at the steering wheel , but then as usual had driven like a maniac in his little red toyota. He considered himself invulnerable after praying, and then drove accordingly. One could only hope that when he did eventually crash he would not take any innocent bystanders with him. In fact one of the Brothers had indeed been killed a few years earlier in our area. He had taken the Brothers truck on a late night visit to see a girlfriend in one of the villages. On the return journey the truck had overturned and the Brother had been trapped and left bleeding badly on the deserted road. Rumour had it that his cries for help had been heard but no one had dared to respond to them (Zambians, particularly villagers, were generally afraid of the dark). He had been found dead in the morning. Perhaps Michael rationalised this by believing the unfortunate brother had neglected to say his pre-drive prayer.

Soon after my parents had visited and returned in January 2005 I was horrified to see what looked like the same bus we had used, now by the side of the road. It was completely mangled, almost comically so, like it had been crushed by King Kong. I found out it had also had a tyre blow out at high speed, but had sped off the road and rolled several times. Being in one of these crashes was always a great fear of mine, particularly in a country with no real ambulance service. As well as the chance of being killed or dying on the spot, there was also the prospect of being mashed up in a blood bath with a group of people of whom a significant proportion were HIV positive.

I hoped fervently that I would get through my two years without being involved in such a deadly smash. Luckily I did, but I heard tragically soon after I had finished that a Japanese volunteer had not been so lucky. He died in a coach crash in Luapula province. The young man had completed his two years service and was on his way to Lusaka to the airport, and home. In that particular crash there some 16 fatalities and for once the government had taken firm action ; the company ' CR ' was closed down. I'm not sure if that particular company was worse than the others; they were all pretty bad. I knew from having regularly travelled on all of them. A cynical part of me couldn't help thinking that the government had only been pressured into closing this company because a volunteer had died.

It was not just potholes or large animals that could cause a bus crash. One of the more spectacular incidents apparently occurred the year before my arrival in eastern province. A particularly bad thunderstorm had resulted in floods and washed away a bridge near the Luangwa river. At night, a speeding bus had no chance of spotting the danger in time. One bus had flown straight into the river where all its occupants were instantly swept away and drowned.

Some of the justifications for speeding would have been hilarious if they hadn't been so tragic. Massina told me : ' Ah, but you have to speed – in case something faster smashes you from behind'. It was difficult to even start arguing against such a point as the exasperation and anger choked you.

THE DEATH OF MUMBA'S WIFE – June 2005

I returned to the UK in my first Easter, to attend a friends wedding. I spent a blissful month eating and drinking myself fat again, catching up with old friends and then returned for the new school term. Despite some misgivings about the obvious problems in Zambia, I was left as cold as ever by the materialistic lifestyle in England and had no great desire to return yet. I noted with particular disdain that a riot had occurred at the IKEA store in London, as people had fought each other to get the latest bargains in cheap soul-less furniture. I still believed despite all that I could yet make a difference at Chassa, and I certainly didn't relish teaching in the UK again just yet.

Upon my return to Zambia the weather began to cool and the last term at school saw the onset of the southern African winter. It was of course nothing as harsh as a British winter (noon still saw t-shirt weather), but nonetheless did get very cold at night. One of these cold nights I awoke with a start. The wailing outside was somehow a little different than usual. It was about four in the morning, still dark. I cursed, anticipating another tragi-comedy bout of chasing dogs around my house with bricks. Some dogs liked to stand right outside my thin bedroom window and howl, waking me up at depressingly regular intervals. Eventually I would get up, and enraged, race outside in my underwear trying to hit the dogs with desperately thrown bricks from my garden. With practice I became so accurate with bricks the dogs would stop when they heard my front door open. I will never forget a spectacular long distance shot that followed a dog's run and estimated its ETA at a particular point. Fifty yards away the shot slammed into a stunned dogs hips and spun it right round, where it stared at me stupidly as if to say ' how can you slap me from all the way over there ? After shots like that the packs of dogs learned to run when they saw me. Nonetheless I would still have to get up initially. Banging on my window did not intimidate them. Now, blindly struggling through my mosquito net I peeped through the curtain and saw some movement at Mumba's house, where sometimes dogs hung around on the porch. It wasn't too loud actually, so I sighed and collapsed back into bed.

I awoke again at a more reasonable hour in daylight. It was a weekend and I half dozed blissfully. And then through my semi-consciousness my ears caught the wailing again. But with a shiver I now recognised it as definitely human. A shudder suddenly ran through me ; that cold hand at the back of your neck that tells you that this time the shit has really hit the fan. The howling and shrieking was still at Mumbas. Now I suddenly remembered his heavily pregnant wife had been taken to hospital the day before with high blood pressure. Pre – eclampsia was it they called it in pregnancy ? With a sickening feeling I got up and again looked through the curtain over to Mumbas house. I saw what I had hoped not to. All the teachers sat around on the low wall, with a dejected Mumba collapsed in a heap, limply smoking his trademark menthol. The women sat on the floor, heads down too, some of them comforting the wailing group of small children and wailing along with them ; less raw but in a more accompanying tone like a choir trying to comfort. Mumba's children occasionally shrieked and suddenly I heard one cry out ' Maaaa- maaa !!! ' So, the worst must have happened then. I threw on my clothes and shuffled meekly out the front door. I did not want to go over there, to have to look into my friends eyes and tell him I was sorry to hear his wife was dead. I stood there frozen, unable to walk round the back to Mumbas. Instead I walked mechanically straight over to the Phiris opposite me. I asked them what I knew and what I should do – should I go over as well ? They said I should, so I reluctantly about turned and traipsed slowly over the long garden, pacing awkwardly to the patio where Mumba sat surrounded by friends. To my relief he looked up and smiled gently when he saw me. His eyes met mine for a moment as we shook hands and then I looked away quickly. He seemed grateful for my presence and gestured for me to sit with the others. The wailing continued, punctuated with the periodic shrieks of ' Mama !'. At one point Mumba lay back on the patio floor, and hearing his young children shriek yet again, his stout little chest rose and fell as he sighed.

It turned out that Mumba's wife had started bleeding heavily at the clinic. The clinic did not have enough blood and plasma. For some reason the clinic staff had decided to put her in a truck and take her to Nyanje hospital, nearer as the crow flies but over dirt tracks, and a poorer hospital than St. Francis in Katete. The hospital in Katete was indeed further, but faster because the road was tarmac, albeit potholed. It was also probably the best hospital in Zambia, receiving substantial western aid and staff. In fact halfway to Nyanje apparently the staff had re-thought this and turned back for Katete. By then it was too late and Mumba's wife died en route, comforted by her helplessly watching husband in the back of a truck. Sometimes for a volunteer Chassa could seem like an idyllic if boring rural retreat, and an event like this was a rude reminder of the kind of society we really lived in. In Zambia child-bearing was less a pleasure and more a duty, and a dangerous one at that.

I also reflected that despite being my neighbour, I had hardly known Mrs. Mumba. She had generally been tucked away in the house cleaning and looking after the kids, or at best sitting on the doorstep with a friend ; the furthest many wives seemed to travel on a regular basis.

That evening Sarah passed by to see if I was ok. She had started to drop by more often and I was finally becoming comfortable around her. She must have thought me rather odd before as I still always seemed ill at ease with her. I'm sure she was used to the attentions of men and I must have baffled her for some time with my stand-offish nature round her. But how could I explain that I had feelings for her when I was not sure they were not reciprocated and she had exactly this trouble with the previous male volunteer? At last however it seemed we were becoming genuine friends. I realised when I got to know her that there was nothing between us and my attraction was a physical infatuation, not helped by my isolation here. There weren't many other ladies around and I never contemplated a relationship with a Zambian ; I could never be sure their interest in me would be genuine or more motivated by money. I even felt uncomfortable being regarded as a sort of 'novelty' by Zambian women and stayed clear of any potential 'situations'. I knew other volunteers who had gotten involved with Zambians and it had usually ended badly. Paranoia about HIV was also a factor. In VSO training we had learnt of two VSO's who had contracted HIV in Zambia, and had died soon after returning to England. With the virus having a 3-6 month incubation period before it could be detected, it would be a long time before you could be absolutely sure your partner was clear.

Sarah and I soon learnt that we could always rely on each other at work whereas others might let us down (a typical example was the whole school Maths and Science quiz on Friday evenings which was usually only staffed by us), and slowly became more used to spending time together. This was also helped by Stacy, whose company Sarah particularly appreciated. The three of us eventually became regular companions at the bar, usually with myself trying to calm down the hard drinking women.

A few days later I dropped into Mumba's house to drop off some Simpsons videos for the kids and some books for Mumba. He was a keen reader and was often borrowing books off me and getting through them quickly. Now I was welcomed into the lounge whilst Mumba ducked into the back to retrieve an old video he had of mine. I stood there rather awkwardly whilst what seemed a multitude of children gaped up at me. Some of them were his children, others were dependents as was common in Zambia ; cousins orphaned due to Aids that were sent to live with uncles like Mumba. It suddenly struck home what a responsibility Mumba had. As if life wasn't hard enough already with children and dependants, he now had to face this tough task alone.

The death of anyone in this community was rarely regarded as a straightforward biological matter. The other wives worriedly speculated about who had cause to strike down their friend. Rumours abounded that Mumba had played around in Sinda and that a jilted girlfriend had thrown a curse on his wife. The deputy's wife hounded her husband to apply for a transfer from Chassa, claiming there was too much 'Ju – Ju' around here. At least this province did not have the tradition of 'coffin-chasing' ; a practice in north-western province whereby the coffin was held up and like a giant ouija board directed its carriers in a crazy chase around the community. Finally it would settle at someone's door ; the guilty party who had allegedly thrown the curse. The accused would then have to settle their debt with a heavy fine.

When our heavy drinking registry clerk, Amos Banda, finally drank himself to death one day, Brother Michael decided on a thorough autopsy to dispel rumours of witchcraft or poisoning. The autopsy revealed Amos had not eaten for a long time. One last session on kachassu, the legendary local spirit that regularly blinded and brain damaged people, had proven too much for the aging drunk. He had fallen into a coma and passed away. Still, I wondered what rumours of Ju-Ju would circulate, about people Amos had wronged in some small way and who wanted revenge.

I later reflected that organisation of the funerals and burials was by far the most efficient undertaking I saw in Zambia. Everybody came together to play their part in good time and lay the deceased to rest in an appropriate manner. The workers at the workshop built a fine coffin, people travelled from far and wide and arrived in good time, and the attendance was usually huge (seeming to involve most people in the community) and well orchestrated by clergy and headmen. No doubt I reflected grimly, Zambians had plenty of practice at funerals. But it was also frustrating to see how the community came together so efficiently for someone's death, but would rarely emulate this goodwill and efficiency to actually help people whilst they were living.

OUR ENIGMATIC LEADER

I never really had a lot to do with Brother Michael directly as I was not senior management or a department head, or involved in any school admin apart from the tuck-shop. Michael wasn't exactly chatty or approachable either, and many of the teachers feared him. His style was dictatorial and it was hard to guess what he might be thinking. He had a peculiarly impenetrable facial expression and it was unnerving sometimes when he fixed you with eyes that were either blank or secretly calculating. Brother Michael was originally a village boy done good, but his manner these days was far from humble. He strode around the school in an imperious fashion, but at the same time he had an almost comical obsession with cleaning and was particularly proud of his toilet cleaning abilities. On Saturdays when the boys had their dorms inspected he would sometimes roll up his sleeves and show them how to get the stains off a toilet pan. At first I thought he had seemed a serious and motivated young man (he was only 31, another reason why some resented him being Headmaster) and he always seemed busy. But as time went by I started to have misgivings about him. I began to realise he spent an awful lot of time out of school, driving his car around the province on trips of questionable necessity. The boys mocked his usual Monday morning assembly speech (if he was there) which invariably started with : ` This week, I will be travelling....` . It was particularly annoying when in staff meetings Michael talked about the importance of `teacher presence` and once rebuked me for missing a day of term due to a UK wedding. As well as the fact that he wanted us in lessons all the time (no argument there) he also wanted us to check regularly on the boys even if we weren't on duty. `Why not get up at 3am occasionally and spot check the dormitories ? Then we might stop these night-time incidents happening. ` he advised. Getting up at 3am and checking the dormitories would not be a problem if we were all as well rested and fed as Michael, who tended to stay up late and sleep in late, probably after messing around on the internet all night. And if Michael had actually been around during the day and tried to educate the boys on drug use and HIV, maybe they wouldn't be running around at night getting into mischief in the first place.

It was on a trip to Chipata with J.Banda and Magomba that I first heard teachers discussing Michael and whether they would leave the school as they were so disgruntled with him1. Most of the discussion was in Nyanja, but I got the gist of it and discerned that Michael's grip on school finances was also a major issue. Since I had once given Michael a donation of 1.8 million kwacha from the Hurworth Lionesses and never had it's expenditure explained, I vowed to keep my ear to the ground and monitor this. On a superficial level I picked up on some other clues as to his attitude to money and it worried me slightly. When he turned up at the bar he always drank an expensive cider if it was available, and bragged about how his favourite energy drink was four times the price of a Coke. At the time the comment just seemed bizarre, but later it acquired a sinister significance as I kept a suspicious eye on his attitude to spending.

MY NADIR

The end of term saw yet another journey back to the UK for me. My best friend Pete from University was getting married and I was given the honour of best man. It was pleasing to again to catch up with friends, family and enjoy western luxuries temporarily, but I still appreciated the simplicity of my life at Chassa in comparison to the hectic stressful lifestyles that everyone in Britain seemed to lead. It was heartening to see my best friend wedded to the woman he loved, but I felt no desire yet to return to those aspirations. In passing through London I had dropped into my old school and seen Anna, now heavily pregnant with another man's child. The sight left me indifferent. I was over her it seemed, but now a 'committed loner'.

Returning from Pete's wedding, I had the package I thought could transform my work and even my life at Chassa. My sister had earned enough spare money during her tour of duty in Iraq to buy me a top of the range laptop and printer. The school computers and printers were notoriously outdated, unreliable and virus ridden. I couldn't ever see myself getting sustained work done on them. Power cuts and viruses had destroyed my previous attempts. But with my own computer and printer I could produce the revision guides I wanted, produce work for the Anti-Aids club, and teach others how to use it. The laptop at my house would be protected by my surge protectors (many electronic appliances were regularly destroyed by Zesco's chaotic management of supply ; after a power cut the surge when power came back regularly blew up appliances if the unlucky owner had forgotten to switch them off) and with the battery I could work to some extent around lengthy power cuts. Only occasionally would a power cut last more than a day. A couple of times the main transformer was blown at Sinda and this took several weeks to rectify. The laptop having its own printer meant I could avoid contamination with the viruses that seemed to permanently jump between the school computers. It was the ideal solution to my work problems. Finally, I could leave it with T.T as an asset for the maths department ; I would probably need an upgraded one anyway after returning.

On a personal note my stereo had packed in, so the laptop could replace that as a music player. I could also watch DVD's and the VCD's that could be bought cheaply here. And with my free time I could try writing, something I had meant to do for years but never found time. There was even the possibility of getting a phone line installed and getting (albeit very slow) a connection to the internet. It's hard to put into words how much I looked forward to a simple machine like that, when I was stuck in the bush with nothing to do and facing such challenges at work.

In England I had balked at the canvas bag it came in. It looked to me like an advertisement for muggers. But my neighbour argued most Zambians wouldn't recognise the bag as a laptop carrier. I wasn't sure, but accepted. I was wrong. The bag wouldn't fit on my lap, so on the bus to Chassa I stowed it directly above my head. When I got up at Sinda to leave the bus I couldn't believe my eyes. The laptop bag was nowhere to be seen. Somehow, someone had gotten it off right under my, or rather above my nose. I remembered just before setting off from Lusaka- someone had jabbered Nyanja into my face whilst someone else shuffled luggage overhead. Maybe it had gone then.

Whatever happened, I was so enraged that I almost got on the next bus back to Lusaka and bought a plane ticket for England. Zambia, and Chassa in particular, was starting to wear thin on me. I had leant so much money, books, videos and had people avoid me on returning them that I was beginning to feel I had very few real friends in the community. It was only Sarah, Stacy and maybe Sondashi and JL I could trust. Everybody else it seemed constantly wanted to borrow money and things which they had no real intention of returning. I felt less like a human being in their eyes and increasingly more like a dollar sign. There was an irrational hoarding tendency amongst Zambians too, a greed which bordered on insanity because it so poisoned relationships. A simple and petty example was the loss of one of my videotapes. At the deputy's one day I noticed the missing tape on their shelf and remembered they had borrowed it. It had now Mrs.Banda's writing in permanent marker across the case : ' Property of Mrs. Banda' . When I asked for it back, Mrs Banda said Audrey had sent it over. Indeed she had sent a copy over I admitted ; that was why Mrs. Banda now had two copies of the same film on the shelf. One of them was clearly mine, and what could Mrs. Banda want with two copies of the same movie ? But Mrs. Banda would not budge, though she could not explain how she had the extra copy. After the hours I had put in giving her free maths tuition she could still not find it in herself to return my possessions, even when they were not needed. I lost some 20 videotapes in this manner. A petty loss, and one which did not bother me materially ; I was going to give them all away when I left anyhow. But the incidents to me showed how Zambians regarded me. I found it profoundly disrespectful, when I had never been anything but helpful to the very people who were now effectively stealing from me.

It was attitudes like this which gradually led to my increasing isolation at Chassa ; I now depressingly reasoned that the less I had to do with Zambians the less they would disappoint me. The less I was around in public, the less I would be bothered for money. It was the fact that it got worse as time went on which rankled with me. I had naively thought that in time as people got to know me and saw how relatively humbly I lived, they would accept me more and see me less as a dollar sign. Yet even in my own locality for instance I still found myself charged double for simple items unless I could show I knew the real price and bargain them down. Even Audrey, who had spoken the language and lived here for five years, had been regularly ripped off. Later on in my service due to housing pressure the woodwork teacher Mashowo was placed in my house. He slept odd hours and we didn't see much of each other, but he was amazed when he saw what prices locals were charging me for charcoal. I protested that Audrey had always paid a hundred thousand for a sack of charcoal. Mashowo was flabbergasted ; the real price was five thousand. Somehow it wouldn't have been so bad if we really were richer, but I was surprised to learn that several senior teachers even earned more than me.

Zambians themselves it seemed had an image of themselves that was a self fulfilling prophecy. There was a younger generation, those who did not remember the horrors of colonialism, who bizarrely saw whites as intrinsically more moral people than Africans. They had grown up with the whites who were volunteers and aid workers, and meanwhile saw around them the narrow minded self -interest of the natives. It was not uncommon for me to be asked by a boy ' What do you think of Africans ? Are we not selfish ?' But it never seemed to occur to them that they had a choice, they just seemed to regard Zambians as inherently selfish. The Phiris whose VCR had broken came almost daily to borrow mine. Eventually I tired of not being able to use my own machine, and occasionally asked that they borrow someone else's instead. Everybody else had VCR's too, so why always borrow just mine ? This produced a look of complete incomprehension which I will never forget. 'But these people are your friends and neighbours, they're Christians'. I would argue. This had no effect. The idea that a fellow Zambian would lend them their VCR seemed utterly ridiculous to them. Yet I was an aetheist whilst they were supposedly devout Christians ; still this as well seemed utterly irrelevant whenever I was approached for help. It did not even have to be material help. Even favours at school were always directed my way ; the idea that a fellow Zambian would give their free time to help another was dismissed as unrealistic.

My major worry began to be being constantly hassled for money by all and sundry who refused to believe I was not rich. I must have appeared rich because I was initially so generous with my loans. Nobody must have realised that sometimes I literally ran out of money completely and sometimes contemplated borrowing money off Brother Michael just so I could buy bread. Various teachers borrowed money, along with other members of the community, and before long my door was always being

knocked on for this purpose. The worst was `farmer Banda `, a local drunk who led me to believe his sons and wives had died and he needed burial money. I gave the money, but later found out that they were all alive. Worse, I discovered Banda was only using the money for drinking. When he turned up at my door one day complaining of hunger and having nothing for his family, I offered a small bag of maize I had bought.
` Oh no, I've got plenty of that ` he said : ` I need money`. Later that day I found him at the bar, although I didn't doubt that his family probably were hungry. A shaken Banda later turned up to my house and apologised, his hand trembling as he reached to shake mine for forgiveness. Someone powerful in the community must have found out about my inquiries and seriously rebuked him.

Another semi-dependent I seemed to have inherited from Audrey was Mrs Phiri the fruit seller. Unlike Banda she did at least intersperse her `loan` requests with selling me oranges and bananas, always a welcome addition to my diet. But I was particularly irked one day when she plonked herself down on my sofa and nonchalantly asked me for 50,000 so she could buy a suit for church. These weren't exactly starvation loans. I wouldn't have minded so much, if there had been some balance and some people had actually shown an interest in socialising with me for other reasons. It was quite a psychological weight to feel that you were an outsider and only valued as a source of money because of your skin colour. Only Sondashi really seemed to enjoy my company, and we often watched a movie together whilst Sondashi rambled on with stories about Johnny Cash and other country music heroes. It was quite strange to be a westerner in Africa listening to detailed stories from a Zambian about American country stars. Sondashi also loved the Clint Eastwood movies I had sent over, and before long he was reciting the Good, The Bad and the Ugly from memory, delighting in the dry dialogue between Tucco the Mexican and Eastwood. Most afternoons for me however eventually became about sleeping through the knocks at my door and then blaring them out with music on an evening. Sondashi noticed my increased isolation and asked often about me, but what could I say ? It seemed most people here, even with time, still viewed me as a source of loans and little else. It was not uncommon to be troubled for these `loans` several times a day. Others began to notice my increased withdrawl, and I became increasingly greeted with ' Ah Burke, but you are not seen these days'. Since many people were ducking me to avoid repaying loans, I had assumed this was a good thing for them.

At least all this was less true of the pupils, still a delight to teach and the main reason I kept going. They would trouble me at the end of term, when many claimed they were stranded and needed transport money (which I later found out was usually beer money for the trip home), but in general they were less financially demanding and I enjoyed their company more. I even started sponsoring a few orphans who were in dire straits and needed help paying school fees. But now I looked at my second year without the laptop and printer, when I aimed to produce sustainable resources and systems, and I couldn't see it happening. What was I doing here ? The laptop thieves were cursed almost daily as my attempts to write maths booklets and HIV posters were frequently lost to power cuts, computer viruses and printing problems. Furthermore I was unable to work comfortably at home, instead having to work in the mosquito infested school office at awkward hours. The couple of times I did go down with malaria it was probably contracted in the school office at night.

I was still largely tolerant of the teacher's small children that came to visit. They were always curious to see what a white man lived like, and they would inspect everything in my lounge to check anything that might be different to their own houses. Every little trinket was inspected and then held up to me with the request : `And Burke – what is this ? And Burke, this ?` I always had some spare chalk and paper which sent them running away in delight to their porches where they would spend the afternoon drawing. If only all my visitors were so easily pleased.

THE BOTTOMLESS TUCKSHOP

The tuck-shop was also becoming a constant source of frustration to me. Despite my ploughing all profits back into stock, the shelves became ever emptier. It soon became apparent to me that the staff of four boys I inherited were stealing. All income from the shop I ploughed back into purchases, so the stock value should have continually risen. Instead it shrank. Audrey came back to visit for a week, and assured me that no boys would ever dare stealing from the shop. Yet I had receipts that proved all cash handed to me was spent on stock. If the stock was decreasing then it could only mean part of the takings were being stolen before they were handed to me at the end of the day. Yet how could I prove exactly which boy was stealing ? I was reluctant to physically oversee them all the time – I had not travelled 5000 miles to keep track of penny sweets. I knew a new gang of boys would take over next term, so I let it slide and concealed it in my first report, rather than smear all four boys and risk their expulsion.

In retrospect this was a mistake. Had I known the new boys, and any future workers would steal I should have blasted it into the open asap. Once it became apparent the new group of boys were stealing as well however, I had to report it. Yet Brother Michael seemed curiously reluctant to act ; he insisted I carry on as usual but just keep a closer eye on things. I resolutely refused to do this ; I was not going to spend my time working in a shop just to stop others stealing. I later learned that the boy I named as my chief suspect had a father who was close to Michael. The pupil was of course a particularly pious church-goer. He was regular performer in the talent shows as a melodramatic gospel singer. And, as usual the culprit was well-off. His family were wealthy and he appeared to be using the money for hair products and other useless crap. A school shop that could have sponsored needy orphans was thus effectively sunk.

Eventually it was decided that breaking long years of tradition, pupils would no longer work in the shop. Instead we would have a single paid worker. Since I would be able to prove with receipts that all income was spent on stock, any stock discrepancies would only be explainable by the single worker stealing. Surely in such a situation the worker would dare not steal, when they could be so easily pinned for it ? It seemed I was still naive.

At first all seemed well and the stock value increased roughly in line with predictions, based on average percentage profit. Then after a while, stock takes revealed that yet again the worker must be stealing. I couldn't believe it. Again my spending receipts showed I was using all the income collected on stock purchases. Therefore again, the worker must be stealing cash before

I collected it at the end of the day. Since I had the keys, and the doors were very noisy if opened, it was highly doubtful any third party was involved. The worker, a young lady called Stella, rather pathetically kept pushing me to raise prices, as if that would cover the thefts whilst the stock base was rapidly declining. Again when I presented my arguments to Michael he prevaricated for weeks. There may have been some embarrassment as Stella's father had once worked for the school. Eventually I took it to the police myself. At this provacation the admin suddenly took alarm and worked out a deal with the worker whereby she would work off her debt (it would take her about two years). By this time I was near the end of my service and very relieved to hand over the tuckshop to another member of staff. But the tuckshop would always rankle in my memory because I saw it as a micro-cosm of the Zambian economy. It should have made a healthy profit and this money could have been put to good use such as sponsoring school projects or some other social use to benefit the community. Instead the selfishness of an individual prevented this and strangled the economic growth before it could take off. Again, like many instances here the theft was committed not by someone desperate, but by someone relatively well off. The stolen funds had been used to buy expensive clothes and beer for her boyfriend. I had already `lent` her half a million kwacha so that he could study to be a nurse at Katete (more money of course that I now had no prospect of getting back). The reluctance with which the authorities dealt with the theft was typical. And the deal worked out, rather than any kind of punishment, was also typically Zambian. Some may argue that the money was not recoverable anyway, but in the long run I'm sure this culture of compensation rather than punishment encouraged people to risk stealing.

TROUBLE AT HOME

The wranglings over the tuck-shop irked me all the more as I was having similar money trouble at home. I had inherited a housekeeper from Audrey, a local man, Mr Soko, who came every other day to clean. I didn't consider him necessary (although having someone to draw water was convenient) but was reluctant to get rid of him as I was his only source of cash income. He had depended on Audrey and I couldn't just pull the rug from under him all of a sudden. For a modest fee then, Soko washed my clothes, dishes, and swept the ever dusty floors. I was suspicious of him from the beginning whilst Audrey was still around. I had hidden my holiday money (fifty US dollars) at the bottom of a box of malaria pills on my desk (in my first room I had neither a wardrobe or door that would lock). Soon after arriving it had disappeared. I was naturally suspicious of Soko, but Audrey was adamant he would not risk doing such a thing. She suggested it may have been a pupil, as they were briefly let in by her every day to borrow books. I found this highly unlikely as the money was stolen from such a place that would take time to find. The pupils may have been unsupervised only for a matter of seconds as Audrey retrieved something from another room. I was 99 % sure it was Soko, but Audrey was adamant. I let it go, and in time my suspicion of the man lessened.

After Stacy had been staying awhile, she began to question quite regularly if she was miscounting her money. After this happened several times we naturally began to wonder if indeed Soko was stealing from her ; he had the keys and the time to do so. It led in the end to Stacy stashing her money in the lockable wardrobe in my new room, and writing exactly how much she had at any particular time. For a while all seemed fine. Until we returned from holiday to find that her money had nonetheless gone down, despite my room and wardrobe being locked. As I had found the doors still locked it was obviously someone who had spare keys that I was unaware of. Since Soko baby-sitted the house whilst I was away he was naturally the suspect. He probably had old keys that opened the door, and had the time to unscrew the padlock on the wardrobe and then reattach it. Most annoyingly, this coincided with my parents visit. Visiting Stacys village, I left my parents case with money locked in my room whilst Soko was cleaning. We returned whilst Soko was still there, and when he had gone we re-checked the money. Some had indeed been stolen ; the money my mum had brought from our local primary school. The well-intentioned pupils at Croft school had spent a day cleaning cars and raised £120 for the beleaguered Chassa primary. At last I was sure I had enough circumstantial evidence to accuse Soko and promptly went to the police. If he could be caught with English pounds then it would be easily solved. Nobody else had English pounds around here.

The police response was predictably farcical. They brought Soko in for questioning, but at first merely accused him and then let him go, at which point he presumably hid the evidence. However, I managed to convince the police that the only logical explanation for the thefts was that Soko had a key for my bedroom. The next time they brought him in I was there too and found out Soko had unwisely brought all his keys with him. I asked that we all go to my house and try Soko's keys on my bedroom door. At the house I instantly spotted a key on Soko's chain that looked suspiciously similar to my bedroom key. I tried it, and demonstrated that it could indeed lock and unlock my door. Soko grabbed the keys off me and lamely tried showing with his own attempt that actually it didn't work. But the police tried the keys successfully too and then angrily dragged Soko off to the station. As he was escorted up the path he looked backed at me bewildered ; he seemed surprised that I had figured it out and resorted to police action (Audrey later related how she had suspected him of stealing many things but had always let it go ; I would have been grateful for this warning beforehand).

The deal worked out was that Soko would pay back the money promptly and in return we would not press charges. I had half a mind to go ahead and press for punitive charges anyhow , but was mindful that Stacy needed her money back quite urgently. Soko it turned out had also just stolen even larger sums of money from Sarah (she had been keeping boys saving safe – they could put them in the school account but often found them difficult to withdraw from the Brothers). As she was about to leave Zambia, Sarah dropped the issue and accepted the money as lost, paying back the boys out of her own money. I reasoned that as Soko was getting away with that he should have plenty of money left with which to pay me and Stacy back. Nonetheless Soko still dodged us for about a year, after which the money eventually started coming in dribs and drabs. Like the tuckshop, I should have just gone all out with the full force of the law from the outset. Having said that, apparently Soko had actually paid back half the stolen sum quite promptly I later found out, but the police had held on to this. After I pressured the police via my friend Kalonde, the local Officer for the President (a kind of political Commissar who wielded considerable clout in the area) they returned this sum and finally began badgering Soko for the remainder. But I left a full eighteen months after the incident with still some money owing, which likely ended up in the police pockets.

After I had left Africa I later heard that Soko's beloved young daughter had died of malaria. I reflected grimly that even with all his thieving, Soko could not bring himself to spend a measly 10,000 kwacha (2 dollars) on a mosquito net for his child.

THE BANDA'S HIV AND GENDER WORKSHOP

At times, struggling against corruption, disorganisation, and apathy it was tempting to give it all up in frustration. But there were moments, glimmers of hope, when I could yet see the potential for change. JL and his wife, a nurse at the clinic, ran their own HIV and Gender workshop later. Thankfully it was a refreshing change to the earlier one run by Sister Angela. It was largely fact-driven as opposed to ideological speculation against condoms, and was frank in its criticism of those who refused to be tested. ' If you are not sure you are negative and are still having sex, then you are potentially murdering others. You have a duty to others as well as yourself to be tested'. It was a point that needed to be made more often in an Aids ridden country that was so fond of Christian moralising. Brother Michael attended and thankfully did not challenge the Bandas when they confirmed that in general, condoms were in fact very reliable. The questions raised at the workshop showed that in fact it had been necessary and useful, but again I had to wonder – why were not more such workshops were being run in schools or generally amongst the youth if the country was serious about controlling the epidemic? Half of these teachers were maybe infected anyway (official estimates were staggering – it was thought 40 % of secondary school teachers were HIV positive) and the workshops main usefulness for them was in recommending testing and use of ARV's. But what of stopping infections in the first place, particularly amongst our boys ? It was almost tempting to yield to conspiracy theories about western pharmaceutical companies and the failed abstinence programs of the Bush administration. ARV's were free for now, but once 'debt-relief' was over – would it be replaced with new charges for a generation dependent on ARV's ?

Education about HIV could only go so far anyhow amongst men who had deeply ingrained sexist attitudes. In conversations in the staff room the epidemic was usually blamed on a new generation of westernised women who wore short skirts and tempted men into behaviour that they would normally never contemplate. This argument even extended to the girls who were impregnated by their teachers. The tragic results were blamed on wicked temptresses, rather than men in positions of authority abusing their power. This led me to reflect that Gender Equality education could only go so far. Educating women about their rights could only succeed if the men were willing to concede these points too.

DAN AND BABY HEADS

Occasionally the monotony of life at Chassa was relieved by visitors as well my odd trips to Chipata. Dan came to visit once after being relocated to nearby Katete hospital. He seemed pretty happy about it. There was less corruption and he preferred the town with its numerous shops and close proximity to Chipata. We had a quiet weekend strolling around the grounds, cooking, and drinking at the bar. At one point he related to me a horrific story that was apparently a regular occurrence in Katete. Walking back from the shops he had seen two dogs fighting over something, and was surprised to see that it was a realistic looking doll. Not often you saw such toys out here. Until suddenly the dogs tore the doll in half and Dan saw the tiny purple organs spill out. It was a human baby. Dan stood stunned as one dog triumphantly trotted off with the head, and the other made off with the torso. Back at the hospital he related the story to other volunteers and eventually found out that the local women buried their babies in shallow graves if they had died in childbirth or pregnancy. It was believed that if a baby was buried deep this would somehow prevent the mother from conceiving again. Obviously hungry dogs could sniff out these tiny corpses when they lay only a foot or so below ground.

For me, it was another of those moments that slapped you out of your reverie and reminded you of where you really were. Sometimes these grim reminders would cross my own doorstep. Another 'hanger-on' I inherited from Audrey was a single young lady with a baby. At first she would appear asking for any food or spare cash just to get by and I duly obliged. She herself didn't appear to be in bad shape and I was more alarmed at the condition of her baby. He appeared to have some sort of parasite eating away his head. Sections of the scalp were eaten away almost to the skull. I could only guess that it was some sort of advanced ringworm condition. Despite this she insisted on him wearing a wiry wool cap, and the fibres stuck like velcro in the raw wounds ; they restarted the bleeding whenever she pulled off the hat to show me his condition. I gave her money so she could take him to the clinic but he never seemed to improve. Later she asked me for a hefty 110,000 so she could buy a sack of fertiliser for her maize field, pleading that if I granted her this she would need no more. I gave the money and she was back a few days later asking for another 60,000. At last, hearing that her maize crop failed, I tired of her constant requests and thereafter insisted she go to the Brothers for help. In my second year I still saw her around and the baby looked much the same. No doubt they had received short shrift at the Brothers.

T.T AND THE NEW MATHS DEPARTMENT

T.T had been a problem whilst A.G was the head of the maths department. He rarely showed up for lessons or to invigilate exams. After a government inspection however A.G had been relegated, as the inspector had deemed T.T better qualified (he had a college diploma whilst A.G had only a high school education). T.T was a new man after the promotion, suddenly driven and conscientious. He became the ideal partner in my drive to raise exam results in the maths department. Any initiatives before had fallen flat against the inertia of A.G. But T.T seemed newly motivated by his promotion and was receptive to my suggestions and initiatives.

The first thing he agreed to was the maximum usage of our numerous albeit old textbooks. They were falling to bits and outdated, but surely better than nothing. The boys could get some use out of them and we began distributing them more freely. Secondly, more meetings where scheduled where we could teach each other the difficult higher level topics that some teachers struggled to teach. T.T became a much more enthusiastic teacher and exhorted his colleagues to work harder. I pondered his earlier lack of motivation and wondered if it was largely down to personal clashes with A.G. It was unfortunately rather typical to see this kind of behaviour ; personal clashes that affected the pupils. I remember a public year nine exam that was postponed at a basic school because the invigilators had not turned up (after widespread corruption the invigilators had to come from different schools, so local schools would swap staff). Apparently the invigilators had been insulted the previous day with a sub-par lunch from their hosts (rice had been provided instead of nsima ; another opportunity for me to curse the white paste that blighted this province). Because of this petty staff dispute an entire year nine at the host school were unable to write their exam that day, indeed any more exams until the conflict was resolved.

The same exam time revealed problems with that other great Zambian public service, the police. I was invigilating an English exam at a local primary school when I noticed a boy at the back drop something. When I strolled to the pupil he had retrieved a piece of paper from the floor and was looking very nervous. I demanded the piece of paper, and unravelling it saw that it was a list of answers to the exam. The pupils English was so bad I realised he had somehow gotten hold of one of the infamous exam leaks and smuggled answers into the exam. When we looked more into his background we found out he was the son of a police officer. The police had recently caught thieves breaking into a school and stealing exams. Obviously not all the papers had been returned to the proper authorities. Selling exams was big money and a big temptation.

'NOBODY HAS NORMAL GUTS IN ZAMBIA'

Meanwhile my hermit like existence continued, as stomach problems led to my avoiding the bar. My stomach hadn't been the strongest since my heavy boozing University days. One last tremendous bout after my Finals had involved me drinking a bottle of Listerine. It had gradually recovered with my somewhat more sober years in London afterwards, but was never really the same again. Like most volunteers, at first I was subject to periodic bouts of diarrhoea as my stomach adjusted to the new foreign bacteria. After a few months however I seemed to have adjusted tolerably well. But there came a time when my limited diet, based largely on white bread, inevitably began to tell on me. Finding ways of relieving constipation became a kind of hobby of mine. When the usual remedies of coffee and cigarettes failed, I began to look around for alternatives. One letter was sent home containing the rather awkward sentence 'please send fybogel'. In the meantime I tried the liver salts at the tuck shop. When these stopped working I discovered Coca Cola could sometimes trigger the desired movement. Eventually I discovered a drink that did the job rather too well. This beverage eventually triggered a long running stint of loose bowels which took nigh on a year to get under control. It's name ? The strangely innocent sounding, yet viciously potent ' Milk Stout'. Sometimes available at the bar when we could get it from Mozambique, this creamy Guinesss-like drink was a delight in the evening. But the cheque was in the post. And in the morning it was always cashed. The said victim would always awake suddenly at about 5.30 with an impending sense of doom. I have never had the urgency as when waking from a Milk Stout night. It was not long before only two cans would get me out of bed rather fast, and eventually I only had to hear its name whispered for my colon to start twitching nervously.

Avoiding Milk Stout seemed to largely control the problem but I began to suffer more now from stomach upsets of a general nature. The local bread I bought was sometimes the trigger of this when it did happen. It was invariably handed to me by grinning, snot covered kids whose principal hobby was playing in rubbish tips. I carried the bread home with my hands and was mocked by others for not wrapping my bread `cleanly` in the paper provided (usually taken from a rubbish tip). In my last year I suffered a lot of acid reflux that continually plagued me. My stomach after this seemed to open up at any opportunity. Eventually antacids, ulcer treatment and a careful diet seemed to clear up the problem. Sarah had suffered similarly at times, probably set off by daily doxycycline which was provided to us in an acid gel capsule form.

We were far from the only volunteers plagued by such stomach troubles. As Sarah once said : ' Nobody has normal guts in Zambia' . How true. The Peace Corps had invented a club ; those that were in 'the club' were those that had inadvertently shit their pants in Zambia. Apparently 'the club' was very much in the majority amongst volunteers. I never joined myself, but by God I came close on many an occasion. Some volunteers could never adapt their stomachs to Zambia. I had to laugh ruefully at the story of a volunteer who had lasted a gruelling six months with constant problems. The poor volunteer had shit themselves daily for months and never discovered the cause. One day they were on the way to the latrine for another 'session' and not for the first time never made it. They happened to be carrying a plastic bag which they managed to drop the business into just in time. Then the urge to vomit as well came on suddenly, and the stricken mzungu instinctively turned and hurled into the bag. At the sight of the hellish mix held gingerly in the bag, they decided enough was enough and decided to quit Zambia there and then.

It wasn't just volunteers who suffered such problems. The state of toilets I visited suggested people had often spontaneously detonated in them. My doctor friends at Katete assured me that constipation, ulcers and general stomach upsets were very common in Zambia and nsima was often to blame. So even the natives were afflicted by these problems, and often due to maize. As for myself, after eating nsima I always suffered the kind of flatulence that wilts flowers. It was another reason to be disgruntled with the staple food. Yet the hallowed plant continued to retain its almost mythical status amongst Zambians.

After my return from Africa I was interested to stumble across an article on 'pellagra' ; a disease caused by a corn-based diet. The nutritional deficiencies of such a diet caused skin lesions, stomach upsets and even dementia and death. It had been recognised in Italy since the 1700's and was prominent in the southern U.S in the early 1900's. Although now a largely a forgotten disease in the developed world, I wondered how many Zambians might be currently afflicted by the disease. There certainly were a few 'madmen' wandering around my locality, although these cases could also have been the result of untreated syphilis.

THE PHANTOM GETS A 'SLOW PUNCTURE' ?

My second Christmas in Zambia saw my goodbyes to my visiting parents, and Sarah who left from Livingstone after joining us on holiday there. Sarah had become my closest ally at work, someone I could always rely on, which was not always the case with my other colleagues. She was an excellent teacher, and when all around at work was malaise, Sarah set the example that kept me going. I would find it very hard after her departure to maintain my motivation ; I became generally the only teacher who went to all timetabled lessons and taught consistently from bell to bell. My colleagues would marvel at the speed at which I covered the syllabus, as they sat in the staff-room and complained that there was not enough time in the year. Over time I had gotten over my crush on Sarah and been grateful to have such a friend at Chassa. I would still have Stacy around, but I would greatly miss having a western colleague at work. Sarah was also a bridge for me to the other teachers. Having been here four years she understood them a lot better than I did, and when I did socialise with them it was usually with Sarah. Sondashi was a great personal friend but could still be frustratingly Zambian sometimes in his attitude to his work. A week spent on duty with him showed he did not think our friendship prevented him from sloping off and leaving the bulk of the work to me.

My second New Year in Zambia was spent in Katete with Sichande and Dan. An uneventful evening was spent in Kings Night club, as my now even dodgier stomach prevented me from drinking at all. The Zambian beer Mosi in particular churned my guts, and Castle beer was little better as it set off stabbing pains in my stomach. I sat in the corner of the nightclub watching prostitutes dance with farm workers and bus boys, and wondered cynically how many more HIV transmissions would take place tonight.

At one point an animated drunk plonked down next to me and began jabbering about mobile phones, seeing me check mine for the time. ' Ah you people, you are incredible' .

' What ? I responded, half-nervously. There was something a little manic beyond drunkenness in the man's eyes.

The man continued : ' How do you come up with these ideas ? To make something, where you talk to someone on the other side of the world, it's incredible'.

' Well er., it wasn't me ..'I started uncomfortably, but the man cut me off.

' No, but you whites, its like magic what you can do. Us blacks can't do these things,'. I struggled to articulate something about the course of development, about how we had a head-start with agricultural and industrial revolutions and whole societal reasons such as education and good governance that made such inventions possible. But where do you start ? I wanted somehow to tell the man that there was nothing intrinsically superior or magical about ' white 'societies ; they had certain geo-physical advantages and a competitive environment. I was always uncomfortable with the inferiority complex that some Zambians seemed to have, but then how do you explain several centuries of history and geo-physical determinism in a nutshell? Although this particular individual was drunk and, Sichande asserted, a little bit demented, his sentiments were by no known means uncommon. It was usual to attribute success to magic rather than hard work and organisation. Many Zambians were jealous of the commercial success of Indian traders, yet both mocked them for working so hard (always counting stock and checking the books) whilst alleging that they had their own powerful magic. A primary Headteacher I spoke to told me of Indians in Chipata who had huge stashes of cash stowed away under their floors. The fact that they did not bank the money in Zambia was also resented. ` How do they keep the money safe there ?` I asked.

`Ah , magic – those guys have extremely powerful magic ` He replied.

The next morning after New Years, Sichande and I awoke in the spare nurses accommodation that Dan had arranged for us. Sichande seemed grateful for my presence the previous night, claiming that having me around had stopped him getting too drunk and cheating on his wife. As we got dressed, he tutted and pointed sheepishly to his now baggy trousers. The belt now was pulled to its tightest rung, and even his previously athletic shoulders and arms now seemed rather weedy ; a classic sign of HIV infection.   He caught me looking and grinned awkwardly with embarrassment. ' Ah , Burke, maybe... *this thing*... is eating me... maybe I have ...a slow puncture '. I looked away, struggling for something useful but sensitive to say. We both knew what *thing* he was referring to ; 'Slims' the Zambian nickname for HIV because it s most obvious symptom was persistent weight loss. The `slow puncture` also referred to the wasting away that seemed to characterise the disease when it got going in someone. Often people would say about someone : ` Ah, but they are too thin ` and this a was a coded reference to HIV. ' I have not always used condoms Burke' Sichande continued. I paused, struggling for the right response.

' Well, if you really think that, get tested and get ARV.s : people live for twenty years on those, and in future maybe they find a cure....' I advised him. But he seemed unconvinced and lost in his own thoughts. He had two small sons, and his wife had no prospects of a job. I hoped he would think about what I said.

140

THE NEW ACCOUNTANT- January 2006

It was in my last year that the school acquired a government appointed accountant ; a long overdue move I was later to discover. Gertrude was a young woman from Lusaka and we got on well, both of us city people and neither of us feeling at home in the bush. Gertrude seemed to perceive my increasing isolation and understand the cultural challenges a westerner faced in rural Zambia, feeling some of it herself as a Lusaka girl. Through local gossip Gertrude soon discovered how much money I had lost to 'loans' and seemed more outraged than myself. Unlike me however, she had the means to do something practical about it. As school accountant she handed out the bonuses to teachers at the end of term. Gertrude demanded that I hand her a list of my debtors. I couldn't remember all the loans ; in the early days I didn't write them down , naively expecting that pious Christians would be eager to repay the favour I had done them. Nonetheless come the end of term a lot of teachers received sharply reduced bonuses and I was largely repaid. I was glad for the money; my finances were often very tight ; the flights back to England were paid for by my parents and advances on my VSO resettlement grant. On the other hand many of my colleagues seemed greatly put out that I had dared to remember what they owed me. My isolation seemed to increase.

I didn't really discover what a hard time Gertrude herself was having at work until she came to my house one day to talk to Mashowo, who had to retire receipts because he was the Procurement Officer. They spoke loudly and in Nyanja until I asked what they were discussing. Gertrude explained the financial reports she had been told to write. ' Burke !' She exclaimed in her usual barking, goggle-eyed style ' there are hardly *any* receipts or records of spending for anything – I have told them to budget , they haven't listened, ...' She trailed off in exasperation. I probed her rather naively : ' You mean money is being ...' wasted? ' I asked tentatively. She looked up at me with her trademark scowl and continued : 'Burke, they spend money like you wouldn't believe... and on what ? What exactly ? They paint a few buildings and think that is doing a good job !' It was true. Brother Michael made a very big deal indeed about buying a few tins of paint and making the buildings look nice, but we never had any textbooks or other resources purchased, despite the rumours of generous sector pool funding from foreign donors.

Gertrude continued : ' and now *I* am the one who is answerable to the government accountants ! Things are changing here – the donors are tired of corruption and demanding more accountability. People are being *arrested* Burke ! Teachers are running away !' She related to me the story of a teacher who had been handling the finances of a Lusaka school. Upon hearing that donor accountants were coming, the teacher had simply fled and was never seen again. Others had been caught and even jailed for a change. Perhaps the age of tolerating theft was finally beginning to end. The donors were beginning to realise the sums being lost were just too large and important to let go lightly. One incident in particular had enraged some donors inspecting a school they had generously funded ; they found pupils sitting on bricks in bare classrooms, whilst teachers lounged in plush armchairs in the staffroom. Now, Gertrude began bickering again in Nyanja with Mashowo, and I realised they were now talking about the hot issue of the Housing Allowance.

The Housing Allowance was an ongoing issue of dispute between the Headmaster and the teachers. At first I sympathised with the headmaster's position. He explained in staff meetings that the Catholic Secretariat would not push the government to pay housing allowance because teachers were provided with free accommodation in Catholic schools. This seemed reasonable enough to me, until now the accountant told me that the government had in fact already distributed the housing allowance. It had been given to the Catholic secretariat, who refused to pass it on to the teachers under them. Such a case seemed simply theft and corruption on the part of the Catholic Secretariat, and yet no one seemed to challenge them directly on this.

It was instructive indeed to be close to someone who had an insiders look at the school finances. It was several months in fact, nearer the end of my service before I began to learn a lot about the school finances, but it was depressing to say the least. The first thing that struck me was how much money we actually had. Each term the school had an income of about 300 million kwacha (about 100,000 US dollars). I learnt we had three main sources of income. A lot of money came from western donors (60 million kwacha per term) ; countries such as Finland and Norway were particularly generous in this respect. The Zambian government provided a portion of school funding from its own tax revenue, (40 million a term) and lastly the boys fees made up the bulk (200 million) as they paid substantial fees each of 350,000 kwacha per term. This was obviously the sorest point with the boys as they saw little, if any return for their money. It was a high fee for eastern province and Chassa had a notoriously poor diet even compared to other schools here. The boys received meat twice a week but otherwise it was beans and nsima every day for lunch and dinner, with 'sample' maize for breakfast. After spending a week on 24 hour duty and sharing their diet I certainly sympathised with the boys, especially the poorer ones who could not afford to bring or buy extra food.

More galling for me was the fact that the school hardly ever bought any academic materials for the boys. From my very first meeting in 2004 the maths department had been requesting textbooks for at least the exam classes ; grades 9 and 12. We were knocked back with feeble excuses every term. All other departments suffered similar treatment. Only the Religious Education department, in which the Headmaster taught, ever received textbooks during the entire two years I was there. (I was however lucky to have my friends the Mitchells visit and bring a stack of A-level textbooks, each one would have cost a hundred thousand kwacha here). As if these boys didn't receive enough religion instruction already. Worse, the fees had already gone up from 250,000 to 350,000 whilst I had been at Chassa, and every staff -meeting it seemed Brother Michael was ever keen for more increases. At the same time however he lauded the Marist Organisation for creating a school in the bush and ' going where the action is' i.e helping the poor rather than the privileged. Yet Chassa was increasingly losing its way ; being now primarily for the children of government officials in Chipata, and increasingly even Lusaka. At one of my last staff meetings I was delighted to see Sondashi look Michael in the eye and tell him pointedly that another rise in fees would be immoral because : 'We should go where the action is'. Perhaps Michael half sought the increases to help cover up his own reckless expenditure, much as Stella at the tuck-shop had pressed me for price increases to cover her thieving.

When Brother Michael did seem determined to buy something for the school it was usually oddly irrelevant. He had an illogical infatuation with unnecessary luxury technologies, as opposed to those that were really useful. One typical obsession of his was trying to procure a wireless handset for our landline. That way he reasoned, some thirty seconds might be saved per phone call as people would not have to come to the office to receive the call.

I was sorry to hear later what everyone knew or at least suspected ; that school funds were indeed paying for the luxuries of the brothers. The accountant confirmed to me for example that the school did pick up the hefty phone and TV bill that also covered the residence of the brothers. As she was often at the residence herself she also told me that many donations from wealthy parents were dropped at the Residence and never made it to the school. Large containers of food and drink from parents who might be managers with food companies were left at the Brothers. But instead of supplementing the poor diet of the boys, the donations were used to spice up the three course meals of the missionary monks.

THE NOTORIOUS RED CAR

Meanwhile vast amounts of money were spent on 'the Administration' which was basically the largely unexplained expenses of the headmaster. In the past it seemed the school had been relatively well managed, with substantial sums saved ; the last Head had not received clear guidelines from the government on how exactly money was allowed to be spent. Consequently he had erred on the side of caution and built up a large surplus. But the current Head suffered no such qualms and the savings built up had now been rapidly squandered. Since Brother Michael had become Head, the school also now failed to produce yearly financial reports to parents. Annual PTA meetings were becoming increasingly heated on this issue. The last such meeting I witnessed saw the resignation of the parent chairman in despair at the repeated failure of the school to account for their spending. Irritatingly, Michael would lament in staff briefings the difficulty of these meetings and the burden on him. Yet it was all of his own making.

The most obvious symbol of the Head's abuse was his gleaming red car which sucked vast amounts from the school account in petrol charges. There was usually a general worker occupied with soaping down and polishing what was an average Toyota, but obviously the pride and joy of Brother Michael in poverty stricken Eastern province. Though the car was provided by the Marist brothers, the school account was used to keep it running. This was on the excuse that the Head was travelling on school business, which was sometimes true but usually unnecessary. Instead of posting something and making a phone call, Michael would insist on travelling in person to either Katete, Petauke (half an hour away) or worse , Chipata (2 hours away). I often pondered his motivation for this. Perhaps he just didn't like being around the school (he became notorious for being virtually an absentee Head). Perhaps Chipata had other diversions. At the very least the Head certainly had a childish love of driving. I once watched in amazement as he drove past me whilst I spent yet another lunch-time collecting water from a neighbours outside tap. He drove to the parish (a two minute walk) then soon returned. There could hardly be a more appropiate picture to symbolise the absurdity of how money was spent at Chassa. Whilst I wasted my mealtimes collecting enough water with which to flush my toilet (because the admin failed to resolve even this fundamental problem − not even long-drop backup toilets were built) Brother Michael took every opportunity to waste our precious resources on unnecessary driving. Perhaps even more ludicrously, Michael later decided that 'the school' was spending too much on petrol and that because the workers benefited somehow (?) , they should be the ones to contribute. So general workers who struggled on a paltry 150,000 were docked some 6,000 every month. This move particularly enraged the accountant, who had to distribute the wages to the workers and explain the deductions. Bizarrely, Michael still seemed to regard himself as exceptionally hardworking. Strange hours spent on the road with pocketed lunch allowances were seen as somehow more valuable than a consistent 9 to 5 effort at school.

The accountant indirectly suggested what was probably the real reason for all Michael's travelling. If travelling, Michael could claim an inflated lunch allowance of 50,000 kwacha (he deemed a monthly wage of 150,000 sufficient for our general workers). He would of course wait until an afternoon to travel. I'm reliably told his morning schedule consisted of mucking around on the internet in his office from 9 to 12, then he would organise money for a trip out. He would eat the usual 3 course lunch at the residence then travel immediately afterwards. Michael could also inflate fuel claims, perhaps pocketing another 50,000 by claiming 200,000 when 150,000 was sufficient (he was always careful to use the petrol station in Katete that didn't have a receipt book). If brother Michael travelled every other day (and he did as a bare minimum; in fact every day was more usual) he would be making a tidy profit in cash (100,000 a day) and probably not even have to ever break into his Heads wages. More startlingly, whilst Michael blocked others receiving housing allowance, he was careful to collect it himself. I was stunned one day in the school office to have 3 officials arrive from Petauke and ask for the Head (he was of course out again).When I asked if I could take a message, I was amazed to hear the officials respond that they needed to give the 'housing allowance' in person to him. Perhaps he was even 'collecting' others allowances for them and not passing it on. It wouldn't surprise me from what I now knew about him.

When the finances were not being misused, they were sometimes just directly stolen. The accountant had come to a department previously run by Chama and Brother John. Gertrude generally had found no records or receipts (despite John and Chama attending numerous workshops away from school on how to run the section). She did know however that Chama had stolen at least half a million on at least one occasion. Like my experience at the tuckshop, she found the Head curiously unreceptive to such information. Until she realised that he too was abusing the school finances. How could he pull Chama up about theft, when Chama knew so much about what the Head was doing ? Like the tuckshop, I began to see the school as a microcosm of the Zambian economy, where corruption could not be tackled by the leadership, because they themselves were the biggest thieves.

At times the handling of the school finances seemed downright bizarre rather than just corrupt. Our lone school secretary took maternity leave. Looking for a replacement, we found a suitable candidate who demanded

250,000 a month, whilst the school indicated it would pay 200,000. Actually 250,000 was a very reasonable demand, given that unskilled general workers received a paltry 150,000. But Michael wouldn't budge ; he wouldn't pay an extra 50,000 a month for an essential worker, despite the fact that he himself often took 50,000 *a day* just for an unnecessary lunch allowance. So for some weeks the school limped on with no secretary at all, with all the resulting chaotic delays. To my great irritation, Sarah and I were often drafted in again to do the typing. Most of the other teachers didn't want to learn and would chase us down when a document needed typing. My protestations that they must learn, that no one taught me, I taught myself etc, fell on deaf ears. I would often be approached at something like 3.30pm.

' Burke. We need this typed' (hands me a long letter to an official in Petauke, etc)

Me : ' Er, Ok, when do you need it for ?

' Er, …today ,.. at 1600.'

Me, irritated : 'How long have you had it ?'

' Ah, but that one …(grins awkwardly and looks away, still thrusting paper at me).

In fact the general handling of paperwork and approach to deadlines was worse at the top of the school. I was fairly relaxed myself and tended to leave projects till late in the UK, though they always did end up done on time (albeit sometimes just). But here I looked like a paragon of efficiency by comparison. I remember passing by the brothers one afternoon. Michael was drinking beer and watching a Nigerian movie on his laptop. I was consulting him on some project papers that needed typing (again given in too late to be typed by the secretary). He himself was helping type an equal number of projects to help meet the deadline tomorrow morning. So I was a little puzzled to see him spending his afternoon like this. The next day was the staff meeting. Michael began by theatrically apologising for his lack of alertness ; he had been up typing the projects until 1.30 in the morning sacrificing his sleep for the good of others, etc. I bit my lip and refrained from blurting out that I had finished mine at 1700 with the genius idea of starting earlier than him.

ACADEMIC SUCCESS

Whilst the money being wasted by the admin was maddening, at least T.T was helping me drive forward the maths department. Vastly improved exam results after my first year gave him faith in my methods, which quite simply involved providing pupils with study skills and accessible resources, a detailed knowledge of the syllabus, and consistent, interactive teaching. The grade nine results, whilst hovering around a 55 % pass rate year after year, had now jumped to 80 %, and more boys were opting to do Additional Mathematics in their senior years. I had decided to get around the intrangsience of the admin on textbook purchases by producing my own concise revision guide ; a resource that could be easily photocopied at low cost. It would be a painfully laborious process on the school computers, and had to be done at lunchtimes and evenings when the secretaries were off work. T.T constantly encouraged me in this and badgered the admin relentlessly for a photocopying budget. He was also much better than A.G in letting pupils borrow books, and he agreed to put up photocopies of syllabus requirements in the classrooms so pupils would know exactly what they had to do to pass. Also, personal maths books I donated to T.T actually stayed in the department and were used , unlike those I had given to A.G Zulu which had mysteriously disappeared.

Near the end of my service I finally produced a detailed 30 page booklet that covered the whole senior syllabus and was photocopied for free for every pupil. Like wise I produced similar booklets for Additional Maths and Junior maths. I was less successful in teaching T.T how to write such booklets himself, largely due to the problems with the school computers. Here again I lamented the loss of my laptop and printer, and wondered bitterly about the ultimate sustainability of what I was doing here.

DAGA AND 'BONGO LAND'

I was less successful with the older boys and maths results, and later reflected that they had been 'lost' a long time ago. Whilst they generally still behaved well in lessons, I was quite shocked to learn what they got up to outside of lessons. One spectacular incident in town involved a group of boys getting seriously drunk and all sleeping with a whore, then being nabbed by a bunch of teachers who had received a tip off (One of the pupils involved in this incident was the 14 year old son of a Cabinet Minister. They were all expelled, although curiously the son of the Cabinet minister returned a year later after a 'private appeal'). This kind of behaviour was apparently relatively common. They had changed an awful lot since being keen little year 8's. Years of being patronised and abused by a corrupt, hypocritical admin and prefecture body had left the older boys cynical. They invented alternative names for themselves, 'Big Elk', 'The Mask', and an entire subculture developed, a dark mirror image of the pious young singers in Church services. Their game was to indulge their fancies and outwit the Administration, and many 'Disciplinaries' were held often involving break-ins (at the School Office and Computer labs) and 'out-of bounds' in which we heard testimonies and often tried to pin the real culprits. Parents might travel from far to attend these disciplinaries, and would often on their knees beg the embarrassed Teacher Committees for forgiveness.   Threats of expulsion were made and sometimes executed, but there were many older boys on ' Final, Final Warnings'.

More directly affecting their studies was the alarmingly widespread use of 'Daga', the Zambian weed they smoked. They usually smoked by sneaking off into the bush or 'bongo land' as the daga smokers often labelled it. It was stronger than regular marijuana it seemed, and the boys were adamant that it endowed them with wisdom and confidence. My arguments with them that it slowed down their thinking were laughed off. It was often smoked it in the middle of the night, which explained why many were so groggy and useless in lessons the next day. Occasionally we randomly searched their possessions and caught a few who were subsequently expelled, but the problem remained widespread. Those year 12 's who were notorious for their use of daga did indeed do particularly badly in exams, but nonetheless the myth persisted that smoking daga somehow boosted mental performance. In the general atmosphere of jealousy and fear that often prevailed here it seemed daga was greatly prized for its confidence boosting properties alone.

THE PEACE CORPS AND HIV/AIDS

It was the Peace Corps rather than the admin who helped the school finally have some sort of whole school education on Aids. I wanted something free of bureaucracy and wrangles over allowances, a characterisation of all workshops in Zambia. I didn't want to go through the interminable wranglings of a VSO funded workshop which would involve piles of paperwork and negotiating over how much money would be needed to bribe people to attend. Spare me please another workshop at huge cost which would go mainly on t-shirts and booklets that people didn't read afterwards. I wanted hard talk and something which would cover the whole school.

I had been continually plastering the staff-room and classrooms with Aids awareness posters as a feeble substitute for lack of sex education lessons. But still, what I was learning about the boys and their behaviour was alarming and showed the pathetic inadequacy of sex education in Zambia. Last year all basic (primary) education had been made free (although schools did not exist in many areas) and all pupils were supposed to be educated about sex in the latter years of basic school. In practice however that rarely happened, as I learnt after questioning my own grade class of year 8's. I believe most teachers felt ill equipped to teach sex Ed and were culturally disinclined to do so anyway. In Zambian tradition a child was educated by an uncle or aunt about the facts of life. For various reasons I'm not sure if that was happening anymore. Perhaps increasing urbanisation and migration had fractured the large extended families that used to educate and look after each other.

It was only in my second year that I learned just how many of our boys were contracting STD's. JL and Jumbe eventually revealed to me that as Senior Teachers they were sending batches of boys every morning to the clinic for treatment of STD's. Depressingly, they also said such cases were on the increase. The 90's had seen a big drive on condom distribution, but these days a church backlash against them (in Zambia most churches, not just the Catholics, were generally opposed to condom use) was beginning to tell. Every day a clutch of guilty looking boys would hover around the Senior teacher's office, each in turn quietly explaining their 'problem' of burning urine etc, that needed attention. Many of them were younger boys, grade 8's and grade 9's, averaging 14 years but many as young as 12. If they were contracting chlamidiya, syphilis and other STD's (and they were), then surely some of them were also contracting HIV. It was a disaster. I knew that some of our boys were already on ARVs but who knows how many were also unknowingly infected with HIV and even spreading it. Many of them were contracting STDS whilst at Chassa, finding ignorant but willing girls in the villages who knew no better.

The tales I heard about the Cadets and their dawn ' road runs' were worrying indeed. Apparently the older boys posted the younger ones as lookouts, then sneaked off to the villages to do their business. Eventually the school properly investigated the cadets. They were supposed to be a sort of backup prefecture also responsible for discipline, but like the prefects, pupils joined so they could supervise manual work rather than do it themselves. Also like the prefects, the cadets caused more discipline problems than they solved. They were frequently involved in cases of drinking, theft, and bullying. It didn't help that the leader of the cadets was Massina ; eminently likeable, but an irresponsible drunk who was no role model. The cadets were eventually reined in somewhat after the admin tired of their frequent involvement in bullying, boozing, and even whoring. But we could never really stop boys sneaking off into the bush and getting into trouble, especially at night.

One of our worst scandals came to light when an amazed Father Brown at the parish received a phone bill for 14 million kwacha. It turned out some boys had their own phone set and were sneaking out at night to hack into the parish phone lines. A nimble pupil had scaled the telephone pole and connected his own set to the parish wires. Bizarrely, the boys had chosen to call family members, so all calls were traced and almost all the guilty boys caught. Irritating though this may be, it was obviously the sexual activities of the boys I was most concerned about, and I tried to stay focused on organising educational workshops for them on this theme.

With the Peace Corps in Eastern province I planned a day where a group of us could cover all 15 classes at Chassa with comprehensive education on HIV, STD's and Gender issues. They all agreed to come and do the weekend for free. I would be unable to reimburse their transport costs but would feed and accommodate them and throw in a crate of beer. Although only a few of the Peace Corps were specialising in health work, all had been thoroughly educated on HIV during their induction weeks. They had the expertise, and relatively speaking they were on our door-step. For fun the Americans would also play the school basketball team ; the Chassa boys loved basketball and trying to beat the yanks at their own game. I wanted a Zambian teacher to pair with a volunteer so that in future the Zambians could run such a day themselves. Unfortunately not one of them wanted to get involved. I can only speculate that they were too uncomfortable teaching the sexual material. I hoped it was not just that the `work` was unpaid ; if they had all become that cynical then the country really was in trouble. But curiously, even JL Banda didn't want to be involved in the teaching that day. When I asked him why, he said he believed the boys would respond better to the 'volunteer experts'. He was implying in fact that because the volunteers were Americans the boys would more readily accept their explanations. Again I had to wonder about a certain inferiority complex Zambians had. JL was at least, if not better qualified than the Americans on sex Ed. He had attended numerous workshops and led the Anti Aids club. As a clinic nurse, his wife also had vast first hand experience of dealing with STD's. And surely as a Zambian he would best understand how to convey the material. Instead he limited himself to videoing the day.

The day was quite a success, although I worried ultimately it would only be a one-off. The Peace Corps expressed an interest in returning, but if the Zambian staff never got involved then what were the ultimate prospects for its sustainability? Above all the school administration should be driving a whole school program themselves, but they were not concerned, despite the obvious problems we had with our boys.

CHAD'S VILLAGE

In my last holiday in August 2006 I spent a few days in the village of Chad, one of my Peace Corps friends. I wanted to get a real taste of what is like for a Peace Corps volunteer, and if possible, a greater idea of what life was really like for that half of the Zambian nation who lived in the real bush. Liz and I met in Katete, and a taxi took us an hour into the bush over hilly roads. We arrived at an open clearing of huts, spread over gentle rolling hills. We soon spotted Chad's conspicuous hut with a large tarpulin draped over it ; his makeshift attempt to plug a persistent leak. Chad emerged from his hut, hilariously tall and out of place looking in this village of near pygmies. He walked us round the small village and took us to see his friend Elias. In a tiny dark hut sat a smiling but drawn looking man, maybe in his mid-thirties. Elias beckoned us to sit, and we crowded around him as he sat on his bed. A variety of newspaper cuttings were pinned up on the wooden posts holding the roof up. Most of them seemed to be about TB. There was a crudely fashioned crayoned notice reminding visitors that there was no smoking allowed. Elias was newly arrived from Lusaka, where he had been living for years. It was a sad story. He had a steady job as a security guard and had had a young family. But in the last year Elias had become bedridden with TB which he had struggled to throw off ; a classic sign of HIV infection. As so often happened, the family abandoned the infected member. Elias's wife took the children and fled to her mother's village. With no family and now unemployed, Elias was left to die in Lusaka. He had scraped together some cash and taken the bus to Eastern province to return to his own village where his remaining relatives might nurse him back to health. Unfortunately he now had the rather unusual cancer of the leg. Rare cancers were another sign of HIV infection. Elias talked of returning to Lusaka when he was better, but there was an uneasy unspoken acknowledgement amongst us that he had come home to die. After we had left the hut, Chad confirmed that Elias was HIV positive and was receiving treatment at St. Francis Hospital in Katete. Even on ARV's though, Elias appeared to be struggling and often had trouble getting to the hospital.

Before darkness fell we needed to draw water, so Chad and I grabbed the empty yellow drums and headed down to the borehole. It was quite a short walk, but downhill. We met a small group of women at the borehole, who insisted we draw water first. There were no men to help them carry the big containers. I had kept myself in good physical shape here, but grunting and cursing I struggled to lug my water cans back up the hill, with Chad doing marginally better ahead of me. As we neared the peak of the hill and paused for a rest, the women breezed past us with the 20 litre drums balanced effortlessly on their heads. One of the women was heavily pregnant.

Luckily after our exertions, dinner was brought to us courtesy of Chad's 'amai' ; his village mother appointed to keep an eye out for him. She was delighted to have guests in the village and had insisted cooking for us. Her tiny, permanently grinning son ' Junior' brought us some steaming plates of nsima with green leaves.

A knock on the door later and the local medicine man entered, dressed unexpectedly in a western handout track-suit. He was reporting to Chad about his efforts to get funding and support for traditional medicine from the hospital. The authorities were not forthcoming it seemed, and I was not surprised after asking the medicine man's methodology. He told me he cured his patients with plants, found by dreaming. This shamen examined a patient and then lay down to dream. In his dream he wandered through the bush and was led to a plant, which was the one necessary. He then woke and set out to retrace the steps in his dream to find the real plant required. To his credit, the Shamen did not claim to be able to cure AIDS (as many others did indeed claim), but did insist that his plants could help with the symptoms of the disease.

The next morning Chad took us through the bush to his communal vegetable garden, nicely placed near a small stream. Although his chief remit was conservation and forest management, Chad had started this vegetable garden as a means of improving nutrition and generating a small income to help families with school fees. I wondered how valuable such a project could be in every village, and reflected bitterly that maybe there was one in every hundred villages.

I saw Chad some months later and learnt that sadly Elias had indeed succumbed to his illness. Although he had been on ARV's, he had perhaps started on them too late. The aggressive leg cancer could not be reversed.

TRAVELS AROUND AFRICA

Having returned to the UK no less than three times for the weddings of best friends, I did not travel as much in Africa as I had originally intended. Nonetheless I did have time to superficially see some of Zambia's neighbours and reflect on how they differed from my new home. I have already mentioned Malawi. Although it featured regularly in international papers as in a dire situation and suffering from a mono-maize culture, I thought this far truer of eastern province Zambia, which looked significantly poorer. At least Malawians had more fish and thus protein in their diet and this often was noticeable in their physiques. The roads were far better (a fact for which I was grateful as we were driven at the usual lunatic speeds) and the better stocked shops may have reflected the greater accessibility of the country as compared to land-locked Zambia.

I saw a significant amount of Namibia as one holiday my sister and I travelled down to Windhoek and beyond on nature and desert safaris. Despite the harsh desert terrain , Namibia was far richer than Zambia. I suppose the Germans had left more infrastructure than the British had done in Zambia, and then the country had later been profitably linked with South Africa. Perhaps more of the population was concentrated in the cities and there was a less of a poor village population. The country had modern problems that come with development however ; a medic I talked to in Windhoek told me of the numerous gun-shot and stab wounds he saw every night.

Likewise I saw a considerable amount of Tanzania as I was driven by coach to Dar-es-Saleem. (There was on old Chinese built railroad on the same route but it took 3 days).The country-side preceding the capital was striking for the range of produce they grew, and particularly the hill-side rice. Dar-es-Saleem was a far larger and more developed capital than Lusaka, although I was almost killed by the bricks that fell off the face of the Barclays building. Many wealthier Zambians on the coach were travelling to Dar-es-Saleem where they could purchase goods a lot cheaper and even bring many back to sell ; Zambia was not so cheap because of distances and transport costs. Close to Dar-es-Saleem, the exotic island of Zanzibar was doing well because of tourism and the rich produce, particularly cloves, that were grown there. I was particularly pleased to meet up with some Canadian friends that were visiting, another morale boost for me.

Botswana I saw much less of as I merely visited the famous Chobe park. Again though, the visible signs of better roads and better stocked shops were a rough indicator of development. I'm told the country was doing well with the diamond trade, although curiously despite it's material development Botswana was suffering more than any country with the HIV crisis.

Despite being within throwing distance of Zimbabwe from Livingstone, the 70 dollar entry fee for UK citizens kept me out. I crossed the bridge and had a friendly enough chat with the guards there, but could only wonder at the trouble inside the country. I knew several white farmers from Zimbabwe who had crossed the border and set up farms in southern province Zambia, and their stories were usually the same ; a group of ' war-veterans' (usually too young to have even fought in the war) had arrived on their property and given them a day to collect their belongings and get out, leaving of course all valuable farm machinery like tractors. There were more of these white refugees in Lusaka, trying to scrape together a living and drinking in the backpacker bars. Here they both craved western company, yet simultaneously often mocked the 'Aid industry' for what they saw as their naive and politically correct attempts at development. Their black counterparts were often lining the verges and medians on Cairo road, trying to hawk various nick-nacks through car windows at traffic lights. The teachers at Chassa always seemed reluctant to discuss Mugabe with me, maybe because he was still a hero to some, but this sat awkwardly with his renewed hatred of the British. They always alleged that colonial authorities had ripped off Mugabe's testicles when he was once in detention, and for this he would never forgive the British. They also found it exceptionally funny that Mugabe bragged of having ' a degree in violence'.

The landlocked nature of Zambia, and its' sheer size was driven home to me by my travels, and I became convinced that villagers might be better off with a more self sufficient approach as opposed to hoping for better roads and access to markets. Large distances and high fuel costs would always be prohibitive to trade. Although economic progress is usually the result of specialisation and trade, rural Zambians were usually subsistence farmers struggling to feed even themselves. They had more immediate concerns than finding markets for surpluses. With its decrepit buildings and roads, Zambia was so economically battered it did look as though it had been through a war. Other countries that had actually been in wars (such as Mozambique and Angola) seemed to be recovering fast and overtaking Zambia. Zambia did not have resources that were quite as consistently valuable as others (Copper could crash whereas diamonds and oil are pretty much always reliable revenue generators) but it was rumoured that were significant emerald mines. As of yet it was said that those in power were concealing these mines and using them for private gain rather than making them a national resource.

Zambians such as the teachers were well aware of how their country measured up to its neighbours. They often felt that their chance at development had been irrevocably missed somehow ; Sondashi often spoke of the gift of Independence being wasted and how the notorious President Chiluba had spent taxpayers money on private flights and Italian loafers (an amusing and yet tragic article in the paper one day detailed Chiluba's attempts to retrieve his 70 pairs of loafers from the Anti-Corruption Commission).

THE ELECTIONS – September 2006

My last September saw the General elections. They were viewed with some optimism by most Zambians. Although the last election had probably been rigged (candidates voted in by non-existent voters), new measures such as photo ID had been put in place which would make corruption more difficult this time. Sata, the main opposition candidate, was very popular. He was an ex-government minister who had a reputation for action, hard work and fighting corruption. After the ludricrous excesses of the Chiluba years (the previous President who had wasted so much money on private jets, Italian suits and shoes) could Zambia at last reach a real turning point ? Many thought the current Levy was at best a holding man. Zambia was gradually clawing its way back after the disastrous eighties, but many were divided on whether real progress was being made. The teachers at Chassa said Sata was the one to 'get things moving'. As health minister he had been notorious for disguising himself as a member of the public and visiting hospitals in secret. When he found staff not working he would reveal his true identity and proceed with on the spot firings and warnings. Obviously this could be a problem temporarily with staff shortages, but in the long run it was exactly what was needed in a shockingly complacent work culture, especially in the key public service sector. Ideally of course policies needed to be implemented that dealt with this rather than relying on the personal efforts of one man, but nonetheless anecdotal evidence from my colleagues suggested that the health service had indeed been in much better shape under Sata.

I was slightly disconcerted to hear about opposition Election rallies being 'disrupted' by mobs of government supporters, something that conjured up unpleasant images reminiscent of Zimbabwe. In nearby Petauke, a rally of Sata supporters had been violently disrupted by such government supporters, and nobody seemed particularly surprised or outraged that free speech had been trampled on. Thankfully the head of Police in Zambia publicly stated he would not tolerate this kind of behaviour, but it was worrying to me that it seemed almost to be culturally acceptable. Despite any misgivings I had though, most of the teachers seemed excited about the election and were reasonably confident of voting Sata into power.

However, I should have been suspicious already before the elections, when schools and clinics all over Zambia had their funding suddenly and unexpectedly cut. Sinda clinic was now in dire straits. Although the public no longer had to pay the small fees for being seen, the government had cut it's central funding too. The clinic wouldn't be able to sustain its services for long at this rate. Chassa Basic, being now unable to charge fees due to government decree, likewise now had no source of central funding ; yet basic education was now free for all hence rolls were up. Our own school had its funding drastically cut with the explanation that the foreign donors had cut back their contributions. Whilst passing through Lusaka and the VSO office in August I mentioned this to George, my education manager. Puzzled, he told me that in fact donor money for education had actually been increased, to help compensate for a drop in the value of the dollar. The explanation of course was undoubtedly that the Zambian government (or rather the ruling party the MMD – the ironically named Movement for Multi-Party Democracy) was using the money for the purposes of re-election. Just before the elections took place, the local intelligence officers received gleaming new land-cruisers (whilst the regular police made do with bicycles and no phone system). The chubby, amiable intelligence officer Kalonde had now ditched his old motorbike and was gunning around Sinda in a powerful new off-road jeep. Suspicious timing indeed. We can only guess at the sums used to bribe election officials and presiding officers, whilst schools and clinics struggled desperately. I had to wonder too at the timing of the repairs to the crumbling Great East Road. For years it had been more potholes than road, and now in an election year it was finally undergoing repairs, as if the government was trying to prove at the last minute that it really was concerned about development after all. However, yet again of course the new tarmac was being laid as far too narrow, so that the edges of the new road would crumble under the weight of the large freight trucks that brought goods to Chipata. No doubt much of the official sum allocated for repair was being divided up between the contractors and the local government officials. The job would be done on the cheap again in order to line pockets, whilst buses continued to blow out their tires and slide off the road, taking more startled passengers to their deaths.

On a more fundamental level I had to wonder about some of the attitudes towards democracy. In Lusaka I met again my regular taxi driver James, a man whom I admired for his running of a charity to provide coffins and burials for poor families. He was a government supporter and seemed irritated that opposition was even allowed to exist. He was critical of Sata, whom he saw as an unprincipled opportunist, but was particularly scathing about an ex-colonel who had started a new minor party. ' This man' James would complain bitterly ' he has no chance of winning, so then why enter ? He is just trying to confuse people' . The idea of choice, dissent and debate didn't seem particularly important. The idea of democracy as a useful exercise in itself just wasn`t there. James seemed to think Levy, the present incumbent, was making a genuine effort to tackle corruption but I had to be sceptical about this from what I had seen and heard. Or at least, if Levy was trying, he wasn`t succeeding.

Neither was I impressed with the government's attitude to a free and independent media. There was only one opposition paper (The Post) and yet I learnt that even the editor of this paper was regularly hassled and thrown into custody on bogus charges. He had a lawyer who was constantly bailing him out of jail.

The weekend before the elections I was in Chipata. Karl, a south African cotton farmer who worked in Chipata and was a drinking buddy of ours, called round the Peace Corps house and we headed out to Hills Bar near the station. There was no escaping drinks and clubs if big Karl was in town. As usual Hills was heaving, and being in no mood for dancing I found a spot in the corner and wedged myself in. A smartly dressed young man, maybe 30, forced his way in next to me. After some small talk he demanded a beer. I wasn't very impressed with his manners but was used to this treatment now and feeling generous today, so I went along with him. I was now fairly used to people demanding beer off me simply because I was a 'mzungu'. He asked me what I thought about the elections. I hadn't given it much thought, but when pushed, said I thought Sata should win. He had a reputation for action and dealing with corruption. The man's attitude abruptly changed. There was nothing but acid hate on his now contorted face. He began poking my chest . ' You should watch what you say. Your mother loves you very much, and it would be a shame if you never saw England again' I stood dumb-founded : 'B- But you asked me what I thought !' The man merely repeated himself. I began breathing fast and my knees began trembling as the adrenalin pumped through me. Looked like I was going to have to dance after all. Suddenly a prostitute jumped in between us. She'd overheard the conservation. As the man struggled with her some other Zambians jumped in too and broke up the scuffle. The man grudgingly wandered away. I got another beer and decided it would be wise to rejoin my group at the other side of the bar. Most were dancing, but Karl was there, tall and imposing in a black t -shirt. It wasn't long however before the man was back. He simply stood staring at me, clutching the beer I had bought him. I decided I had to approach him and ask him what the problem was. I needed to know. I pushed my way through to him and asked : ' What's your problem –I don't vote – so what are you so angry about ? Why are you worried ?' He looked like he was so furious he could barely spit out the words. As he moved closer to me the considerable bulk of Karl suddenly blocked my view. He'd picked up the vibe but not the exact words over the blaring music and decided an intervention was necessary. Like two children separated by a teacher we began bickering over Karl's shoulders. The man was almost incomprehensible but was angrily spitting out threats. I hurriedly explained to Karl and then my resolve stiffened. I clutched my empty beer bottle and decided the man wouldn't be deterred by reason. 'Sod it Karl, the guy threatened my life. He's crazy ! And he s got me so wound up now I wanna kill him too! This guy shuts up or he's getting a bottle over his head right now and the broken end in his face.' Karl turned to me to cool me down and suddenly the man attacked. But as he launched himself Karl spun round and caught the flailing arms. The man struggled wildly but Karls big arms had him easily pinned. The man struggled helplessly and comically ' Cool down or I'll put you down ' warned Karl, and then released the man and pushed him back. But the man came again. This time Karl put him down with a big right hand and the man fell awkwardly onto his knees. In a flash other Zambians were upon us and Karl began putting them down too. I recognised the Zambians as those that had helped me earlier. They were just trying to keep the peace. I jumped in too, to try and stop Karl flattening them. After a few seconds of confused scuffling we all managed to disentangle ourselves. Some bouncers had thrown out my original attacker. We decided to rejoin the others on the dance floor. ' Well thank god that's all sorted out !' I commented to Bo, a Peacecorps buddy. He nodded, not having really heard me, and looking at the girl dancing in front of him, and merely said ' this hooker's got a great body !' I laughed at his apparent oblivion and joined in the dancing.

I still have no idea who the man may have been. At the time I could only speculate he may have been an MMD party cadre or someone in some capacity sent from Lusaka to monitor the elections. Now I believe he may have even been someone in intelligence sent out to help with the fixing of the election. It would account for his paranoia and aggressiveness, although admittedly not his rather lame fighting abilities.

It was an odd night all round. Iqbal, our aging, hard–drinking muslim friend, drank himself into the arms of a whore, murmuring about red stones that he mined in the bush and sold for use in explosives. At seven in the morning we stumbled outside into dazzling daylight, and as people began walking to work, Karl took off his belt and literally whipped away the whores that milled around us expectantly. I shambled back to the Peace Corps house, dreading the journey back to Chassa I would have to make later, after a few hours of snatched drunken unconsciousness.

As the day after voting progressed, most people seemed happy that the results were as expected : Sata, the hugely popular, nationalistic opposition candidate, seemed to be pulling well into the lead on the basis of the first known results. He was already 75, 000 votes ahead in the presidential race ; a considerable margin at so early a point and with an electorate of only a few million. I wondered if the government would accept the result or whether we would be in for trouble. Thankfully the government seemed remarkably relaxed about the situation, although later we would see the sinister reasons why. In a newspaper article the main government spokesman confidently rebuked Sata's supporters for prematurely celebrating victory.

Later I wandered into the staff room and found Sondashi again listening to country music through the satellite TV radio channel. He was not yet confident of Sata's victory. ' They can still fix it, buddy'(the government). I asked him what would happen if the government did fix it ; would we see anything like armed resistance ? Would the people do anything ? Could they do anything ? ' No' he replied simply. ' Nothing will happen. Last time Sata appealed in the courts. The process takes four years. But the president is inaugurated the day after results are finished. Then he controls everything. He appoints the judges. And Zambians will not fight.'

That night I passed by the bar. Emmanuel, a teacher from Chassa Basic was there, after helping at the polls. He was utterly shit-faced, having been paid a sizable cash sum for his admin work and had already blown most of it on Castle lager. Contrary to the general mood, Emmanuel, like Sondashi, was not confident of Sata's victory at all. ' Watch out' he hinted darkly : ' expect a late shock – very difficult to defeat an incumbent government in Africa.' I wasn't sure. 'But how will they fix it this time – after the uproar after the last elections and the subsequent new measures for voting ' I asked him.   The procedures for voting now included photo ID and more. Emmanuel's eyeballs rolled lazily in his red sockets as he contemplated this. ' They can't. Not at the polling station. Voting itself was free and fair. But... then the results are taken to a regional headquarters.... by a police officer and a Presiding Officer. The presiding officer is ....government appointed' . He didn't need to say anything about the police officer. With their relatively meagre salaries they were of course easily bribed.

The next morning I was up relatively early (by my standards, not Zambian !) to buy bread. I saw Sgt. Sichande sitting outside the Police post and strolled over to chat. He was excitedly jabbering Nyanja into his phone, wriggling in his seat and stabbing the air with his finger. He eyeballed me sideways like a predator and motioned me to take a seat whilst he finished. Finally he hung up and turned to me. ' Levy - 300,000 votes in front' . I stared disbelievingly at him. 'Says who ?' ' Police in Lusaka.' He replied. 'It's a fix.' I didn't believe it. ' It – they can't steal that many votes- its too obvious for Christsake' I protested. Sichande continued ' And now Sata...'he grinned menacingly ' is a dead man. He will have an accident relatively soon after the election. And then the opposition will be finished.' We talked a bit more, but I privately thought Sichande was full of crap. I had lost respect for him over time and doubted his competence. I repeated the claims to Stacy when I got in, saying again I thought Sichande was wrong and the claims had to be a gross exaggeration.

That afternoon through my thin lounge walls I heard Mumba and J Banda outside, shouting to each other across the road; ' Yeah, Levy 300,000 votes ahead ...' . I jumped up and opened my front door. ' What – what was that – what's the election latest ?' I shouted. They both turned to me : ' Levy Mwanawasa is 300, 000 votes ahead'. I stood dumbfounded ' What - how ?' Mumba gave a wry grin and shrugged his shoulders. ' Africa !' he laughed simply, and walked away. The situation seemed to be accepted with the usual weary fatalism.

Later I dropped by the Brothers residence to see the results come in on TV (the staffroom cable was being sporadically cut due to late bill payments, although the Brothers suffered no such indignity). Even in Sata's homeland the incumbent was picking up a surprising number of seats. Father Fanuel, also watching, turned to me and tapped the side of his head : ' Villagers. They can't think straight. The government gives them a bag of fertilizer and a sack of maize and they're happy. Their headman tells them how to vote. Villagers can't see the bigger picture.' Chiza smirked ironically . 'Hmm, that's not all - even in the towns...my cousin works for the electoral commission. Even he says the government has gone too far this time.' 'Rigging, you mean ?' He nodded, and continued : 'But people – police, electoral officers – fear for their jobs. The voting may have been fair, but the weak spot is in the transmission of results to Lusaka. And see that woman announcing the results for the electoral commisson ? ' I looked at the woman, plain and bespectacled, spectacularly benign looking, in her fifties. Not your usual villain. 'That's the presidents cousin !' Chiza spat.

We continued to watch grimly as most of the seats came in for Levy and further extended his lead. Then came the news of the first riots. Sata supporters in Lusaka and the Copperbelt had taken to the streets, standing off with the cops and looting shops. To their credit the police seemed to remain calm and handled the rioters delicately. Probably many of them had voted for Sata too and sympathised with the protesters. Sata was an ex-police chief and also had a lot of sympathy within the army . Rumours spread that Levy Mwanawasa had become nervous, and fearing a coup, had ordered special commando units to guard the houses of army Generals. Years ago there had been one abortive coup, and a certain Captain Soko of the airforce now languished in prison with a minor cult status. Sata himself appealed to his supporters to remain calm. Most Zambians remained dismissive of the possibility of any real trouble.

A couple of days later the president was sworn in again, with a final majority of close to a million, in a country of only 3 million voters. Amidst widespread allegations of voting irregularities, only one minor opposition candidate attended the inauguration, and his fawning manner suggested he had only do so for TV exposure and to curry favour with the incumbent. The President's slick campaign manager, widely known as the fixer, commentated the inauguration on ZNBC. ' This government has the support of the majority – the villagers – but admittedly we do need to look more at the problems in the towns'. Chiza was again dismissive. ' There are a lot more people than you think in Lusaka and the copperbelt. Several millions. The population is actually close to 50 –50 if you look at the villages and the towns. And it's easier to fix results in isolated areas. No EU monitors and less of Satas' officials to contest suspicious figures before it's too late'. There had been Chinese monitors too, but I'm sure that with the mining concessions they were getting these days in Zambia they had come to an arrangement with the government. Their own interpretation of democracy was fairly loose. Sata had been quite vocal in his criticism of the Chinese as investors who did not pay taxes, so the Chinese were hardly likely to protest about vote rigging against him. Everybody was suspicious about the high numbers of voters in the villages. Like last election, the government in many areas had magically gained more votes than there were voters. But yet again the president was inauguarated and was now holding all the cards. It was too late. Five more years of the same. Chiza was finished with the whole process. He didn't want to say much, but simply said ' I have never been so disappointed. I knew it was all over when I saw Levys campaign manager just quiet and relaxed as the first results came in. I knew then that it had already been fixed.'

I eagerly awaited the arrival of my Guardian Weekly, a renowned liberal paper that focused on international development issues. Surely they would have an article that courageously explored the allegations of vote rigging. When the paper arrived, I saw with dismay that Zambia merited one tiny paragraph. It merely alluded to rioters being 'disgruntled' with the results. Allegations of corruption and rigging were not mentioned.

Gertrude returned from Lusaka, and related how the shops had been shuttered and police had tear-gassed crowds of angry young professionals who had favoured Sata. Then, alighting from the bus at Sinda she had seen Kalonde, smug and smirking, sitting in his land cruiser, obviously happy with the results. He taunted her, knowing she was a Sata supporter ' Ah , you said your party would win Miss Njobvu, but it was ours !' Gertrude had berated him back in the street . ' Shame on you ! I know what you did !' She barked, alluding to the fixing, and perhaps even his own role in this area. He had apparently smiled awkwardly and been silenced with this.

Another incident occurred after the elections that made me wonder if the MMD were indeed becoming paranoid and dangerous. They had lost control of (or rather popularity in) the towns and that would make any government nervous. A couple of weeks after the elections I was in Sinda dropping by the post office. I swung by the motel for a coke to boost me for the bike trip home in the intense heat. I didn't enter the bar ; there was some meeting going on there. ' What this ?' I asked the barmaid ' Workshop for the clinic workers ?' 'No' a man replied for me , also outside leaning on the wall. 'Post mortem on the elections by the party' I turned to look at him. I didn't recognise him but he was well dressed and looked at me intensely. Another man came outside, saw me and then murmured in his friends ear ' Burke, teacher at Chassa'. Unlike most Zambians, these two were in no hurry to introduce themselves . ' So,..post mortem' I asked ' you lost. Which party ?' The man straightened up. ' *Government* party, MMD.' He answered, with particular stress on the government, as if they were the natural ruling party. 'We are analysing why we lost this seat' he explained. ' But this area' I started ' has never been MMD, it has always been er, what is it UPND, or UNIP is it ?'
' UPND' the man replied'
' Oh right ' I corrected myself' the others UNIP , are southern ,the Tongas ?'. The man suddenly looked at me with more interest.
' You seem to know a lot about our politics. I'm surprised you know the names of the parties'
I stared at him, incredulous : ' What - the names of the major political parties ? I read the papers. I've been living here two years.' There was no response from the two men. I began to feel the anger well up inside of me. Were they just stupid ? how could I live in a country for two years and not know the names of the major parties . I'd have to be deaf, bind, and never talk to anyone !' No, these man were paranoid because I was white, an outsider. They were either brought up on tales of CIA interventions and rumours that volunteers were spies, or maybe they knew that as a westerner I would be less likely to keep my mouth shut about corruption and fixing. I jumped on my bike in disgust and cycled off.

Several other incidents occurred during the last months of my time in Zambia that made me wonder if the country was beginning to turn down a dangerous path. Would it go the same way as Zimbabwe ? Or had it always been this way and I was now seeing these things for the first time after being more familiar with the place ? One incident was a high profile multiple homicide in Kabwe on the copperbelt. Actually it was via friends, Zambians in Chipata, who attended the funeral that I first heard of the murders. A white family on a farm there (my friends neighbours and old friends) had been hacked to pieces by machete wielding intruders. The official version was that it was a robbery, but nothing had been taken except the family's mobile phones. My friends intimated that some dispute had taken place with a local politician over land access and cattle grazing rights. But later I heard rumours that the head of the white family had been involved in the copper mines and had uncovered high level corruption.

Later I bumped into the same Chipata friends again. They had been on safari in the bush of South Luangwa , but had to return early because of fears over their safety, something usually unheard of in Zambia. A drunken chief had burst into their camp late at night with armed followers wielding machetes and AK-47s. He demanded thousands of dollars for the privilege of letting them camp on his land, although they had already paid for permits. They had packed up and left. ' Is it me, or this country changing ? I asked Louise. I told her about my election 'incidents'. She agreed ' No, you are right. Something is changing here. I don't know, but it's like it could get like Zimbabwe.'
'Yeah' I agreed ' like Sata was compared to Mugabe, but it seems the MMD party below Mwanawasa are the real ones acting like Mugabe'.

Conversations with Zambians at Chassa however later taught me that Zambian history was not so peaceful as was commonly portrayed. True, there had never been a civil war or serious repression (aside from one 'cult' uprising in northwest in the 70's), but political assassinations, it transpired, were a well established tradition. Lawyers who took on corruption cases soon met with conveniently fatal muggings. The revered first President Kenneth Kuanda himself had had a son who had been a promising Presidential contender, standing against the notoriously corrupt Chiluba. But an alleged botched carjacking had left Kaunda's son seriously injured. In the hospital his condition had mysteriously deteriorated and he had died unexpectedly suddenly. Even Levy in recent times had suffered a suspected assassination attempt. His car had once crashed mysteriously and the President had suffered mild brain damage. A series of minor strokes later on led to the Opposition daring to call him a cabbage, which Levy angrily countered in the press. ' I'm not cabbage, I'm steak' a headline thundered.

The opinion in Lusaka amongst ex-pats gave me a clue as to what had probably happened in the latest elections. Sata had clearly put the willies up the established interests, i.e, the foreign investors who pulled the real strings of power. He was a nationalist who would not tolerate foreign exploitation of resources. Maybe the EU had overlooked rigging in the election because the incumbent Levy played ball with foreign corporations, and no doubt the Chinese observers were even less inclined to defend democracy. Hanging out at the backpackers bar, a half-drunk ex-VSO, now settled in Lusaka, told me simply : ' Well, if it was a fix , it was a bloody good one – Sata is a nutter - and a drunk . You know he tried to sue Coca Cola for a million dollars because he found a cockroach in a drink ? If Sata had got in – it would have been the end of democracy here – so it was better that it was fixed'. The peculiar irony of this statement didn't seem to strike him as odd at all. But then, I reflected with my growing cynicism, this was Africa.

Later at Chassa it almost seemed as if the irregularities of the election had been forgotten. Mumba and a couple of others discussed the western concept of democracy and its failure in Africa. ' Democracy has not worked in Africa' asserted Mumba. I sat half stupified, incredulous. ' But Mumba, you have never actually *HAD* democracy here. Democracy is more than the right to vote. It's relatively honest and above all, responsible and accountable government. When have you had that here ?'. He could not answer. Articles in the press suggested to me that democracy, though forty years old in Zambia, had never really taken hold. It was normal here to see a mainstream paper here for example lauding Mugabe as a 'model of strong leadership in Africa'. It seemed there was either a fawning exaggerated respect for the west, or on the other hand an old hatred and perverse pleasure in defying the west, even when it destroyed your own country.

In fact later the EU did admit rather lamely that they did now consider that numerous ' irregularities' had taken place in the transmission and recording of results. But it was too late. Levy had been inaugurated and could now control the judiciary. Another court case challenge would only take four years again and be thrown out. Suddenly I began to look even more forward to my imminent return to the UK. I had now had enough of Chassa, but the election debacle had cemented my desire to leave the country full-stop. I was now convinced that political change was the necessary precursor to other development. I may still have been disenchanted with the shallow materialistic culture of the UK, but I was coming to appreciate relatively honest government.

I did not have a lot of direct involvement with government myself, though I was massively unimpressed with the officials that had come to brief us on the setting up of the CRAIDS project. This Community Response to Aids was to fund some sort of sustainable project in the area that would benefit all people affected by HIV. As was often said, if you were not infected then you were at least affected. One way or another AIDS touched the lives of almost everyone here. After we had waited for months, the officials gave us a couple of hours notice one Saturday that they would be coming, and there would be a compulsory meeting in the staff-room. I duly cancelled my shopping trip to Sinda and waited in the staff-room at the appointed time. Eventually the officials turned up four hours late with no apology or explanation. No doubt they had enjoyed an ample and leisurely lunch. Their first act was to berate us for the poor attendance. Criticising the people who had turned up at late notice didn't seem logical, but I sat patiently. The patronising manner with which they talked to everybody oozed arrogance, and likewise the deference and even fear with which the general workers treated them (few teachers turned up) made me uncomfortable. It was soon obvious after a short time that these people were idiots, and it was difficult to see them talking sharply to JL Banda, our CRAIDS co-ordinator ; he likely had far more ability and integrity than any of them.

It was also interesting to note that the traditional source of power in Zambia, the chiefs, seemed far more cooperative and punctual than their urban bosses, at least in this case. The chief's representative turned up like us at short notice and on time. He was a well dressed, elderly and distinguished looking fellow who spoke perfect English. Unlike his urban counterparts on whom we waited, he did not turn up in a land-cruiser but instead slowly pedalled an ancient bicycle. Like us, he waited for a couple of hours before leaving in exasperation , citing the many errands he had to run for the Chief.

INTERLUDE : HOW TO CUT MZUNGU HAIR – A BARBERS GUIDE

Welcome pink mzungu into your shop and make a fuss about where he sits. Bark at other bewildered customers to make an entire bench free for your honoured guest . Quieten mzungu when he protests. Answer his anxious enquiries and assure him that you can cut his type of hair no problem, no problem. Just before you begin, leave the shop and say `I'm just coming` as you are in fact leaving. Return from mysterious errand. Seat mzungu in cutting chair. Buzz clippers nonchalantly over mzungu hair and then hide surprise on face when massive clump falls off. Momentarily wonder about asking mzungu if he has alopecia, but then realise from his face that this is normal for mzungu hair. Gingerly buzz clippers over again and hide despair when scalp is exposed. Maintain composure and steadily buzz all of mzungus hair off, reasoning that this must be all how mzungus have their hair cut. Leave a few random clumps to dispel the allegation that mzungu is now totally bald. Charge mzungu twice normal price for your special expertise in mzungu hair cutting. As mzungu leaves, stand in doorway and smile reassuringly to maintain illusion that all is well. When mzungu is safely around the corner, turn around and laugh your ass off.

CHIZA , BOOKS, AND THE TROUBLE WITH ZAMBIA

Near the end of my last term one afternoon Chiza passed me as I was marking books in the staffroom. 'Oh , Mark, I got your note about those books, I will find them.' He promised. I had lent him some history books, although he no longer taught history. I wanted them passed on to Sondashi, Head of history, ASAP where they could be of most use. Chiza had borrowed them and held on to them for nigh a year despite the fact that he now only taught IT. It was a minor thing but it irritated me as it was so indicative of many of the teachers' attitudes. Books would be hoarded and not used, as if some perverse gain was to be had in denying them to others. Meanwhile Chiza was bemoaning the lack of IT textbooks for teaching. I knew of this situation and had brought several from England for the department, even before I began teaching IT to the younger boys.

' Brother John' Chiza explained ' The books that were in the department before belonged to him. He has taken them with him to Malawi.' Brother John had gone to Malawi to be a farm manager. I was rather puzzled.

' But he`s not teaching I.T anymore is he ?'

' Well no ' Chiza admitted ' but those books were his personal ones' he said ; as if it needed no further explanation. I laughed , half in exasperation : ' This monk pledged his life to the education of the youth, and he can't find it in his heart to leave a few books at a needy school ?' . Chiza was silent. Wait a minute' I continued ' the books I donated to the IT department last year, I gave them to Brother John : I hope he hasn't taken those as well ?' Chiza looked away awkwardly. Furthermore, I knew that John came from a rich family ; his brother was a dollar millionaire in the construction industry. Brother John had become legendary at Chassa for his selfishness. He had once refused to use the Brothers truck to take a malaria stricken child to the Clinic, arguing that school fuel should be used (this despite the fact that the school account probably was used to fill up the brothers truck anyway). When people were occasionally directly critical of the Brothers, they would respond that they didn`t actually own anything personally – the car, the residence, these things ultimately belonged to the Brotherhood. But the point was that even the way they used resources denied them to others. I sighed, got up and walked home. It was becoming an increasingly common response of mine after dealing with my colleagues, with the general exception of my new Head of Department T.T Ngoma.

I was finally beginning to crack under the continual disappointments of people who put their narrow self interest before others, even when there was no obvious benefit. I rankled particularly when it was combined with religious self-righteousness. It was becoming more usual for me to stomp home, slam the door and angrily spit out another such small tale to Stacy who would usually be waiting on my couch. She had similar tales of petty jealousies and rivalries from her village. Each of the incidents may have seemed relatively trivial to an outsider, but because we saw them continually from almost everybody we dealt with, we began to see them as symptomatic of much that was holding Zambia back. Inevitably, volunteers like us had a developmental agenda to everything we did, and this was the moral prism though which we viewed events. Understandably to some extent however, Zambians were just trying to get by and didn't seem to see the bigger picture. People here just couldn't appreciate that by withholding something from others they were ultimately only hurting themselves by impoverishing the overall environment they lived in. There must have been a sort of mercantilist mentality in which they believed there was only so much wealth and opportunity to go around. More for someone else meant less for you. There was no appreciation that by enriching your neighbour you also improved the chances of enriching yourself. A teacher like A.G Zulu, who irrationally hoarded books rather than let pupils use them, not only held back achievement in the maths department, but also contributed to the impoverishment of his own country by playing a part in the poor state of education. The role of education in development seemed little appreciated by those teachers who had the biggest role to play. Teachers would skip lessons, instead sitting in the staff-room bemoaning the poverty of Zambia. They would even bemoan the state of education whilst leaving their classes unattended. In an extreme example the deputy once complained to me about the current calibre of pupils finishing school in Zambia. Yet he himself was notorious for never going to lessons and teaching.

One of my most disappointing and frustrating experiences was trying to get the Chassa teachers to help me translate HIV/AIDS material into local languages. The situation for villagers was quite appalling in this respect ; most information was limited to a few posters in English in the towns. At one time there had been some sort of `outreach` programme for the rural areas, but it seemed to have fallen by the wayside. I wanted to produce simple posters in local languages that could be given to the headmen of each village or perhaps the very rural basic schools (whilst Secondary school was for the relatively wealthy, most people could still afford to attend Basic school at least). I approached several of the Chassa teachers on this issue many times. They always lost the posters I gave them and never returned anything. I thought I would get more help from Mr.Nyoni ; not quite as active as J L Banda on the issue but nonetheless someone who expressed interest in the subject. One morning he was in the staff-room reading the paper and chatting as usual. I approached him with a short paragraph I needed translating. It was literally about 8 sentences which covered the essential facts about HIV. Nyoni was a local man and would be better qualified than others in translating the material. He fobbed me off however and insisted he was busy, but once again just chatted over the newspaper. Eventually it was down to the boys from the Anti-Aids to help me with this project, which they did partially successfully. Upon reflection I now believe some of the teachers were a little uncomfortable writing about sexual matters. However I made the material fairly bland and I think most just weren't particularly bothered. Villagers were beneath their concern, despite being literally on their doorstep.

Too many Zambians seemed to think that development somehow happened magically or was just given like a sort of economic `organ transplant` ; once a few McDonalds were set up the country would progress just fine. Their concept of development, probably as much our fault as theirs, was a strictly material one that overlooked the actual people. Development was DVD players and satellite TV. It was not highly educated people of integrity who could serve their country and create sustainable systems of production. Money when acquired was often spent on useless luxuries rather than invested in sustainable projects. A small but typical example might be the teachers' wives, who baked bread for extra income, then used the money to buy make-up to lighten their faces. Meanwhile their children walked around in rags, un-shoed, wasting time sweeping the surroundings of the house whilst they should have been doing schoolwork. And volunteers it seemed were here to do what Zambians would not, rather than share skills. I was incensed to be drafted in for extra exam invigilations in my first year. The extra work didn't bother me ; it was rather because I was doing it because Massina had gotten drunk and not turned up for work. Yet the solution was to send in the VSO because they knew I could not abide the boys missing exams. The idea that Massina could be held accountable did not seem to be even considered. No-one was even sent to find him, nor was he rebuked afterwards. How could anything ever change this way? It was this kind of incident that convinced many of us volunteers that our presence may have been doing more harm than good. We were often used this way to paper over cracks that should have been confronted and dealt with by Zambians. The now decades long concept of western Aid had created a generation of Zambians who could not conceive of solving their own problems. Even Mwale, a motivated and trustworthy teacher, told me seriously : ' Burke, when you are a big man in England you must come back here and solve our water problems at Chassa'.

So often I saw the anti – corruption posters with the slogan ' Corruption holds back development' but I don't think many Zambians really believed that. They couldn't, as it was rare indeed to find anyone who would not abuse public funds or even do their job properly. The idea for instance that someone stealing from a hospital was therefore contributing to disease and death never seemed to take root. It seemed a given that disease and death would be rampant anyway. Perhaps Zambians didn't really believe in progress and development. Unlike my generation in western Europe who had grown up amidst a relentless rise in living standards, these Zambians, particularly the professional and urban classes, had grown up in an era of decline. In the early seventies it had all been going swimmingly as the copper industry boomed and public servants enjoyed an almost first world standard of living. In those days it had been normal for a Zambian teacher to own their own vehicle, something almost unthinkable now. But Zambia had bankrolled the freedom fighters in the neighbouring countries and had gotten nothing in return. Then the price of copper plummeted, the IMF and World Bank swept in, privatised and asset stripped Zambian industries, and the state began to fall apart.

Perhaps Zambians had never had a good government before and so didn't believe it was possible. They had had tribalism, then a colonial government based on exploitation, then finally their own national governments who viewed power as a privilege and most certainly not a responsibility. They had never experienced the benefits a relatively honest and accountable government could bring, so they didn't believe in it. Better to grab what you can, when you can for yourself, because nobody else was going to help you. And why work for future generations, a legacy ? The world markets and the IMF could come in and blow it all to hell anyway. Besides which there was apparently a glorious afterlife waiting for you anyway, as long as you prayed. Because a majority probably believed this, the country was trapped in a Catch 22. Who would stick their neck out and sacrifice their time and effort for others ? What were the chances of that being reciprocated ? Bitter experience had taught them, and to argue against that was difficult. Seen from this short-term view the behaviour of most Zambians was eminently logical. But nonetheless from a developmental perspective the country was stuck was on the starting line, and no one wanted to be the first to start the race. Corruption had arisen because of the circumstances after Independence, and now it was viewed as the only real way of making money. People needed feasible alternatives to corruption, but corruption strangled any development of an alternative economic system. Like the HIV virus that targeted the very T-white cells that could have fought it, corruption killed off the development of the economic system that could have been a viable competitor. Thus corruption seemed thoroughly entrenched in the life here. And yet it was not a complete inevitability.

Teachers and policemen might bemoan their wages, but this was by western standards. In fact given living costs in Zambia, their salaries were perfectly adequate. They had no problems getting satellite TV and running mobile phones. Actually I was better off financially in Zambia than I was in the UK, although of course my attempts to explain this were met with ridicule by my colleagues. They could not appreciate the cost of living in the UK, and took it for granted that all of their income was disposable. They paid no rent or bills, and the houses might have been in bad shape but they were larger than any British schoolteacher could have afforded. The chief difference and advantage we had in the developed world was access to credit. Added to this, the slight demands made on teachers at work in a Zambian school could not compare to working in a developed country. The Zambians might put in long hours at work but they were not actually doing much whilst there. Brother Michael frowned on my not being around in the afternoons but I was still way ahead of my colleagues at work and never missed deadlines. My colleagues may have hung around longer at work, but it was more appearances and little substance ; the culture seemed little concerned with concrete results.

The outside world might have a picture of rural Africa as comprised of community minded villages, but the reality in Zambia was sometimes worse than tribalism ; people were generally unwilling to help anyone outside their immediate family. Indeed the fear surrounding HIV meant even immediate family were often abandoned. Certainly in-laws were often not well treated as the phenomenon of `property grabbing` showed ; if a man died his relatives would often descend on his new family and forcibly claim all possessions. Widows and orphaned children were left with nothing. When men survived longer, husbands would commonly infect their wives then abandon them when the wife succumbed first to the sickness, and finally move on to another wife. Even orphaned cousins were treated poorly and often abused. It was common to treat them as indentured servants and leave them uneducated. I even heard the Massinas arguing one day over an orphaned cousin in nearby Petauke. Mrs Massina wanted to take the small child from a relative and use her as a housemaid in her house. To his credit Masina was more forward thinking than many others. ' No, it s not right' he protested 'if she comes here, she deserves an education – she must go to school. I can't afford that, so she will have to stay where she is'.

It was in later staff meetings that I vainly tried to argue the importance of doing our best for our boys, by appealing to people's own self interest : ' When you are old and retired' I would argue : ' Who will be running this country and looking after you ? We must attend all lessons and educate these guys as best we can. They are your future leaders and guardians'. It was an appeal that fell on deaf ears. Chassa was the best school in Eastern province, and one of the best in the country . As I too often moaned to my Peace corps friends ; ' If this is one of the best schools in Zambia, (and reputedly it was, excepting of course the private schools for expats and the very richest Zambians) ' then Zambia is screwed. End of story'. There was never going to be enough educated professionals to help lift the country up. I was particularly concerned because as the boys got older I saw them becoming like the role models above them. The boys started out as good because they actually believed the pious crap they were being shovelled. It was maddening when teaching the Year 8s to realise I was one of the few teachers who ever did so. So often I would walk past the grade 8 classrooms and see not one of them with a teacher. As much as I shyed away from the Bible, there was no doubt ' the devil makes work for idle hands' was at play here. I often pondered how many boys started to drift of course after hoursof being unattended in grade 8. The teachers focused their limited efforts on the grade 9s and 12's as these were exam classes.

Later, as the boys were older and some were prefects, they had indeed learnt that power here was privilege, not responsibility. As a teacher on duty I spent most of my time chasing up negligent prefects and protecting the other pupils from their abuses. Bullying and theft were rife in the dormitories. They had learnt that all the self-righteousness talk was a charade. Even a special workshop for the prefects on Leadership had no impact. The school admin pondered curiously why the boys they chose to lead as prefects so often turned out to be the very source of discipline problems. To me it was painfully obvious. They had learnt by example from above. A weekend workshop could not compete with the actual daily practices the boys saw. They were far from stupid. They saw the hypocrisy, and had figured out long before I did how the admin was wasting money. This was a source of several 'almost riots' that were quelled at the last moment at Chassa (often due to the timely intervention of the popular and respected Brother Jumbe). Riots were a yearly occurrence in Zambian schools as normally exemplary pupils finally snapped under the regular abuses they saw above them. The schooling that boys had here only increased my admiration for those who stayed true to their principles despite the environment they lived in. Many boys, despite their experiences expressed a determination to do things differently for their children. This minority gave me some hope for the future, if they didn't give up and find a way to emigrate. There was Mwale too, a new Chemistry teacher who was conscientious and taught full time, no matter how much the admin ripped him off (and they did – after moving he was allocated a moving allowance but this mysteriously was never released by Brother Michael – ditto for the housing allowance) . Not all the teachers were neglectful of their duties. But most were. And apparently other schools were even far worse in this respect. It was difficult to fight against the tide and the prevailing culture.

THE PROBLEM WITH AID AGENCIES

To be fair the Aid situation sometimes struck me as little better. The fractured nature of Aid was particularly striking. I always found it exasperating that the vast myriad of various NGOs all focused on the same or similar goals (especially Gender and HIV) and yet rarely, if ever worked together. It was always an aim of mine to work with Peace Corps and JOCVs (the Japanese version of VSO) where our objectives overlapped. JOCV also placed maths and science teachers in schools, and when VSO announced it was terminating its education programme I was appalled to discover they had not discussed this at all with JICA. All the work VSO's had done was not in any way to be continued at all through JICA. Incensed, in Lusaka I arranged for some JOCV friends to come into the VSO Office and discuss the possibility of some sort of handover. I then badgered VSO to include JOCV's in the workshop where we discussed the termination of the education programme. What was the most frustrating aspect to dwell on was that for all the time our programs had run in parallel there had never really been much or official collaboration between the two agencies, even in situations when JOCVs and VSO's worked in the same schools. The Japanese volunteers were usually excellently qualified in science and maths but struggled with their English. It was obvious to me that VSOs could help JOCV's with writing revision guides, lesson plans or whatever they were doing. No doubt this happened on an individual level at some schools but it should have happened at an overarching official level above all. VSO's and JOCVS should have officially collaborated and produced resources together that could be distributed to all volunteers and all schools. It was the lack of vision and ambition that enraged me, and the lack of appreciation of what could easily be achieved at relatively little cost.

The general lack of coordination and cooperation even seemed to exist within agencies, as if mirroring the faults of the society it was trying to help. I was stunned to walk into the VSO office one day and see an excellent maths revision guide that had been produced by an earlier volunteer. It had probably sat in a cupboard for years and then been stuck on the shelf one day as an afterthought. I asked if I could take a copy but they insisted I pay the full hefty price. Why hadn't the following VSO maths teachers after this volunteer been given copies ? Why hadn't JICA been sent copies ? Why weren't VSO using their contacts in the publishing industry (and they had them) to mass produce this for cheap and get it into as many schools as possible ? Pupils would certainly buy it at a low cost price.

Stacy was delighted to pick up some Gender and HIV manuals that VSO had produced and I had picked up. She got my copies, and with another volunteer ran a workshop at a local girls high school. It was apparently a great success, and one could only ponder what other NGO's would have appreciated the manuals. The areas where VSO and Peace Corps could have worked together but didn't was criminal, particularly given their similarities in methodology, let alone subject material.

My predecessor at Chassa had produced an excellent textbook which taught about HIV through mathematical topics. To their credit on this occasion VSO did organise with the government for all maths teachers in Zambia to receive a copy. But it was long before I saw a copy ; no one seemed to know where they were. After nagging VSO and the school repeatedly for a copy and never getting one, I eventually found out they had already been distributed to schools, but it was a bit of a mystery where they were exactly. Finally it transpired they had been sent without instructions. Our copies had been passed on to J Banda, the patron of the Anti AIDS club, and they had duly sat on a shelf there for a year. They were sent without instructions and he had not understood they were to be used in maths lessons. It was another example of the common under-use or misuse of precious resources in Zambia. Too often money was pumped in, rather than first assessing what resources were already there and how they could be used better. The simple sharing of information would be the first place to start. Next would be a frank assessment of what was already there and a commitment to certain priorities. The most spectacular example of disorganisation in Zambia was probably water management and agriculture ; drought and hunger regularly afflicted a country that had several huge rivers and an abundance of water along with fertile soil.

As for the maths and HIV books, T.T was keen on using them when we finally got copies, but the other teachers didn't mirror his enthusiasm. Again, the cultural barrier was there when it came to discussing sexual issues. This was disappointing, because if one actually bothered to talk to the boys they would find them eager and willing to discuss such vital issues. Many a time I would teach about HIV through a maths topic, and then end up being side-tracked into a full hour-long discussion about sex and STD's.

At the Peace Corps house one day I noticed some excellent US manuals on sustainable agriculture in Zambia. Later when I met a VSO volunteer who also had the same remit in agriculture he confessed he had never seen the manuals, and didn't know where his local Peace Corps headquarters in northwest province was. I swiftly asked my PeaceCorps friends where their HQ in northwest was, and told the VSO to get directions to go and exchange resources and ideas. Again, the idea that there was all this knowledge out there and it wasn't being shared was greatly distressing to me.

Occasionally the Aid agencies even mirrored the corruption of the government. The Peace Corps volunteers were constantly complaining about being paid late and I had to help Stacy on several occasions when she literally ran out of even money to buy food. I was suspicious, and I had now seen enough in Zambia to suspect theft rather than incompetence at the Lusaka Office. Months later it did indeed emerge that the Peace Corps Accountant had been siphoning off huge sums of money ; some 39 million kwacha at least (ten thousand dollars – a vast sum when each volunteer received about two hundred dollars a month). Eventually somehow the accused escaped a prison sentence which I had also come to expect. A smaller sum stolen, but more saddening in a way was the 750 dollars that was the personal savings of a volunteer and entrusted to the Lusaka office for safekeeping. Despite being in an office safe it soon disappeared. When such thefts occurred they were demoralising not just because volunteers felt betrayed by people they were trying to help, but also because they were usually committed by the Zambians who were relatively well off, and done at the expense of the genuinely needy. Stacy and I sat watching the movie Full Metal Jacket one night and turned to look at each other pointedly as a marine who had just had his camera stolen complained : ' You know what I don't get ? We're here to help these people, but they just keep shitting on us' . Soko had been a prime example in my own experience. I had always been generous to him, paying him more than Audrey did, bringing him a camera from England amongst other things, and neither was he was badly off. He had used my freezer to store his meat and other food – usually ten kilos of beef or other (more than I could afford) – whilst at the same time stealing from me so that he could buy luxuries.

In the great scheme of Aid agencies perhaps there was a sinister logic to their general lack of cooperation between each other. They were as much a job industry as anything else. Ultimately by their own stated aims they should have been trying to work themselves out of a job, but of course like self-preserving bureaucracies they sought to do the opposite and expand their sphere of influence. If Aid agencies had pooled their resources and cooperated more, this rationalisation would have led to reduced numbers of employees and budgets. In Zambia, like the church and the government, the Aid agencies were major employers. Not only that, they were generous employers. I was stunned to find out the common wage for a middle ranking NGO worker was 20 million kwacha a month. I was doing fine on 1 million a month, and even a large family could do well on 4 or 5 million. Aid agencies were spending an awful lot of money on high wages and excellent SUV's, and not an awful lot on the essentials that would have actually helped the needy. They had indeed breed dependency, not only in the mentality of the people they purported to free, but also with the reality that they must now comprise a sizeable section of the economy itself. Many volunteers, eventually disillusioned by the culture of dependency in Zambia, advocated a complete with-drawl of Aid. This was the only real long term solution, painful in the short run though it might be. Tempting though it was to agree, I couldn't see how such a thing could be achieved without a catastrophic economic crash. Direct budget assistance and a huge NGO sector were such a large, integrated part of the economy that they could not be withdrawn now without dire consequences. And such economic consequences tended to throw up precisely the kind of brutal leaders that made things worse and perpetuated a nations' decline.

Zambia was like a patient that had unnecessarily been put on a life-support machine instead of being given targeted help, and had now give up using it's own organs. Random Aid continued to be thrown at the patient in a sporadic manner (and often not followed up) but there didn't seem to be any long term plan of how to restore the patient to full health. Neither treating symptoms nor withdrawing treatment was the answer. Restoring the proper functioning of 'organs' such as the law and the public services was necessary, but this would require harsh accountability. In the end the solution to many of the problems was probably quite simple and unglamorous ; send in the accountants. It had started now, though why not sooner I had no idea.

None of the aid agencies tackled head on what was the overarching cause of most of the problems ; population increase. Some of them tiptoed around it by addressing women's rights and touching on family planning, but it was never a topic challenged head on. And yet since Independence in 1964 the population had more then trebled whilst poverty had become more entrenched. Of course poverty has many causes, but population increase arguably perpetuates poverty by leading to a hugely under-educated workforce in a country where education requires a degree of wealth. Zambia was a large country with only around 11 million people, but it was family size rather than 'population density' that was affecting development.

Neither did the agencies fully embrace sustainability in terms of renewable resources. Recent books I had read on Peak Oil and the environment convinced me that Zambia was in for harder times like the rest of us, as the world approached the natural limits of economic growth and the end of cheap fossil fuels. What was the point in building systems that would crumble so quickly if the world was to experience, for example 'Oil Shocks' again ? Even the villagers, seemingly so removed from the developed world, would be deeply affected if US AID could no longer supply cheap fertiliser and seeds.

On a side note I had to wonder why VSO had placed me at one of the better-off schools when so many other secondary schools in the area were far needier. Was it just for historical reasons ? Were they really not that bothered ? Perhaps they thought a westerner would not have coped at the other schools, but again it seemed NGO`s were not really focused on the neediest.

RACIST MYTHS AND POLITICAL CORRECTNESS

Too often foreigners would berate Zambians (and Africans in general) in racist terms, but their logic was way off the mark. Zambians, at least the so called `professional class` were indeed generally `lazy` by western standards (it might be more accurate to say disorganised and de-motivated). It was true, at least of the professional classes at this time in history. Even the other Africans believed this (the Kenyan and Ugandan VSO's indeed, as is most often the case with neighbours, were the most vehement in their criticism of Zambians). But it had nothing to do with genetics or race, as I was once stunned to hear an apparently intelligent Dutch engineer try to argue with me. To me it was obvious why many educated Zambians were `lazy`. It was not to do with skin colour or even culture, but was simply because they were allowed to be lazy, and generally lived in a work climate where effort was not rewarded. Arguably, most humans are lazy if they can get away with it, unless they fear consequences and /or have a positive motivation to work. The teachers didn't go to lessons because they didn't have to. No one was ever punished or fired for not working. Once you had a government job it was almost like a job for life in some old communist system. Likewise the right people were rarely rewarded for doing a particularly good job ; the bonuses they received could not compare to the perks Brother Michael raked in through corrupt measures. Combine this with a lack of belief in education and its role in development, and their thinking becomes understandable. But these qualities were not fixed or permanent, they were the work culture prevailing at the time. A real effort to properly make people accountable could have changed the culture.

Likewise Zambians were often labelled as thieves, again even by other Africans. The only people who seemed to have a worse reputation were Nigerians. Again, unfortunately this was largely true of the professional classes at this time. I knew only 2 staff at my school who had never stolen school funds. All the others had at some time or other been implicated in incidents. And yet all these incidents were always awkwardly overlooked. And of course they had to be, because those in charge were even bigger thieves. When someone was caught red handed the only consequence usually was returning the stolen money. Thus there was an incentive to steal ; it was worth the risk – the worst that would happen is you would break even if you were caught. Seen from this point of view ,you were stupid *not* to steal. Somebody else would get it if you didn't. And they wouldn't be punished. Think back to your childhood. Who never stole anything ? But you were punished and in future feared the consequences. Eventually, when you matured a bit, you appreciated the hurt it caused other people (especially when it was done to you) and why it was morally wrong. But initially as a small child you needed to be punished to put you on the right track. But imagine if you had never been punished, had found that something was tolerated, and everyone else was doing it. You would have grown up different, no matter what a geneticist or right wing thinker will tell you about fixed personality traits.

Corruption is a sensitive issue in development debates because it used by right wing thinkers to argue against Aid. Yet it has been too overlooked by even eminent economists such as Jeffrey Sachs. In his recent bestseller ' The End of Poverty?' Sachs argues that because Asia developed despite corruption it is not a significant brake on development. There are other factors, such as geophysical ones holding back the unique case of Africa. Indeed there are, but I would say this only makes corruption all the more damaging in Africa. Because Africa faces so many unique challenges, corruption is even *more* devastating there, where public funds are even more valuable. Likewise Sachs berates western leaders for being stingy with Aid (and relatively speaking this is true, despite the sums of billions given bemoaned by right wing thinkers). He says that even relatively small sums can do wonders in Africa, therefore not to help is a crime. Absolutely right, I agree. Relatively small sums of money *DO* go a long way in Africa, so how can Sachs overlook the significant sums that are lost to corruption ? When such an eminent economist, feted by infatuated stars such as Bono and Geldolf , applies such ill thought and childish logic it is difficult to be positive about the future management of Africa. Perhaps if Sachs and co had actually lived in Africa instead of zipping through in air-conditioned land-cruisers, they would have a clearer picture of the reality on the ground. But history shows us that such theoretical 'experts' will patronisingly dismiss people like me as ' missing the bigger picture' ; because I haven't eaten caviar in 18 different embassies around the world. I did agree with one thrust of Sachs argument ; that what much of Africa needed was one `big push` to get it up and running. Too much Aid had been piecemeal and unfocused, too many ill conceived projects started and then abandoned.

The issue of promiscuity and sexual deviancy is a touchy one, particularly amongst AIDS campaigners who don't want promiscuity to be used an excuse not to help Africans with the pandemic. Again, it is unfortunately true that most Zambians are relatively promiscuous. They may be no more promiscuous than westerners often are in their twenties, but the difference is the Zambians were often married and continued this behaviour well into their forties. I knew just a few teachers who did not cheat on their wives. A traditional culture of polygamy helped tolerate this, but it was also a general tolerance of a broadly masculine culture and the lack of empowerment of women all round. There were many other factors spreading HIV too, including of course the lack of condom use (education) , a health care system that couldn't cope with STDs' (untreated sores from STDS cause far easier transmission of the HIV virus) and cultural peculiarities around sex (such as the use of herbs to dry a woman's vagina and increase friction) . However, for Aids campaigners to deny promiscuity is a factor in spreading a sexually transmitted disease (as sometimes they do as a reaction to right wing criticisms of Africa) is patently absurd and discrediting to their own cause. It is also deeply disrespectful to the many women who have been infected through the transgressions of their husbands alone. In Zambia the highest risk factor for a woman to be infected is to be married.

It has sometimes been asserted (by Geldolf and co again) that education on Aids has failed and thus it has been proved that Aids will continue to spread until poverty is eradicated. No doubt poverty does remove choices and forces more women into dangerous prostitution. But the key point is simply : why would men insist on not using a condom?   Cost and accessibility was not really an issue. Even in the bush condoms were often available at clinics or at stores for the price of a penny sweet. Condoms were not used chiefly because doubts have been spread about their effectiveness and women feel a lack of power insisting on their use. Women's rights and education are as crucial factors as poverty, but have not been stressed enough sometimes because of 'cultural sensitivity'. I encountered a huge amount of ignorance about Aids, particularly amongst villagers who did not have access to information. It was too often available only in English. Education has not failed ; it has barely even started. Get out of your land-cruiser Geldof and smell the shit on the ground. And while you're at it ; why don't you actually let some Africans perform in the next Live Aid concert for the beleagured continent ?

As the African Journalist who filmed the shocking 'Dispatches : Aids in Zambia' has asserted : political correctness, whilst having many good points, is in danger of causing us to overlook the real problems in Africa. A Zambian tendency towards fatalism, perhaps engendered in them by their recent history, is encouraging tolerance of fatally damaging behaviour. Thus for example I would have arguments in the staff-room about teachers having sex with pupils. It turned out that several Chassa teachers had been transferred to this boys school because they had impregnated girls in other schools, and often after more than one offence. I knew for sure that this was the case with at least two teachers. Again, this probably happened precisely because it was historically tolerated. Chassa was one of the best schools around, so the reward for impregnating a schoolgirl was to be sent to a better school ? In anger I explained to my colleagues that such behaviour in

England resulted in a prison sentence and probably trouble in the showers, and this was one of the reasons why it rarely happened (it was depressingly common in Zambia). S. Zulu, such a seemingly benign and jolly character, would protest to me : ' Ah, but we're only human, to have such temptation...'. Even the normally mouse quiet and seemingly straight-laced Moyo backed S. Zulu against me. Only the ever reliable JL Banda (also one of the only teachers the Accountant trusted with school funds) would take my side in such arguments. Again, if they had grown up in an atmosphere where such behaviour was taboo, it wouldn't happen. To me, a pupil was a child entrusted to my care. To abuse that trust was a gross crime, no matter how attractive or old they were. I like to think I'm that way anyway, but it only takes a bit of thought to imagine how you might be if you had been raised very differently from a young age.

Some of the traditional attitudes seemed in plain denial of the reality of the situation. Brother Michael once walked in the staff room and saw the wedding photos of our new secretary. She was a town girl and the ceremony was quite westernised. She had worn a white dress and there had been a big cake. In the pictures she had been snapped kissing her husband. Brother Michael tutted in disgust at this; a traditional taboo in rural Zambia. He was a village boy himself. Husband and wife didn't hold hands in public, let alone kiss. Michael looked up, directly at me . ' See what things are coming now into our culture ? Things didn't used to be like this before'. Then he haughtily walked off, the self-righteousness in his stride almost tangible. I was flabbergasted. What western culture accepted in public was not the problem. It was what Zambian culture deemed acceptable behind closed doors that had caused the HIV epidemic. There was no HIV epidemic in my country, where lap-dancing was legal and sex was on the TV all the time. Michael's own sister had slept around as a teenager and contracted HIV. She had been staying at the residence, and whilst Michael was away, it was all the other Brothers could do to keep her away from our somewhat naïve and ill-educated boys. Chiza had caught her kissing prefects and worried about what she got up to when no one else was around. And correct me if I was wrong, but hadn't villagers walked around with their tits hanging out before the corrupting white man brought Victorian morality and cotton bras? That was the problem with people like Michael – their moral vision, if they had any, was a confused mix of Christian Victorian morality and traditional Zambian values. They didn't even realise any more what was their own culture and what were outdated Christian values.

Occasionally traditional attitudes to sex and women reached farcical proportions. The Catholic Archbishop of Zambia had been caught cavorting with a secret wife. When the Pope found out he ordered the suspension of the

Archbishop and that the man report for interview. The Archbishop however simply went on the run and refused to relinquish his post. At around the same time the Archbishop of Zimbabwe was caught having secret affairs. The episodes provoked little but whimsical amusement amongst the Brothers, only Jumbe looking suitably uncomfortable as I tutted at the TV coverage.

All of these problems with sexual behaviour and corruption were not inevitable and not due to any fixed personality or cultural traits that Zambians had. The corruption was likely more a generational problem that had arisen with the virtual collapse of the state in the 1980s. The sexual habits admittedly were more deeply rooted in native culture, but even there the major problem was a fear of HIV testing and a distrust of condoms, rather than any inherent problem with traditional polygamy (distasteful though it may be). Like the stubborn adherence to maize, it was all changeable and not inevitable, and this was why it rankled so with us volunteers. We could see the potential for change, even see it desired by some, but it was usually blocked by those with power and authority who could afford to live without it.

At first in Zambia I had appreciated the respect and deference people generally had for each other. Society here may have been more strictly hierarchical than Britain, but there were advantages to this, particularly in the classroom of course where I benefitted. But now I seemed to see that first official in Chipata everywhere, the one that had typed up my letter to open a Bank account and had so harshly dealt with the native teacher. Even when I looked at children playing I saw how a four year old learnt to bark and order around a two year old like a personal slave. Here was magnified that most crucial of human failings ; compassion was mistaken for weakness, and people thought aggression was the same thing as strength. It was an attitude I had seen in Anna particularly and despised back home, and now I seemed to see it everywhere here.

My frustration with aspects of Zambian culture was magnified due to my own personality. I had an obsession with starting projects, getting the broad brushstrokes done and the momentum going ; the rest would follow in time. Many others, Zambians in particular, often had a fascination with detail that I clashed with ; I viewed it as delaying the real work. They never seemed to have the sense of urgency that I thought was necessary ; for me everything was too late already, for them nothing would ever change anyway. Their obsession with neatness as opposed to substance was also doubling maddening to someone of my temperament. A small example might be my patching up on an old envelope and using it to mail something via the registry office. The clerk stopped me ;

' Ah, Mr. Burke, we will put this in a proper envelope for you.'

Me : ' No thank you , I've already stamped it.'

Clerk : ' Ah , we'll just use another stamp.'

Me : ' That's a waste of money ! (It cost the same as a loaf of bread). It's an envelope man. They're going to rip it open and throw it away. It's what's inside that's important.'

Clerk : ' Ah no, but you can't post a letter like that. It looks dirty.'

I never ceased to be amazed at the wastefulness and inefficiencies in a land of such poverty. There may have also been a habit of concentrating energies on trivial problems precisely because those could be easily solved. The other problems sometimes may have been so daunting that people avoided them out of fear of failure.

INTERLUDE II : CONFUSIONS WITH MZUNGU SKIN (A CLINCIAN'S GUIDE)

When Mzungu arrives at the clinic, tell him that he looks like Wayne Rooney, David Beckham and Steven Gerrard. Assume his puzzled look is gratefulness for the compliment. Add anyway that all mzungus tend to look the same anyhow. When mzungu complains of pain and swelling on his backside, ask him to turn around and drop trousers. Immediately reassure mzungu that what you see is a temporary 'nodal swelling' caused by a blow to a nerve, probably by riding his bike. Send mzungu home with painkillers. The next day pretend not to hear when mzungu tells you that actually he had a giant blister on his ass ; it popped in the middle of the night and he thought he had wet the bed.

HELP FROM THE UK

Some of the help I received from the UK bypassed the usual problems of Aid in Africa. My neighbour ran a charity called International Humanity which had been set up by a Czech doctor in the wake of the tsunami. Whilst mainly concerned with Sri-Lanka, they expressed an interest in helping my local health clinic ; a small set-up that had to cater for a staggering 33,000 people. To my surprise they managed to raise a considerable sum of money for buying modern medical equipment, which I was then able to give directly to my clinic. I returned to the UK for friends weddings on no less than three occasions and each time I was able to pick up medical equipment donated by International Humanity and give it direct to the clinic upon my return. It wasn't an ideal solution – I wasn't going to be around for long, and the clinic needed expertise above all – but at least Aid was going direct to those who needed it, rather than being spent on dubious workshops and t-shirts.

Likewise I was fortunate to get a response from a primary school in England when I wrote to them asking if they were interested in a link with my local Zambian primary, Chassa Basic. Thankfully the primary in England responded and managed to raise sizeable sums of cash which again I was able to give directly to Chassa basic. Although I was by this time becoming wary of giving cash, I was at least relatively comfortable this time giving money to Sister Angela, who was the deputy head of Chassa Basic. I might disagree vehemently with the nonsense she spouted about condoms, but I was fairly sure she could be trusted with donated money. Weeks later I visited Chassa Basic and found they had been able to do extensive renovations on the buildings using the money. All the buildings' foundations had been shored up with concrete, an urgent priority as little or no money was forthcoming from the government in an election year.

On the other hand a large donation I secured for my own school was unfortunately in all probability mis-used. Soon after my arrival I had asked my local Lionesses club in Hurworth for assistance with what I thought was the dire condition of Chassa Secondary. They were kind enough to donate £200, a sum which would go a long way in Zambia. Unfortunately this was early in my service when I was ignorant as to the true wealth of Chassa Secondary and assumed the Head could be trusted. I converted the money to kwacha and cheerfully handed over 1.8 million kwacha in cash to Brother Michael, benefiting from a favourable exchange rate. Despite numerous requests I never received a satisfactory explanation of how the money was spent. A full two years after, Michael eventually mumbled something about the money being spent on a classroom renovation. Questionable indeed, given that the renovation could have probably been done for a tenth of the cost. Likewise he ignored my repeated requests to write a thank you letter to the Lionesses club. It was shenanigans like this that eventually prompted me to write to the Anti-Corruption Commission amongst others and try and give them enough circumstantial evidence to start looking into the finances of Chassa Secondary. I later learnt that even Brother Jumbe had become suspicious of Brother Michael, but it seemed nothing could be done. Brother Michael was the head of the Marist order in Zambia and the head of the Brothers at Chassa. He was holding all the cards. And the Catholic Church was a powerful institution. The issue of the Catholic Secretariat holding onto Teachers Housing Allowance suggested even high level collusion when it came to Catholics stealing money.

On a personal level the longer I was in Zambia the more packages I received from friends and family. It was always a joy in the afternoons to discover a parcel on my desk at work, and I regularly hassled poor Ziyambo about whether he had picked up the post that day. Inside these treasures were news, packet food such as instant pasta, and my old CDs and videos. The occasional evening felt like a mini-Christmas as Stacy and I would settle on the couch with a melted chocolate bar and a fresh movie. The Lord of the Rings trilogy was great, but you could only watch it so many times (even so , I reckoned Stacy watched it about 100 times). Even better for morale of course were the visits from the UK. I was profoundly grateful that my parents had plucked up the courage to visit Zambia (though the bus journey to Eastern province made me rather nervous) and likewise the visit of my sister and my friends the Mitchells was a big morale boost. I crossed over with more friends at Livingstone, and even bumped into an old university acquaintance in Lusaka. All such meetings helped keep my spirits up when I was dwelling on the difficulties at Chassa too much. The financial help I received for flights back home was a life-saver, and in the end I have to wonder what would have happened to my mental state if had spent the full two years at Chassa uninterrupted.

MELVIN'S STORY

Melvin was typical of many of the boys I knew at Chassa, in that he was an orphan. I had first got to know him when I ran a Gender workshop in the evenings. It started out as a real eye opener. As I went through the nature/ nurture debates I argued with the boys that most of the qualities we assign to women are in fact false, and when they are evident it is because we raised them in that fashion. If for example girls are poor at science it is because they are discouraged in that subject and encouraged to focus on other things. Hence women, particularly in Zambia become self fulfilling prophecies of what men want of them. But their original potential is as much as any boy. Arguing this at first with the boys I got some astonishing responses, such as : ' girls are stupider than boys. They have smaller brains. It is scientifically proven and written in encyclopedias.' This might of course also say something about the quality and age of the encyclopedias in our library ! Over ten or so sessions I managed to sway most of them to thinking more analytically about what forms a personality, and what women were capable of. Most of all I persuaded them that involving women more in decision making was the key to developing their country. Zambia faced enough challenges already before writing off 50 % of its potential talent. Empirical evidence suggested women in developing countries often spent household budgets more responsibly than men, and educating women tended to result in fewer teenage pregnancies and better prospects for all. An educated mother tended to result in a smaller more secure family, as they tended to have fewer children and later in life when they were better equipped to look after them. In this respect many development experts believed Gender Equality was the key to progress.

Melvin became one of the more vigorous exponents of this, a real 'convert', and when the PeaceCorps ran their HIV and Gender day at Chassa, Melvin and David (another prefect) ran their own gender sessions with the younger boys. They thoroughly enjoyed it and excitedly told me afterwards how they hoped to work for NGO's in Gender Equality work. Melvin had hinted at his background in the earlier gender sessions. The more I dealt with him I learnt how difficult his life had become. Both his parents died whilst he was young, leaving himself and a younger brother to be offloaded at the home of an unwilling relative. Like many children in such situations they were treated like the awkward burden of a wicked stepmother. It was a tragically common story. Eventually they went to live instead with an ancient great grandmother. Like many poor people in Lusaka this lady had no cash income and lived hand to mouth doing small jobs for richer neighbours.

Melvin was a prefect who I could actually trust ; he didn't seem to be corrupted like many of the others. It was always a relief whilst on duty to meet Melvin and know I would have some genuine help in keeping tabs on the boys that week. Despite his prefecture duties, Melvin studied hard and did well in his finals. His situation in Lusaka was poor however ; I later helped him with funds for some short college courses but was unable to organise longer term help. I left him in uncertain circumstances, trying to support his great grandmother and keep his younger brothers on the right track. It was the courage of such individuals like Melvin who gave me some small hope for Zambia. Their quiet determination, against all the odds, to make things better for the next generation was inspiring, although I had to wonder if the tide they were swimming against was too great. Even quite brilliant boys for example might fail to get scholarships for UNZA (the national university) because corruption and nepotism took all the places. Job prospects were such in Zambia that even academically successful pupils would look to emigrate, or at least work for a western NGO or the church. But there seemed to be little support for genuine wealth creating enterprise of Zambian origin.

THE WHEELS ON THE BUS DON'T GO ROUND

There was one more major debacle with the management of school finances before I left Chassa for good. As a nearby secondary school had procured a school bus, Brother Michael had suddenly decided that we too needed a bus. In the long run this was true, as the terrible accident the previous year had meant we could no longer transport large numbers of pupils on the back of trucks. In the immediate future however it meant the bus was to be purchased with unnecessary haste and disastrous consequences.

First of all it meant our large flatbed truck was sold. This was done with no problem. We had a large Toyota which was in good condition and fetched a decent price. This raised some 17 million kwacha. A good bus would cost us 80 million apparently; 65 million for the bus itself, with transport, admin and other fees coming to 15 million kwacha. The considerable shortfall was made up with a steep one-off rise in fees for the boys. Since the boys finishing this year would not get to use the bus, this particularly annoyed them.

Now came the problem of where to purchase the bus from. Most vehicles were actually bought from Durban. This large South African port received many cheap second-hand vehicles from Europe. It was often worth the trek down to South Africa, although one had to be careful of car-jackings. Eventually two members of the PTA went down to Durban and brought back a bus that was smaller than the one we had wanted. Brother Michael travelled to Lusaka to evaluate it, staying over a week and of course claiming considerable overnight allowances (150,000 a night ; the monthly wage of our general workers), despite no doubt staying at the Brothers HQ there for free. Eventually he decided unilaterally to accept the bus, despite the opposition of the staff who deemed it too small, too old, and in unacceptably poor condition (it needed extensive refurbishment). The oldest boys' near rioting one night (citing amongst other grievances the late arrival of the bus which they had largely paid for) may have influenced his decision. No doubt Michael knew that he and the Brothers would be the main targets in any riots (which did not usually result in harming people intentionally but did involve burning down buildings and a lot of brick throwing).

The bus eventually arrived from Lusaka, old, ugly, but allegedly endowed with a good motor. It promptly blew up on its first trip. The diagnosis was a major write off. The boys as usual were the quickest to remember the Heads patronising words and turn them against him. In an Assembly he had justified the hike in fees necessary for the high priced bus by patronisingly explaining that ' Cheap is expensive'; if a cheap bus was purchased it would become a liability and cost more in the long run. Now the boys realised that this was in fact exactly what he had done. ' He, himself, was the one telling us that ' Cheap is expensive, but look what he did ' they complained to us.

Rumour had it the bus had been overheating badly on the journey from Lusaka (which explained how it suspiciously took all day) but the PTA members who brought it concealed this out of embarrassment. Mysteriously it had been given a clean bill of health by the mechanic in Lusaka.

Sondashi had been instantly suspicious upon seeing the bus. He said he had seen similar vehicles advertised for sale in Lusaka for about 25 million. The idea that we had spent 80 million getting it from South Africa didn't make sense. Whatever had happened, it was another calamity and an utter waste of school money. The school eventually declared their intention to begin legal proceedings to get their money back, claiming the milometer on the bus had been tampered with.

UNSUNG HEROES : THE NZP+ : October 2006

Unfortunately it was near the very end of my time in Zambia that I met the people I came to admire most, and the ones I could have worked most productively with. They were those HIV positive people who had come out in the open and were actively trying to combat the fear, prejudice and ignorance around the condition. It was a hot afternoon in October and I had just returned from Sinda on my bike. I was rather irritated to see 3 Zambians crouching on my porch, a middle aged man and 2 young ladies. No doubt they had come to the white man for help – despite my relative poverty compared to the Brothers and other individuals involved in the Church, I was regularly hassled by all manner of people who refused to believe I was not rich. Beggars would still come to my door and in vain I would point out the new TV Satellite dishes on teacher's houses and insist they look for help from Christians and fellow Zambians. But now these people ignored me. They seemed to be waiting for someone else.

It was only after I entered my house that eventually they timidly knocked on the door. My now usual apprehensive half scowl faded when they said they were looking for Stacy. They knew I was a friend of hers and wanted to get in touch with her. But when I asked them if was to do with her work in community schools, the man replied that actually they were looking for Peace Corps because they needed help with HIV issues. Interested, I asked them in. I didn't have money to spare but I had knowledge, resources and contacts that could help them. They settled on the sofa opposite me and introduced themselves as Jeremiah Phiri , Margaret Mbewe and Loveness Phiri. They were members of the Network for Zambians Living Positively (commonly known as the NZP+) . I had heard of the organisation but didn't know much about them. They now told me they were people who had come out in the open about their HIV status and sought to live with their condition and educate others, to advocate testing and the use of ARV.s. I had never met any such people before – I had always been seeing denial. I quickly explained who I was, and that I had some knowledge of HIV and maybe could help them. Painfully noting that their sole resource was a small ragged book on nutrition, I offered what I could. First of all I had a spare folder of HIV/Aids information that I could give them ; a huge resource of UN educational material that friends back home had printed off the web. I also had some spare VSO books and other pamphlets. But most of all I was interested in them and what they did. They showed me a list of names. They were a small group of locals who had tested positive, and bravely accepting their condition had formed a support group. I saw with a sigh that one of the members was a 12 year old girl. Most of them were on ARV's which thankfully were now free due to US assistance – one good thing that had come from the Bush admin. Many it turned out had literally been brought back from the brink of death due to such medicine. In many cases they had only agreed to testing when things had become desperate, but upon seeing the remarkable results of ARV medicine they then agreed to live openly with their status and seek to convert others to testing and medication. This, despite the fear and discrimination they encountered.

What I wanted most of all was to link the NZP with JL and the Anti-Aids club at the school. To my mind too much of the Aids education in Zambia was focused on slogans, poems and t-shirts. Too much talk that was meaningless and not enough action. Too many people walked around with the slogans on their t-shirts but acted otherwise. To some extent it was even the same at the Chassa Anti Aids club. Many of the boys had indeed lost relatives to Aids, but even so I wondered if the education was still not direct enough in addressing this.

As I had hoped, the NZP made quite an impact when they turned up one afternoon at the Anti-Aids club. I hadn't warned the boys exactly who was coming, so when I turned up later I found the boys sitting in stunned silence as the ladies each stood up in turn and told their story. For too long the boys had read about Aids and written songs and poems about it. They may have suspected that relatives had passed away due to Aids but might still deny it on some level. Now a lady stood in front of them and told them how she had been abandoned by her husband and left at deaths door. There could be no arguing about the reality of Aids with such people. There could be no doubts as to the efficiacy of testing and ARVs, as each lady related how they had been brought back from the brink of death whilst typically their husbands died in denial, often after running away and infecting other women.

I left firmly convinced that the NZP had the key role to play in turning around the epidemic. It was their living example that could finally persuade people to get tested and get ARV's (now free). Too often I had seen the messages that were preached not being practised, something that only undermined the message. I had even heard of HIV workshop advocators who themselves shied away from testing. Indeed in nearby Katete where Liz worked, the Tikondane centre (active in HIV education) had even had a deputy director who had refused to get tested despite showing obvious signs of the illness. Even being next to St. Francis hospital, with many friends even as doctors, she could not accept her condition and passed away. Because she was unmarried she had been unable to admit that she had had sex. The church had created an atmosphere where it was shameful to have sex before marriage. Despite this, because of the ignorance around sex there were countless unmarried women who had had kids in their early teenage years. It was like a reversal of my childhood ; I seemed to have spent my high school days desperately trying to get laid (I half thought American Pie was a documentary). I had talked about sex all the time and never gotten any. Here, it seemed nobody was talking about it but everybody was doing it, with dire results for sexual infections and unwanted pregnancies. With their teaching and living example the NZP could potentially turn this around, and without the vast sums of cash that were currently being spent with dubious results.

Jeremiah Phiri, one of the few men of the group, was a particularly inspiring man. He had gone through TB twice, something very few survived, before he had been tested for HIV. He had lost his job as a manager with Sable and was reduced to subsistence farming like so many others. I explained to him that I was having trouble finding people to translate Aids information into local languages. I wanted to set up a scheme whereby the school helped me produce posters and pamphlets for local villagers in their own language. The boys had been rather disorganised but at least partly successful in helping me with this ; the teachers far from cooperative. It took several months to eventually get a few posters done at school. When I gave Jeremiah several lengthy posters in English, they were presented to me the very next day completely finished. Such efficiency and motivation was rare indeed in Zambia. I had little time left here myself, but tried to link the NZP up with as many useful people as I could. Stacy vowed to help them with proposal writing, and JL would try to procure CRAIDS (Community Response to AIDS) funding for them.

TIKONDANE COMMUNITY CENTRE

Whilst waiting for the other teachers to finish marking so I could send off my final reports, I spent a few days in Katete with Liz at the Tikondane community centre. I had visited before but had never actually spent time observing lessons and seeing what really went on there. Elke, the founder and director was running a health education course for villagers and I sat on in the lessons. Elke was direcly addressing the issue of nsima; the course covered basic nutrition and the villagers were stunned to be told that nsima was not a source of complete protein necessary for growth and repair. Elke also addressed the issue of disease at a microbiological level ; the pupils were taught about micro organisms and the importance of hygiene. She even took pupils to the neighbouring hospital to view germs through a microscope. Such simple direct addressing of vital issues showed more faith in education and human nature than anything the church ever did. Anecdotal evidence from Elke suggested villagers responded well to the courses and were eager to learn if given the opportunity. Two villagers from each village were trained as home carers and teachers on health issues. The Catholic church ran a similar home based health care program but that was limited to teaching people how to care for sick relatives ; there was little thought given to prevention and change.

Tikondane was largely self sufficient as it functioned as a motel, but also had craft shops where villagers learnt skills such as carpentry and metalwork and then sold their goods. There was a garden where a variety of vegetables were grown and used to teach crop diversity. A new solar powered cooker represented another step towards self-sufficiency. However, Elke was keen to employ as many locals as possible, and Tikondane struggled with a huge wage bill. Meanwhile the fall of the dollar was reducing the real value of any donations. Ultimately Elke aimed to set up mini Tikos in the area but she would always struggle with funding. I was now cynical enough as well to wonder how the finances were handled whilst Elke was away on trips.

LEAVING CHASSA –Deember 2006

The boys left in early December after finishing exams. The previous year I had supervised a year 12 tutor group and spent a lot of time in disciplinary meetings, after incidents with booze, whoring and daga. Many of these boys had wealthy parents in Lusaka and I was not overly concerned about their prospects. At the end of my second year however I was saying goodbye to a tutor group of year 8's amongst others, and felt both more hopeful and yet more apprehensive about their prospects. There were more village boys in this group, a group I had grown fonder of as I had become disdainful of the snobbery of Lusaka boys (whose heroes seemed to be increasingly American gangsta rappers). These younger boys had potential, and yet if they continued to be unattended they might go off the rails like their older peers. Even in this group I had had to send a couple of boys to the clinic for STD treatment, and suspected already that some had started smoking daga. If they did well in year 9 exams however they might enter senior school more motivated and on the right track. Above all I urged these boys to look after each other, and fight for their rights ; if they were being unattended to by teachers, let the Senior teachers know, tell their parents ; just do something positive to get their money's worth out of the school rather than resort to rioting later on. Who knows how much money was spent every year on repairing schools after riots ; something which can only have exacerbated the funding problems. If rioting occurred at a co-ed school the results could be bitterly tragic ; when boys rioted violently at Liz's school in Mambwe, the terrified girls fled into the bush where they were raped by villagers. Apparently if women wandered out of their own locality this was always a risk in rural Zambia ; something which made trekking around for water and firewood also dangerous.

I was mildly surprised to find a Christmas party was being thrown and was to be a leaving party for Father Fanuel, Jumbe and myself too. At the party Michael gave a brief speech in thanks for my time at Chassa. He had given a similar speech at Sarah's leaving do, in which he had acknowledged the good work of volunteers and hoped that they would also one day find God, because their work showed God was surely in their hearts, even if unacknowledged. Now however, a year later, I wondered if he even believed his own words anymore. I had always found his blank expression difficult to read but had half believed that he meant what he said. Increasingly though there seemed to be a distinct hollowness to his words and tone. Did he even believe what he said anymore ? Shortly before the speech he had told me of his Marist trip to Kenya, and how he had enjoyed the buttock waggling traditional dancers in the expensive nightclubs there. ' Oh, it was wonderful !' he enthused. Perhaps he thought that as a westerner I was impressed with his tales of high living. In fact I was merely disgusted with his lack of concern for the needy. He then stood and delivered a brief, dry speech before returning to his beer. I left the party as soon as was reasonably polite. When I found it hard to read what Michael might be thinking, a slightly paranoid part of me wondered if he resented me for the godless example I set. Despite being professional at work and generally helpful to my neighbours, I was a well known atheist. People would usually come to me for help before they would a Christian and I wondered if this sat uneasily with Michael, as if I was undermining the message of the Brothers (although they did that plenty themselves). Whilst vainly trying to retrieve allowances for Mwale (a newly arrived teacher) Gertrude had angrily exploded, and proclaimed ' What is wrong with you Brothers ? I should just stop going to church and become an atheist like Burke !'

As I might have predicted, my departure caused some ill-will amongst my colleagues. They were all scrambling to be first to buy my various valuables such as TV, stereo, etc. They expected I was hoarding vast quantities of these valuables, despite the fact I was a single guy. This attitude had always been there, as my neighbours had come over on occasion to request to borrow '9 eggs' or 'a bag of sugar'. In bewilderment I would explain I considered myself lucky to have two eggs to eat. And why would a single man have more than one bag of sugar in his house ? (Sometimes I went without sugar completely, and this particularly astonished my colleagues ; in Zambia sugar and salt were regarded almost as staple foods. Tea was often served with ten sugars and meat so heavily salted it made my eyes water). Perhaps they thought because I was running the tuck-shop I was also skimming the goods like previous managers had done. But my real suspicion was that because I was white they thought I naturally had everything in abundance. The Zambians had their own TVs and DVD players of course (in fact most teachers now had their own satellite TV since the dishes had dropped in price) but they had an exaggerated respect for any electronics brought from the UK or bought at a reputable store in Lusaka. My DVD player I had promised to the accountant, whilst I promised JL my parents would send another to him. Even the normally good natured JL became tense and thought he should have the current DVD player I had, angrily snarling at the accountant that she should relinquish her claim. My last weeks were often spent trying to calm disputes between people who somehow claimed moral first rights to a particular item. One visiting teacher had heard a mzungu was leaving and practically barged me aside on my doorstep, demanding that I sell the clothes on my washing line. I patiently tried to explain that I would need some clothes to take to England ; the authorities would probably not look kindly on my naked arrival at Heathrow. Likewise my last week saw frequent badgerings from the wives about selling my cutlery and dishes. Presumably again they thought I had many spares of each item. Again I had to explain I did not, and I still needed to eat up until the last day (which did indeed see a virtual mob of chattering wives descend on my house and clean it out).

Audrey had once told me of how a previous volunteer had some 'issues' with the school or VSO, and in anger he had burnt his remaining possessions rather than pass them on. It sounded bizarre at the time, but now I saw what Audrey chose to overlook ; he had probably lost a lot of money and possessions on 'loans' and was spectacularly denying his neighbours any more benefits.

My last morning was spent with the NZP. I took their pictures and we made a video of them at the Anti Aids Club, recording their ordeals and their hopes for the future. I intended to use this evidence to help me secure help from charities in the UK. Disillusioned as I might be with a lot of the Aid industry, these people were amongst the most deserving and effective in actually seeking to change attitudes. They pledged their experience and help to the Anti Aids club ; to educate the boys and get involved in whatever Anti-Aids activities occurred at schools. JL promised he would try and involve the NZP in HIV projects in future at the Chassa club. The government had funded a CRAIDS project (Community Response to Aids) at Chassa that had turned into a bit of a farce. Millions of kwacha had bought sewing machines, cloth and bicycles for local villagers who were supposed to set up sustainable businesses manufacturing chitenges (the African version of the sari).They had never been heard of again. It was a little bit of a mystery to me why CRAIDS funding had gone to people who still shunned testing. It was a nice project to help poverty stricken villagers but wasn't exactly specifically relevant to HIV (unless it was directly aimed perhaps at keeping women from turning to the risk of prostitution). JL had been much more impressed with the motivation of the NZP and promised to try and redirect the project towards them.

My last speech to the NZP was heartfelt. I told them I considered them the real heroes of Zambia. They were the first people to come forward and stand up in a meaningful way to the prejudice and fear of HIV in Zambia. Their courage in coming forward could be the beginning of the victory against Aids in Zambia. Though illness might break their bodies, they had a strength of spirit that remained unbreakable. I urged them to look after each other and I would do my best to secure help from the UK. I hoped that the personal stories and knowledge I brought with me might be more effective in fundraising than the usual anonymous statistics.

As I said my last goodbyes to the brothers at the residence, I left Jumbe and Chiza on the steps to the front door. Jumbe was being sent to Malawi. He was generally regarded as the only 'genuine' brother (in that he practised what he preached) and I had to wonder if he was being moved out after becoming increasingly critical of Michael's management and suspicious about school finances. Likewise the popular Father Fanuel was being sent out to another parish, far into the bush. He was older than the brothers and I wondered if he had tried advising Michael. I was suspicious about their reassignments. Brother Michael's hold on the school would now be stronger than ever. The perpetually crestfallen Chiza was as usual looking sorry for himself. He looked genuinely jealous that I was returning to a relatively well-governed country. Yet he himself was part of the same mindset that kept Zambia trapped in poverty. As a Brother at the Residence he lounged around in luxury, unconcerned with the difficulties of the school, and taking comfort in premier league football and cold lager as villagers around the area died of hunger and disease. Nonetheless I thought Chiza was becoming increasingly disillusioned with the Brothers even as he shared in their abuses. Recently some white monks had visited from the original founding seminary in Canada. Chiza told me they were a little shocked with what they found ; they related how when in Canadian management the school had several farm vehicles and generators, long since sold off.

There was one final goodbye to my loyal cats. After initially considering them as mewling, irritating nuisances, they had become my constant companions – invaluable to me both practically and psychologically. The feeling of being safely guarded from rats and snakes gave me an almost Pharoah-like contentment. I gave them a final treat of tinned sardines. I had been fattening them up with milk for months, anticipating they might be on their own after the departure of the last volunteer. Mashowo, my newly acquired Zambian housemate, grudgingly accepted to keep Rhino, though he could not stand the wild and black Fink. I wondered however whether Mashwo's new wife-to-be would tolerate a cat, even Rhino. I had managed to convince Edwin Banda, the deputy's younger brother, to take Fink to his uncle's farm near Chipata. Edwin was persuaded that she was capable of clearing the rat-infested house there. So bad was the problem that Edwin said rats even jumped on his mosquito net at night. I had doubts however whether Edwin could capture and transport Fink without me. Our first attempt to put her in a thick cardboard box had resulted in the swift shredding of the box by the TasmanianDevil-like creature within. Edwin would have to try some other way next time there was a lift to Chipata. I removed the cat's collars. The ticks would come back, but sometimes the cats got a leg stuck in the collar and no Zambian would ever dare handle them and free them. Whatever happened to them I knew they could survive if abandoned ; I just hoped nobody would stone them to death, especially of course Fink who would be widely seen as a witches agent because of her colour. Zambians in general were not noted for their kind treatment of animals ; Sondashi had seen on the BBC that the British police were hunting a teen who had shot a cat with a cross-bow. He found it ridiculous that a society would divert resources to such a task. I could half appreciate this, but also pointed out that how a society treats animals often reflects how humanely it deals with people. He was not convinced.

My last few possessions were given to Michael, my part-time, humble gardening boy. In return for using my land for growing maize, Michael had kept the yard tidy. He had never asked for anything except when he was obviously in dire straits. I left him as much food as I had saved, clothes, bags and my spare petty cash. He had recently been married and no doubt would soon have the responsibility of children. It was frustrating to leave him knowing he faced such an uncertain future, like all the subsistence farmers here. The weather looked set to become more unpredictable each year and population pressure could only degrade the land and environment further. Crop yields were likely to decline and even developed nations would soon have their own energy problems ; seed donations, gas based fertilisers and oil based pesticides and other such Aid might not last much longer.

The last teacher I said goodbye too was Mwale, a relatively recent addition from Petauke. He stood with me whilst I threw my bags in the back of the truck. He had always been a dedicated teacher, despite the allowances he had been denied by Michael's shady financial manouverings. Whatever the administration did to him, unlike many of his colleagues Mwale did not take it out on the boys by sitting disgruntled in the staff-room when he should have been teaching. He always taught a full lesson, from bell to bell, and often beyond if necessary (the other teachers at best interpreted the bells as a rough guide only ; as long as some teaching was done in between bells that was considered good) . I wished him well, feeling genuinely torn. I was very ready to go indeed, but felt some shame at leaving individuals like Mwale and the NZP behind in such difficult circumstances.

I was less enamoured with most of the other teachers than I had been on my arrival, but harboured little real bitterness. In a way I understood some of their attitude to work ; they were not single and unburdened like me. I could 'give my all', knowing that soon I would be back in the UK. They however, were here forever and often supporting extended families, so 'rationing' their energies and resources was understandable to some extent. Toward the end of my service I too had begun to feel the long term tiredness that sets in after a persistently patchy diet. My fat reserves had long since melted away and I was now being more extravagant with my money, buying Cokes and tinned beans to try and keep my energy levels up. I was finding it increasingly hard too to maintain my motivation and wondered if I had stayed on longer as the only VSO I would have eventually become like many of the teachers I was critical of. On the other hand, this was their country and home, and they did not seem to appreciate that as educators they had a crucial role to play in improving the nation. They knew what was the right thing to do. Sometimes they had spoken admiringly of an old Headmaster who had taught a full time-table, and even turned away his superiors if they interrupted him whilst teaching. After teaching forty periods a week and marking, this particularly legendary man would head to the fields for labour. ' Ah, he was a *man*' the Chassa teachers would say proudly, even whilst they sat in the staff-room ignoring their classes. The legendary Head had died at age 40 of Aids, as had A.G Zulu's predecessor, the previous energetic Head of Maths. Somehow it seemed HIV often took the very people the country could least afford to lose.

I had said my goodbyes to Gertrude earlier. She was away on a course now. As Sondashi now had a small family, Gertrude had become my closest Zambian friend at work. I often brought my western movies to her and she helped me with food. She had a rich boyfriend who regularly brought her supplies from Lusaka. I was often able to get a half kilo of beef from her, which was taken proudly back to Stacy and incorporated into our miserable 'tomato and onion sauce with white bread' dishes. Together Gertrude and I shared our exasperation at the way Michael spent the school money. To her credit though she had fought him all the way and already had made a difference. In my last term the school had ended with a healthy 50 million still in the account, something which astonished the Deputy. Usually we completely ran out of money a few weeks before the term ended. However, though she might limit the wastage of money, Gertrude was powerless to dictate what it should be spent on. I still had little hope that any useful materials like textbooks or a generator would ever be bought.

Throughout the year Gertrude, like many others I knew, persistently lost weight. She was extremely thin when I last saw her. The obvious had occurred to me long before of course, and I had broached the subject tentatively whist talking of my work with the Anti Aids Club. She seemed well informed on the issue however, once telling me that HIV was now a manageable illness because of ARVs. I knew her boyfriend was a married man and probably had other girlfriends. He was an educated man from Lusaka so perhaps he was careful with condoms. Her weight loss was steady and unabated however and I wondered if like others she was infected and in denial. Possession of the mere facts was not enough in the atmosphere of fear and discrimination created by the churches. On the other hand she was a city girl and she had suffered repeated bouts of malaria whilst at Chassa ; perhaps this explained the weight loss. We exchanged email addresses but I half expected her, like others I knew, to drop off the radar next year. I anticipated visiting Zambia a few years later and finding many of my associates such as Sichande and Gertrude had passed on.

I had lots of mixed feelings about Chassa. I had some regrets, mainly wishing that I had tried harder to integrate more into Zambian life and learn the local language. Then again, apart from with Sondashi, not once had I been invited to a colleagues house for dinner or other social reason. Avoiding boozing at the bar and hiding from `borrowers` had pretty much completed my isolation. It took a long time to settle in ; only toward the end of my second year had I felt I was really getting to know the place. But I was unwilling to stay any longer. I had initiated some of the major changes I had wanted to at work , and somehow felt like I was cheating VSO if I had elected to stay longer for no particular reason. Besides which, VSO was winding up their education program anyhow. Some volunteers might opt to stay on in Zambia by other means, but the General election had left a sour taste in my mouth and I was ready to go. When chatting to a traveller in Chipata he related the tale of a VSO in Guyana who had stayed on for 5 years with little management. His battles with corruption had led to him developing a conspiracy mentality and he had gone slowly insane. I wondered if that would have happened to me if I had stayed on as the only VSO and not had PeaceCorps around or other western colleagues to vent to.

In the end the bitterness that I would take with me was due to the realisation that no matter how long I stayed here , no matter what I did, I would always be viewed as an outsider because of the colour of my skin.

My last bus journey was thankfully uneventful. I had made it out of Eastern Province and survived my last trip on the notoriously dangerous roads.

LAST TIME IN LUSAKA – December 2006

I was soon out in Lusaka, drinking with a group of white Zimbabwaean immigrants I often bumped into in the bar at the backpackers. Near the end of the night we drove out to town to get a takeaway. As we waited for the others to return with the food, Rory and I looked at a kid outside who was staring mournfully at us, tiny hand timidly outstretched. ' What do you reckon will happen here, with all the crap going on ?'I asked Rory. I suppose I meant in general, although I was also referring to the recent debacle of the obviously fixed elections, and all that implied for the future of the country.

Rory sighed, paused, then turned to look at the kid outside. ' See that kid out there Bru ?' The boy was dressed in brown rags and stared mournfully in at us. Rory continued : 'If I told him to..... learn French and.... and follow me barefoot to fuckin Egypt . He'd fuckin do it man ! And do you know why ?' He grimaced and tapped the side of his head. ' because his head is fucked ! And its not his fault ! His head is fucked because of *where* he is ! This place is fucked man, and it fucks the people.' Rory shook his head in exasperation and we waited in silence for the food. Eventually Rory rolled down the window and in pity gave the kid some money. That 'drop in the ocean' feeling I believe was felt by both of us.

A taxi driver I chatted to later that evening told me that he thought Zambia was mis-ruled because Zambians had curly hair and that reflected the confused nature of their brains. I waited for the laughter but then realised he was absolutely serious. Such was the lack of self-belief that many Zambians had about their abilities, and the crazy theories that tried to explain why a resource rich country was so poor. The simple truths of corruption and lack of cooperation were too often not seen.

Back at the hostel, I now noticed the owner stressing about book discrepancies and cursing her staff, and reflected bitterly on my own experience with the tuck-shop. It was difficult to be positive about the prospects for business here.

More of my initial illusions about the peaceful nature of Zambia were overturned when I dropped into Lusaka Central Police Station. I needed to get criminal clearance for teaching in the UK. Being directed upstairs to the fingerprints office, I waited my turn in the small dusty room. I noticed a huge collage of photos pinned on the wall opposite me and thought I could make out a picture of a man hanging. My curiosity piqued, I stood up and examined the pictures more closely. They were dead people. Suicides and murders. A picture in the middle particularly caught the eye ; a large portrait shot of a macabrely grinning man with a huge cross section smashed out of his forehead. A scribbled annotation noted that the murder weapon had been an axe. I was particularly shaken by a shot of a naked white woman bent over in the doggy position, wrists tied behind her back, drenched in blood. Was this Louise's friend, whose family had recently been slaughtered on the copper-belt ? Or perhaps it was actually a black lady, but completely drained of blood. I didn't know enough about corpses to judge. There were certainly plenty of other corpses it appeared that had lost so much colour after death it was difficult to tell if they had been black, white or other. Another dead woman in another shot, plastic cord wrapped around her neck, appeared to have a miniscule head. I stood goggle-eyed at this particular shot for a full minute, uncomprehending. Eventually I realised it was swelling ; the limbs had blown up after death and the head had not. All the pictures were clustered together with no obvious order or purpose. There was no title or nearby files attached. It appeared to be for all intents and purposes just a random collage of saved pictures ; maybe even private photos that had been extra to evidence requirements. Suddenly I was shaken out of my stupor by the call of the clerk. It was my turn to be fingerprinted. I turned and saw the smartly dressed young man grinning at me. ' How are you ?' he beamed, revealing his bright white teeth. I snapped myself out of my stupor and we began the fingerprinting.

As I strolled down Cairo road the next day, I noticed a headline on a Vendors paper. ' Satanist crash lands'. The article was in all seriousness about a Satanist who had apparently crash landed on a roof after flying from Dubai on a magic plane fuelled with sacrificial blood. I wondered how far this country could go when such stories were accepted at face value. All cultures retain elements of this ; even a broadsheet in the UK has horoscopes. But when such thinking dominates the culture your faith in the possibility of change is tested. Another article that week commented on the recent elections and showed the failure of our own culture : Apparently the EU now admitted that there had indeed been ' irregularities' in the transmission of results to Lusaka. Of course it was all too late now.

I also picked up a small paperback that I had seen advertised – the latest garbage from an author who espoused conspiracy theories about Aids and the west. Actually most of what he said in his book about the World Bank and the IMF was true – generally these shady institutions did indeed strong-arm poor countries into accepting huge loans for dubious projects. But the rubbish the author espoused about HIV was shocking and downright dangerous (like a bad movie the book was called 'Extinction : This time Africans are the Endangered Species'). With no evidence whatsoever, the author asserted that condoms and ARV's were a western conspiracy to kill off Africans. He exhorted his people to avoid them. I wished he could meet many of my boys who had been orphaned by parents in denial, or meet my NZP friends who were now healthy, whilst their relatives were wasting away or already dead. Worryingly, I had first seen the book advertised in my staffroom at Chassa. My usual Aids information posters had been covered up by a newspaper cutting that advertised the book, complete with it's glowing reviews. Staggeringly, one influential church minister who reviewed the book enthusiastically recommended the author for post of Health Minster for Zambia. Most infuriating, like many Zambians who articulated conspiracy theories about neo-colonialist plots, the author of the book expressed himself largely in the language of the bible. Historically, the Zambian independence movement had been led by Church ministers as they these tended to be the only Zambians educated by the British. This might explain the apparent paradox of anti-colonialists being so attached to the imperialists' religion. Zambia was no longer under direct political domination (although arguably it was still indirectly so, via multinationals who controlled western governments and economic policies) but I left viewing it very much as a country mentally enslaved by the doctrine of Christianity.

In my broad analysis Zambia was a country failed by its leadership and so called professional classes, and our own governments who supported them. A cynical, unspoken deal had been made between the native elites and foreign corporations ; keep things as they are and the elite would be able to lead western lifestyles ; albeit at the expense of the majority. Aid was swallowed up by corruption in the towns before it even reached the illiterate villagers who were left struggling in the Dark Ages. And the government *wanted* the villages left in the stone ages. An educated population would be likely to demand accountability from a government. But ignorant peasants could be bribed with chitenges and made dependent on government fertiliser and seeds. In this way the situation could be perpetuated and hopefully the gravy train of donor money would continue to keep the elites happy whilst western corporations mined away the real resources. It was quite brilliant financial trickery, but it sometimes reminded me of a memorable line from Apocalypse Now : ' It was such hypocritical bullshit : we chopped off their arm, and then offered them a Band Aid.'

Not that of course the cities themselves didn't have terrible problems as well. The gangs of orphans that roamed the streets were a national disgrace and symbolised the abject failure of the government and this so-called pious Christian nation.

Melvin was now based in Lusaka. We met up and I introduced him to some NGO's who might in future employ him. I left him with enough cash to tide him over and pay for some short college courses in computing. But I left with the same feeling of guilt and helplessness that I had felt about Michael my gardener, and the NZP. I promised to look for sponsorship for him in the UK but I had little idea where to start. A charity called ACET that I had seen in the UK headlines made no response to my emails and letters. I would have to see what my neighbours small charity could do. Perhaps there was some way I could organise support for Tikondane, the project I admired most in Zambia ; a small school and motel that focused simply on HIV education, diversification of agriculture, and craft industries to make a living.

My last night in Lusaka was spent with Liz and my Peace Corps friends. I never would have made it through 27 months at Chassa without them, especially Stacy, who had become like a sister to me. After initially feeling very welcomed at Chassa I had gradually become disillusioned with the management and found it increasingly difficult to keep myself motivated, especially when I began to have personal difficulties with my neighbours and colleagues. I had ended up a virtual hermit in my house during the week, especially now that Sondashi had a family (near the end of my service he had finally married and had a baby). Many hours were spent sleeping, and then frustration, rage and excess energy burnt off in comedic marathon press-up sessions. At one point I wondered why I was so tired all the time with aching shoulders, then realised I was doing 800 press ups a day. The odd weekend in Chipata with the Peace Corps and above all the company of Stacy at Chassa , and later Gertrude had kept me sane and sustained me in my work. Almost like soldiers we volunteers had formed a special bond that would probably always be there.

I left 3 letters for Stacy to post, each detailing the abuses I had seen at Chassa and containing, I hoped, enough circumstantial evidence to warrant an investigation into the finances of the school. One was to the Anti-Corruption Commission, the other to the Ministry of Education, and the last to the Bishop of Chipata. To be honest I didn't expect much from any of them. The Anti-Corruption Commission I'm sure had bigger fish to fry. It was largely a gravy train anyway, set up to target high profile figures but in the meantime providing a lavish lifestyle for those doing the investigating. It was also allegedly corrupt itself. As for the Ministry of Education, it was notoriously corrupt ; one of, if not the worst government department. Gertrude had told me about their shambolic 60's style offices in Lusaka and heard the stories. She had also seen and contrasted the better run Foreign Office. I didn't expect much from them, but with the stories of new donor accounting sweeping the country I could hope they might seek some sacrificial scalps at Chassa. As for Bishop Lungu of Chipata, I tried to appeal to his own interests by suggesting the ill repute the Brothers were bringing the Catholic church into was against his own interests and the good of the church. Perhaps he could influence Brother Michael and persuade him to curb his excesses, if nothing else. However, again, the issue of the Housing Allowance gave me cause to suspect high-level corruption in the church. Several times high-ranking Catholic officials had visited Chassa. They oozed authority and arrogance, and easily batted away teacher's questions about the Housing Allowance. In the end I doubted anything would come of this appeal to Bishop Lungu either.

I was leaving Zambia having effected some small change in one academic department of a school, but what was that really in the great swamp of corruption that held the place down ? I left convinced that until the political situation was resolved, all other developmental issues would be unable to progress. VSO told us to stay out of politics, but like population pressure, were they just avoiding another, indeed *the* crucial issue? However, they had now put 'Governance' and civil participation into their program and I hoped this would begin to pick at some of the more structural problems. With the current set up, honest and accountable government was the necessary precursor for change. Until that changed, most organised aid seemed to be just going down the pan.

And how had Zambia changed me ? Had I just come full circle ? I had come to Zambia to be healed of a broken heart, and to gain some sort of satisfaction from helping others. Time had largely healed my heart. The brooding young man, stung by love, had gradually relented in his suspicion of women, although my increasing isolation in the bush had perhaps accentuated a natural tendency to be a loner. On the one hand, seeing the dysfunctional Zambian State, I was intellectually convinced of the pressing need for people to work together to solve problems. On the other hand, my frustrations with often failing to secure this cooperation pushed me further towards a view that humans were inherently selfish, and the less I had to do with them the better. I would never again be the gregarious social drinker of my younger twenties who sought to befriend everyone. I'm not sure the work of helping others actually changed me much in the end ; I came to view it as essential for its own end anyhow, as I suppose it should be. I had come to Africa filled with notions of a noble native people struggling against corrupt international institutions that kept the country on its knees. Instead I was leaving rather more despairing at the native corruption I saw on the ground, and more appreciative of the relative transparency of western governments. The sums of money lost to corruption locally might not be comparable to the vast sums manipulated by the IMF, but its effects were more immediate and evident in poorly equipped clinics and schools. And somehow it was more demoralising to see a people screwing over each other as opposed to being screwed by foreigners, even if they were doing it for survival. Somehow local corruption was more damaging to the culture in that it taught people they should not care about each other. It was as much a corruption of the heart as anything else. People were taught to mistrust each other and that only the individual mattered.

I had also had some naïve notions about coming back from Africa somehow toughened up ; instead I came back with a heightened sense of my own mortality and the precious nature of life. I had seen how easily people can die, either succumbing to disease or in accidents. Whilst before I may have harboured secret ambitions for some sort of fame or power one day, now one of my chief objectives was simply to die an old man in my bed. After what I had seen in Zambia, I realised that globally speaking that was a considerable achievement and blessing. And whilst I remained indifferent to making lots of money, I certainly appreciated more the basic necessities so easy to find in a developed country. The quiet life would do me fine for a while.

One holiday in Lusaka I had met a young American woman travelling to Tanzania to set up an orphanage. Surprised to hear she was not going back to the States, she merely stated `there's nothing there for me `. I recognised in her eyes the same pain I too had carried a year ago. Maybe someone had broken her heart as well and pushed her to this. I wondered if she would eventually leave as I had, almost relieved to be returning home and despairing at native corruption.

In the end I left somewhat disillusioned with the Aid industry, but not completely despairing. If something is broken, it doesn't have to be thrown away ; it can be fixed. Aid does have the potential to help Africa if done properly; such as with the potential of the self -sustaining project at Tikondane. Tikondane was headed by a western woman however, and herein lay the conundrum ; on the one hand it was difficult to trust Zambian leaders with funds, but on the other hand you didn't want to do everything for them and leave them dependent on western expertise. I did not agree with some that aid would have to be completely withdrawn, but was wondering if would be best if donors directly built the infrastructure in one big push and got it up and running, then stepped back and left Zambians to it. When the Great East Road had originally been built by Italians, it had lasted twenty years. Now it was rebuilt in a poor manner every few years with donor funds that were siphoned off. I suppose the key was finding the natives that could be trusted, and the problem here was that you might have to go around traditional power structures., creating all sorts of problems.

In the long run I still thought education of the youth was the key. A new generation of young leaders, particularly women, were probably the best hope for Zambia. Education and the sharing of knowledge was the crucial issue, and I left Africa more committed than ever to education, having at earlier times in my career been unconvinced. Some of Zambia's greatest hopes lay in a new generation of young people and particularly the potential of women whose opportunities were finally being seriously redressed. Here were some real glimmers of hope. For financial reasons I would have to put volunteering on hold for the time being, and instead might rattle around in the International school system as I sought to expand my world view. But I would return to volunteering, and Africa. In the meantime a pipe dream began to slowly form in my mind ; one day in a poor country I would run a school like Chassa for the poor ; but I would do it effectively and charge minimum fees. It was not just what was done at Chassa that had embittered me so ; it was what was not done. The potential of the school to develop not just its pupils, but in fact the whole area was massive. Chassa had a photocopier, library and a computer lab, and more to the point teachers and pupils who could have bridged the gap between villages and the modern world. The school could have been a dynamo, an education and development centre for the entire region if its funds and organisation had been properly managed. Even our own relative success in the exam league tables was probably down to the fact that our boys tended to be wealthy and could afford to buy exam leakages. Ultimately there was very little the school achieved with it's considerable resources.

In the bigger picture what I had seen, particularly with the elections, had opened my eyes to the machinations of international finance and high power politics. Western corporations were pulling the strings of western governments and dictating policies and tolerating corruption in the developing world. The rigging by the MMD had been overlooked by the European observers because Levy played ball with their paymasters. Likewise the western media conveniently overlooked allegations of rigging, and reported only riots as disgruntlement with the result, as if Africans were like children who could not accept losing a football match. It was never mentioned that many of the rioters were actually educated professionals who knew the vote had been rigged. The media too were in thrall to their corporate paymasters. I had read plenty of books on corporate manipulation, the media and high power politics. But now I had seen how in practice it linked the economies of the Developed and developing world, and kept entire nations trapped in poverty and ignorance. I had become more appreciative of the relative honesty and organisation of my country, but saw that this was merely affordable given that instead we 'exported our corruption' and developing nations paid the price for our set-up.

Third World Corruption was the price paid for god knows what leverage western governments had over Zambia. And why were the MMD themselves so desperate to stay in power? Orwellian analysis on the thirst for power notwithstanding, politics was more of a gravy train in Africa than elsewhere. A politician in Africa could be filthy rich even by western standards. Levy was richer even than Blair in absolute terms. And why were there so many of these men, who chose that life-style rather than help their country in any meaningful way ? Common human faults notwithstanding, the fear and insecurity that normally drive greed were magnified ten-fold in Zambia. History and bitter experience had shown that it was possible to lose everything and there would be no State to pick up the pieces and help you back on your feet. The bitter experiences of 'property-grabbing' (where in-laws descended on orphaned relatives and cleaned them out) showed that often Zambians could not even rely on their own extended families. As much as anything it was a lack of faith in the future, understandable in part given their history. Why do you pay taxes and pension fees ? Because you have faith that in a stable society your investments will one day pay off ; the government will honour its commitments to you. That kind of faith in the future wasn't there in Zambia, and I believe it coloured a lot of the behaviour. The country was caught in a catch-22 now, where the government was corrupt and that corrupted the people, who in turn later staffed the government. But to say that Africans are naturally lazy and thieving is not only deeply racist, it is intellectual laziness of the highest order and shows an unwillingness to really analyse what the problems are.

Sometimes you might hear bitter jokes about long term volunteers' gradual disillusionment with Aid work ; a Zimbabwean kicked out by Mugabe might ask you :
' What's the difference between a tourist and a racist ?'
Answer : 'About 3 months'.

The 'very temporary' volunteers, those who might jet in to help out at an orphanage for two weeks, were snidely mocked by some of these white Zimbabweans for their naive and gushing enthusiasm for native culture. In my opinion neither side was right. I had my own reservations about some aspects of native culture (when one lady enthused to me her love of Zambian culture, I was having a particularly bad day and sharply retorted with ' what : you like wife beating and promiscuity ?') but I refused to succumb to the view that it was anything to do with race. It was learned behaviour and it was reversible.

Sometimes, being constantly hassled for money and paying double for everything, a long term volunteer might feel a victim of 'reverse racism' (some of us joked bitterly about the 'melanin tax' we paid on items because of our skin colour) but you had to keep this in perspective. On the whole whites were indeed better off, and if it was a kind of racism then it was largely benign ; at least we weren't being lynched, hosed and having dogs set on us.

Many volunteers might leave Africa more right wing than they had come, believing in the necessity of standing on your own feet and shrugging off dependency. But I left more than ever believing that the social ills that plagued Zambia were rather due to a weak, parasitic State that degraded people instead of than fostering a common purpose and humanity. Right wing economics were way off. Little money in Zambia was being usefully invested by central government, it was in fact being freely spent by corrupt individuals, yet clearly this 'Market efficiency' did not benefit the country. A developing country needs investment in infrastructure and education to get it up and running. The State would have to be rebuilt from the ground up. For now Aid might have to go around governments and create an educated class who take over with the right intentions. Government itself would have to sever ties with business or else the inequality gap would only widen. Politics would have to be free of big business donations. Parties would have to be funded some other way, in all countries, and the role of the largely corporate media needed to be critically re-examined. In the meantime, though people might have reservations about the motives of the Chinese (one almost had to wonder if a second Scramble for Africa was underway) at least they were investing in Zambian infrastructure. They had built a first class high school outside Katete, and a modern health clinic in Petauke. Their record of safety in mining accidents was not so good, and they were the not best teachers on democracy and human rights, but there was no disputing the tangible benefits they were bringing to Zambia in the short term.

I left Zambia feeling that money, along with unaccountable power, was indeed a hugely corrupting factor in human relations. I didn't have an alternative to capitalism, but believed more than ever that the State should exist to regulate its excesses rather than foster them by acting as a front for big business. The State should remind us that the strong exist to help the weak, not exploit them. And a grossly unequal society with a rich elite is bad for all, fostering instability and vulnerability to movements of foreign capital.

I had been sceptical of religion beforehand and my experience in Africa had cemented my poor opinion of Christianity in particular. Christianity was paraded endlessly in Zambia , but I often reflected that I never really met anyone there who I would consider genuinely Christian, most especially those in the employ of the church. One small act stood out in my memory precisely because it was alone. Near the end of my service, whilst tutoring a friend in mathematics at her house, a drunken beggar had come to the door. My host Grace had prepared a full meal of meat and vegetables for the young tramp, and apparently did so every week. I was literally quite stunned, having been in Zambia for two years and never seen any act of charity and thoughtfulness even approaching this.

In the context of Zambia I came to see Christianity not just as harmless nonsense but as positively dangerous. It encouraged irrational thinking and opposed the development of Reason. I had always had this view of religion, but now saw it brutally in action in a poverty stricken country. Opposing condoms for instance because they were' un-natural and man-made' ; one might just as well lead a crusade against socks. My animosity to religion grew as I perceived that its encouragement of un-critical thinking was half responsible for what I considered illogical behaviour. Why did people criticise me for sleeping in on a weekend for example, when they got up early only to do nothing and feel tired all day ? Why did people here spend half the day sweeping but not fix their roofs ? Why did they watch their crops die in poor rains, even when some extra water might be available to water them by hand ? All these aspects of Zambian behaviour and many more I came to attribute to a lack of critical faculties encouraged by the sheepish following of religion. The best that could be said of Christianity in Zambia is that may have contributed to social cohesion and kept a lid on tribal tensions.

The hypocrisy of the religious in Zambia had left me feeling physically ill at times. I came to see religion as something that actually encouraged immoral behaviour because it led people to believe they could repent. Thus they could have the best of both worlds ; cheat and steal, then repent and assuage their guilt. I discerned something perverse in the relieved faces of the repenters − it reminded me of self harmers who cut themselves for endorphins and pleasure. I had a hunch that both actions satisfied similar pleasure centres in the brain.

Religion was also a diversion ; it may have helped people feel psychologically stronger and been some source of hope, but at the same time it distracted from what were the real pressing issues in a poor country. In my second year it became increasingly hard to bite my tongue when constantly asked ' Do you pray ? So many times I wanted to snap back : ' No, I don't pray. I get off my arse and ACT !'.It was not unusual to mark a boy's script and find at the end, when it was evident they had not revised : ' Bless this paper and I pray that God gives me the marks I need' . When people did act it was often to avoid the real issue. Churches were built instead of boreholes. In the end that for me was the biggest sin of religion. Except in how it might sometimes foster unity and aid morale, in general religion was a waste of time and energy. And the importance of time was something that had now been impressed upon on my mind forever. Time wasted was lives lost. The delays in education I saw as akin to murder. Every delay in educating people about HIV, crop diversification, the importance of mosquito nets, family planning ; I now associated such delays personally with the all the people, many of them children, that I had seen die needlessly in Africa. The inertia borne of fatalism and apathy were strong forces to battle against. Somehow people needed to be constantly reminded of the simple truth that *change is possible* ; but this was a message being constantly undermined by corruption.

BACK IN THE UK

I arrived back in time for Christmas, eager to catch up with family and friends, eat myself silly, and immerse myself in an escapist's world of digital tv and broadband internet. Occasionally I would receive a typical SMS text from another world : ' Burke. Trusting God is keeping you safe. We are ok. Only that my brother died last tues and we buried him on Friday in Chipata. Please send the book you promised.' I remained with a strange kind of 'survivors guilt' about having lived in the Zambian bush and then returning to a comfortable first world country. Soon after my return I saw ' Blood Diamond' in the cinema and the hairs on the back of my neck stood up as in one scene I listened to Di Caprio's character deride ' Peace Corps types as only staying long enough to realise they can't make a difference'. I had pretty much had exactly the same conversations with such Zimbabwean drinking buddies in Lusaka. I remained plagued by internal doubts – what good had I really done ? Had I just reinforced the corrupting relationship between donors and dependents ? As an ex VSO in Lusaka argued ; VSO had celebrated over 40 years in Zambia ; the fact that they saw this as something to celebrate showed that something was very wrong somewhere in the mentality of the Aid industry. As for my own contribution, in all the misery, what did the maths scores of a few kids really matter ? It was making agriculture more productive and sustainable that was the really useful work in Zambia.

Other films and programs seemed to pop up and remind me chillingly of Zambia. Africa seemed to be the flavour of the month with movies and TV. The Last King of Scotland, whilst much fictional and far more brutal than anything I had seen or experienced, felt oddly similar to my leaving Zambia, as if I too had escaped a country increasingly losing its grip on reason. Children in Need ran a program on a village in Kenya struggling with yearly droughts. A baffled Adrian Edmundson reflected on the mindset of people who merely said ' God will provide' whilst the government wasted donor funds on irrelevant schemes that benefitted corrupt contractors.

I retained a frustrating sense of helplessness about all I had seen and been unable to change. I sent books to the NZP on nutrition, seeds with the help of my neighbour's charity, and transferred some small funds when I could. But it was difficult to find out what was actually going on the ground. For some reason they were slow to respond to my texts and never wrote. But I would never let Africa go. I might still travel, and would be wary of further involvement with Africa at an organisational level, but I would always believe in the merit of directly helping people on the ground ; precisely because so much good could potentially be achieved at little cost and effort. Another cheesy line from ' Blood Diamond' jarred in my mind and played back again and again as I moved on with my life : ' You'll never leave Africa, Danny'. Africa would always be there in the back of my mind, reminding me that every day I was blessed. I had a chance at a happy and productive life, and I owed it to others less fortunate to help them. In the end, I had come full circle and was left merely asking the same questions that had nagged at me before VSO. How best should we live our lives ? I believed I had come closer to answers, and they had confirmed my instincts. Existential agonising about the meaning of life was way off the mark. The meaning of life was self-evident ; the world had plenty of misery in it, and we should aim to do our part to relieve it. The question was how.

My first month back, as I reflected on the corruption in Zambia, the children and villagers I had seen dying, my chest would heave with sadness and rage. In these moments of frustration and irrational fury I wished for another chance to meet the government supporting fool in the nightclub ; the man who had threatened my life. Never before had I felt such indignation and rage ; being threatened with death for simply expressing an opinion. I wanted to kill him. In moments of madness and fantasy I started thinking I should have tailed him home, knocked him down in a dark alley and pushed a broken bottle through his neck. The lack of forensics in Zambia would have allowed me to have escaped unscathed. Maybe Che Guevera was right. Corrupt governments cannot be reasoned with. Freedom must be taken by force and won at the point of a gun. Calming down later I would wonder that Zambia and the anger it provoked in me was a poison that showed precisely how the people there themselves had been corrupted, now caught in a catch 22 mentality of self fulfilling fatalism. Violent action usually serves to do little else but provoke a vicious counter-Reaction. The decades after Guevera's death had seen the inaguration in South America of some of the most atrocious dictatorships in history. Patience and slow peaceful change were undoubtedly the best option in the long run, but it was difficult to accept this, when in the meantime most Zambians ground their way painfully through life. For the most part they were unaware of how close change was within their grasp, passing them by.

POSTSCRIPT

In the two years since I left Zambia fuel and food prices have indeed rocketed as I feared they would. Villagers in Zambia are finding life as difficult as ever with high fertiliser and grain costs. Although a global economic recession has led to some deflation in these prices, the long term trend is undoubtedly upwards, and with environmental and population pressure there can be little doubt of the challenges ahead. Zambia is becoming better known as a tourist destination, and Chinese investment continues to visibly improve some towns, but there is still a worry that the rural poor are being side-lined. In fact their particular situation may even worsen as the land degrades and rains become ever more erratic. Against this background Aid has now a higher profile in the media. On the one hand Bono and Geldolf are as active as ever in urging donations, and on the other hand there is a growing cry of `Trade not Aid` i.e an exhortation to free trade as a panacea for Africa. As usual there is merit to both sides of the argument ; European agricultural subsidies no doubt depress much African agriculture, yet many Africans live in such dire poverty they cannot wait for a gradual `rising tide` of prosperity. A rising tide of 'trickle-down economics' may lift all boats, but some people don`t even have boats. Most recently a Zambian has released a book entitled `Dead Aid` in which Aid is criticised as feeding corruption and breeding dependency ; indeed it is seen as the very source of Africa`s problems. There is a recommendation that Aid be cut off for the long term good of the troubled continent.

Whilst I agree that much Aid is of a troubled nature, the challenges of living in a rural area are such that I believe there is still merit in helping the poor directly (I agree entirely that direct budget Aid to governments has largely been a waste of time). If you would like to give money to charity and have some concern about how the funds might be used, I can recommend getting in touch with the NZP+, Tikondane Community Centre, or International Humanity UK. This will normally guarantee that funds are used properly and directly by the needy. A charity I have not dealt directly with, but to my mind looks sensibly focused on food self-sufficiency is Send A Cow. Of course, if you really want to be sure of helping the deserving, it`s best you visit yourself and make your own mind up. Just be careful with the buses.

"When confronted with ever-declining resources, the preservation of social order requires more and more cooperation, but individuals are genetically programmed to reduce cooperation and seek advantage. This genetic legacy sets up a positive feedback loop: declining common resources cause individuals to reduce cooperation even more, which reduces common resources even faster, which leads to collapse even faster."

– Jay Hanson
(Essay on Sustainability)

Made in the USA
Lexington, KY
05 December 2011